Building New Communities

New Deal America

and Fascist Italy

Building New Communities

New Deal America

and Fascist Italy

Diane Ghirardo

Princeton University Press

Princeton, New Jersey

**Library of Congress Cataloging-in-
Publication Data**
Ghirardo, Diane Yvonne.
Building new communities : New Deal
America and Fascist Italy / Diane Ghirardo.
p.   cm.
Bibliography: p.
Includes index.
ISBN 0–691–04067–2
1. New towns—United States—History—
20th century. 2. New towns—Italy—
History—20th century. 3. New Deal, 1933–
1939. 4. Fascism and architecture—Italy—
History—20th century. I. Title.
HT169.57.U6G48 1989
307.7′68′0945—dc19   88-23817

To the memory of

Anna Kapetanić Madden,

my grandmother

Contents

Illustrations

Photo credits

Archivio Centrale dello Stato, Rome: Figs. 2.1, 2.2, 2.7, 2.29–2.32, 2.38–2.41, 2.43, 2.44

Istituto Italo-Africano, Rome: Figs. 2.33–2.37

Landesbildstelle, Berlin: Fig. 1.2

Library of Congress, Washington, DC: Figs. 3.1, 3.5–3.11, 3.14–3.18, 3.20–3.22, 3.24–3.29, 3.31–3.33, 4.3

National Archives, Washington, DC: Figs. 3.2–3.4, 3.12, 3.13, 3.19, 3.23, 3.30, 3.34, 3.35

Collection of author: Figs. 1.1, 2.6, 2.9, 2.23

Acknowledgments

I have been assisted in the preparation of this manuscript by Fulbright, Whiting Foundation, and American Academy in Rome grants, and by the Texas A & M University Faculty Research Fund. The staffs of the National Archives in Washington, DC, and the Archivio Centrale dello Stato in Rome also gave generously of their time and expertise. In particular, Dr. Mario Serio, Director of the Archivio Centrale dello Stato in Rome, has been exceedingly generous in more ways than I could name. His staff members have been unfailingly helpful. I would like to mention especially Dr. Marina Giannetta and Dr. Gaetano Contini for their particular help, and the staff members in the Reading Room who always helped make my tasks more pleasant. The libraries at Stanford University, Texas A & M, the University of Southern California, and the University of California at Los Angeles located books and periodicals promptly and courteously. Silvana Palma and Emanuele Zinevrati of the Istituto Italo-Africano generously assisted me in my search for photographs from Ethiopia.

Audiences who heard parts of this material in lecture form at the Ohio State University, the Miami Architecture Club, the University of Iowa, Stanford University, and the College Art Association offered provocative comments and suggestive insights. Portions of the manuscript benefited from readings by David Kennedy, Stanford University; Kurt Forster, the Getty Center, Los Angeles; Henry Millon, the Center for Advanced Studies in the Visual Arts, Washington, DC; Thomas Hines, UCLA; and Mike Davis, London. All made helpful comments and in some cases steered me toward additional useful material. To David Kennedy and Kurt Forster, in particular, who read parts of the material when it was still in dissertation form, I owe a special debt. At various points the following people generously shared time, ideas, and insights: Russell Berman, Stanford; Giorgio Ciucci, University of Venice; Cesare De Seta, Universita Orientale di Napoli; Andres Duany and Liz Plater-Zyberk of Miami; Stephen Ferruolo, Stanford; Riccardo Mariani, Milan; Vincent P. Pecora, UCLA; Jeffrey Schnapp, Stanford; Tom Schumacher, University of Maryland. Kurt Forster, Ghazi Alireza and Ferruccio Trabalzi visited some of

Acknowledgments

the sites with me and generously shared their observations, photographs, and delight in architecture.

Eric Van Tassel of Princeton University Press encouraged me through the long stages of preparing the text for publication; more than that, however, he did a more careful job of editing than one could hope for. Needless to say, remaining errors are mine alone. Thanks also to Aleta Dayton, Sylvia Royston, and Morgan Ames, who undertook to type this manuscript at various stages, and especially Morgan, who readied it for publication.

In different ways, several others made my research and writing more pleasant: TWA, the airline that ferried me regularly back and forth between Italy and the United States, and in particular the staff in Rome, who made so much of my travel more pleasant; Suzanne Balke; Jo Ann Bank; Michael Black; Julia Bloomfield; Stephen Fox; Edward, Priscilla, Steven, Gerald, Natalie, and Larry Ghirardo; Carlos Jiménez; Carol Miller; Margo Morris; Aldo, Fausto, and Vera Rossi; Sergio and Angela Sonza; Lorraine Wild and John Kaliski; and Ferruccio Trabalzi, who considerably brightened the last months of editing. To my parents, Joseph and Margaret Ghirardo, I owe more than I can say; and my children, Rachel and Christopher, merit special thanks for having lived with this book far too long.

Abbreviations

AAA	Agricultural Adjustment Administration
ACS	Archivio Centrale dello Stato (Rome)
AG	Archivio Generale (ONC)
AOI	Africa Orientale Italiana
AR	Archivio Riservato (ONC)
B	Busta
C.O.	Carteggio Ordinario
C.R.	Carteggio Riservato
CWA	Civil Works Administration
Div. Pol. Pol.	Divisione Polizia Politica
Fasc.	Fascicolo
Fed. Prov.	Federazioni Provinciali (PNF)
FERA	Federal Emergency Relief Administration
FSA	Farm Security Administration
GIL	Gioventù Italiano del Littorio
IACP	Istituto Autonomo per le Case Popolari
IRI	Istituto di Ricostruzione Industriale
Min. Cul. Pop.	Ministero di Cultura Popolare
NIRA	National Industrial Recovery Act
NRA	National Recovery Administration
NRPB	National Resources Planning Board
ONB	Opera Nazionale Balilla
ONC	Opera Nazionale per i Combattenti
OSS	Old Subject Series (National Archives)
PHA	Public Housing Authority
PNF	Partito Nazionale Fascista
Pres. Cons. Min.	Presidenza del Consiglio dei Ministri
RA	Resettlement Administration
RG	Record Group (FSA, NRPB, PHA, SF)
SAIS	Società Agricola Italo-Somala
Seg. Part. Duce	Segretario Particolare del Duce
SF	Subsistence Files

All of the Italian archival material is drawn from the Archivio Centrale dello Stato, Rome; all American material from the National Archives, Washington, DC.

Building New Communities

New Deal America

and Fascist Italy

Introduction

"There is something peculiarly subtle in the feeling that a bit of the soil is one's own," mused Secretary of the Interior Franklin K. Lane in 1919. "It makes for a stronger, higher citizenship. It gives birth to loyalties that are essential to national life and a healthy home life."[1]

Lane spoke on behalf of his dream of settling returning U.S. doughboys on their own land following World War I, a dream shared by Italian officials in the Nitti and Giolitti administrations (1919–21) for their own veterans, and later by Italian Fascists and American New Dealers. In each case, the vision of widespread landownership was buttressed by the conviction that spiritual benefits accrued to those who worked the land; that unemployment would be reduced; that landowners had a greater stake in society and hence were less susceptible to the tide of revolution that gripped Russia and threatened to spread through Europe to the United States.

The enchantment with the magical benefits of property ownership coincided with another widely held belief, in the wickedness of cities. Revulsion for industry and the dirty, crowded cities it spawned characterized not only early twentieth-century Italy but England, Germany, and the United States. The distaste for industrial cities reinforced a far more ancient dislike of cities as centers of vice and corruption. At the same time, however, some architects and planners found the density of the city to be the perfect locus for inspired visions of a future world in which technological advances could provide a more efficient and orderly life. In Italy before World War I, Antonio Sant'Elia rendered his Futurist visions of a dynamic city with a vertical thrust; in the 1920s in New York, Hugh Ferriss and Harvey Wiley Corbett offered even more precise renderings of a city of streamlined blocks with tapering skyscrapers and complex, carefully devised transportation systems. Fascination with machine-age movement, dense agglomerations of humanity crackling with energy, and a new world based upon a dynamic technology animated their work, which focused on the city as the appropriate field of action.

In the same year that Ferris published his celebration of the megacity, *The Metropolis of Tomorrow* (1929), Ralph Borsodi's *This Ugly Civilization* emerged with an equally vigorous attack on cities, industry, and the factory system. Four years later, Borsodi published his answer to urban blight in a sequel, *Flight from the City* (1933).* He rejected the city and all its works, and urged a migration to self-sufficient rural communities.[2] This idea became increasingly attractive in the 1930s, particularly when industrial capitalism seemed bankrupt. Just as Edward Bellamy's *Looking Backward* (1888), with its vision of an American society wholly organized on cooperative principles, had inspired Ebenezer Howard to design and promote his Garden Cities in 1898 in England, so Borsodi's ideas may have prompted Frank Lloyd Wright to design Broadacre City as an image of the possible shape Borsodi's communities could take.[3] The idea of a decentralized nation, forever cleansed of slums, congestion, traffic, vice, and disorder, also found a ready audience in Italy. Luigi Piccinato, one of the designers of the Fascist New Town Sabaudia, drew from Wright's proposals the inspiration not only for Sabaudia and its relation to the other Agro Pontino towns, but also for a fully decentralized Italy of the future.[4] In Nazi Germany, the Labor Front built several hundred rural settlements for factory workers in accordance with Hitler's ideas on agrarian stability and Germany's agrarian heritage. The rural villages Ramersdorf (near Munich), Schottenheim (near Regensburg), and Adolf Hitler Koog (in Schleswig-Holstein) usually consisted of a hundred and fifty single-family homes, many with subsistence gardens.[5] New towns were a prominent feature of the Soviet government's Five Year Plan as well: at least a thousand such communities were planned by Stalin's government.

The Roosevelt Administration also found the Sant'Elia/Ferriss megalopolis less attractive than the Jeffersonian romanticism of the visions of Borsodi, Wright, Bellamy, and Howard for an agrarian America. Garden Cities were established at three sites as Greenbelt towns, and cooperative and subsistence communities at nearly a hundred others. Although they represented greatly watered-down versions of the Howard and Wright proposals (both in scale and in aesthetics), the same dream animated them: to induce people to leave urban squalor for the freshness of the country, and at the same time to recover the spirit of cooperation that had characterized the American pioneers. Like their Italian counterparts, the American settlements intended to reward the virtues of order and traditional morality, and they reinforced the role of the family and the small

*Borsodi was not an insignificant figure in the New Deal community programs: his farm colony in Dayton, Ohio, was the first to receive support from the New Deal Division of Subsistence Homesteads.

property-holder in the acquisition of those virtues on a society-wide basis.

Governmental planning on this large scale in both countries seemed designed to reassure citizens that the respective governments would continue, and that they looked toward the future with unbridled confidence and a sure sense of governmental longevity. Both countries drew upon indigenous traditions of community planning and new town plantation, which accounts for some of the obvious differences in their respective programs. In Italy, the tradition of providing discharged veterans with farm land in the mother country and in newly conquered colonies dated back to republican Rome. During the intervening centuries, princes and lords had also rewarded their troops and secured conquered territory by distributing land and establishing outposts of rule according to well-defined formulas. New town plantation and land distribution were predominantly governmental activities, and the public character of Fascist Italy's New Town program followed directly in this tradition. The association of even a small urban center (with provision for future growth) with land distribution, both as a service and administrative center for the colonists and to secure imperial control, dated back equally far and had served as the typical model for colonization long before the advent of Fascism. Because a large reclamation and settlement zone such as the Agro Pontino lacked convenient existing administrative centers, building towns and associated small hamlets also served obvious practical needs.

By contrast, America's colonization in the oldest regions dated back barely three hundred years. As immigrants arrived and the population expanded in the East, families pushed westward, clearing and homesteading new land as they went, some men also receiving bounty land after military service. Cities and towns were laid out by slapping down the same kind of grid Roman surveyors had used for their colonies and farms two thousand years earlier, but (unlike in Italy) with few exceptions it was private rather than public agencies that undertook the enterprise. The government's responsibility included ratifying acquisitions, protecting against Indians, and conferring territorial status and then statehood on the new land. In the aftermath of World War I, Secretary of the Interior Lane developed a national soldier-settlement program to resolve the problem of urban unemployment and the flight from the farm by merging town and country in European-type rural villages. In the face of steady opposition from the agricultural community and a general lack of public interest, and especially with the decline in agricultural income during the 1920s, the plan languished and died.[6] A significant part of the opposition to this program centered on the involvement of the government in a traditionally private sphere of activity, an opposition which was to surface again during the 1930s with the New Deal communities.

But if the communities the two governments established during the interwar period involved nothing more than land distribution and reclamation enterprises, they would not interest us much. Officials in Italy foresaw redemption of infertile land tied to redemption of the citizenry as well. "Redemption" aptly conveys the notion of the spiritual change the colonists were to undergo in their new environment: purged of their urban, industrial mentality, they could develop "healthy rural virtues." In America too, life in close contact with the land and with farming seemed to promise a new way of life with communitarian rather than individualistic values, and for many officials nothing less than a transformation of the populace was the goal. Italian and American government officials shared the same dream of effecting a new society, and indeed both governments sought to give land to the landless proletariat precisely so as to stimulate the traditional and individualistic virtues of the small landholder. The small-scale individualism would be subsumed within the larger community of Fascist corporatism—a hierarchically ordered organization wherein the state would mediate between the various sectors of society to eliminate conflict and produce harmony in the body politic. Despite assurances that everyone's rights would be respected, the Fascist state favored industry over labor and traditional large landholders over small proprietors or sharecroppers. For the purposes of this study, however, it is also important to recognize that the Fascist colonization schemes reasserted traditional capitalist values in lieu of earlier attempts to "socialize" the rural masses.

In America, when some governmental administrators (Milburn L. Wilson and Rexford G. Tugwell, for example) tried to restructure traditional property relations, they met with a solid wall of opposition to anything but fee-simple property ownership. Nonetheless, as Lane had noted in 1919, property ownership remained a cornerstone of democracy, and hence of the New Deal resettlement plans. In either case, both governments believed that in order to realize its goals the state would have to educate and supervise the colonists. The agencies involved in the subsistence or resettlement programs in the United States concentrated considerable sums of money in management and educational programs in the service of the programmatic goals of achieving a new system of social organization, while the United States Housing Authority and local housing authorities that were engaged in providing urban low-income housing spent negligible sums on management. Perhaps the homes offered to homesteaders, especially in the South, would have enjoyed such niceties as indoor baths—which all USHA projects had—if the Resettlement Administration had chosen to spend its money on construction rather than on largely paternalistic management programs.*

In Italy, agencies including the PNF and the recreational-educational Opera Nazionale Dopolavoro (OND) and the Opera Nazionale Balilla/ Gioventù Italiana del Littorio (ONB/GIL)—as well as the agency in charge of domestic colonization, the Opera Nazionale per i Combattenti (ONC, the veterans' organization)—oversaw equally paternalistic attempts to mold compliant Fascists out of the Italian settlers. As we shall see, striking similarities marked the two programs, especially in the supervisory duties the state exercised through its agencies. With each government occupying the dual—and often conflicting—roles of benefactor and creditor, they had the power to reclaim what they had given and to expect and demand conformity to their expectations in labor, behavior, and attitude.

*A number of New Deal agencies were involved in the community program. The Federal Emergency Relief Administration (FERA) instituted its Rural Rehabilitation program, headed by Lawrence W. Westbrook, in 1934; the Department of Interior included the Division of Subsistence Homesteads in 1933, headed first by Milburn L. Wilson and then by Charles E. Pynchon. Both were eventually shifted to the Department of Agriculture's Resettlement Administration, which was under the direction of Rexford G. Tugwell (1935–36) and Will W. Alexander (1937) and became the Farm Security Administration from 1937 to 1946.

1. Italy and the United States During the 1930s

By the winter of 1932, the United States was paralyzed by the Depression. Unemployment had driven hundreds of thousands of Americans out on the road in search of a job, any job. People never before out of work suddenly found themselves without a paycheck, and mortgage foreclosures forced thousands of others to collect cardboard and scrapwood to build shanties for their families in "Hoovervilles" on the outskirts of many American cities. Ford Motor Company, the pride of "rationalized" manufacturing industries, dropped nearly four-fifths of its employees between 1929 and 1931, and by March 1933 approximately fifteen million Americans were out of work, desperately seeking some way to feed themselves and their families. "It was simply a gut issue then: eating or not eating, living or not living," as one man recalled.[1]

At first it seemed just a temporary dislocation that would quickly improve: free market forces would correct themselves if left alone, and life would go on as before. President Herbert Hoover reassured Americans in 1930 that prosperity, or at least recovery, was just around the corner, and the Secretary of the Treasury, Andrew Mellon, also predicted an upswing during 1930. But as 1930 waned and 1931 saw no improvement—and, indeed, as increasing numbers of Americans lost jobs, houses, and savings—the easy reassurances evaporated. Hundreds of banks failed. Labor unrest and union agitation, including actions by newly organized unions of the unemployed, threatened to erupt into violent confrontations—or at least many observers believed that they would, and some even predicted a revolution. Hope began to dim. The Hoover Administration, apparently unable to cope with a crisis of this magnitude, floundered helplessly.

The 1932 presidential campaign saw Franklin D. Roosevelt castigating Hoover for overspending, swelling the federal bureaucracy, and failing to deal with the crisis. Roosevelt promised fiscal responsibility and a "New Deal" for Americans. Once FDR took office, however, he reversed course and enacted a dizzying array of legislation in an attempt to jolt the sluggish economy into life. The programs initiated during the "first hundred days" sought to accomplish several objectives: providing cash relief to the unemployed, stopping bank failures, resolving the problems of agricultural surpluses and low prices, and inaugurating massive public works programs to provide employment and pump money into the economy again.[2]

By 1930, unemployment in Italy (as in England, Germany, and France) had become a serious problem, as the Depression began to affect even less advanced industrial economies. Exports dropped almost 20 percent in the space of a year in Italy, the deficit soared beyond the levels of 1923–24, 20 percent of the employed had seen their working hours reduced, and important industries such as textiles had begun to feel the squeeze. Grain production fell drastically between 1929 and 1930, and (in part as a consequence) many smaller banks failed, especially those associated with agriculture; but not even the larger banks escaped unscathed. At the same time, from 1930 on, increasing unrest bubbled up from the ranks of industrial and agricultural workers in the south as well as in northern centers. Workers in Turin demanded "bread and jobs" during demonstrations in late 1930, and the government and press attributed strikes and protests throughout the country to Communist activity.[3] Given the already serious problems of a country beset by long-standing poverty, by insufficient and inadequate housing for most of the population, by chronic underemployment, and by an almost total reliance on foreign oil, at worst the success of Fascism might be in jeopardy, and at best Italy faced difficult times in its march toward industrialization and modernization. Benito Mussolini, who had come into office in 1922 with promises of crippling the Socialists, restoring order, and breathing life into the country, had to secure his position as Prime Minister and Duce of the Fascist party in a period of serious economic problems.

In comparable situations of economic distress and political unrest, how did the governments of Italy and the United States respond? This study examines the role of government building for new communities in Italy under Fascism and in America during the New Deal. Pairing democratic America with totalitarian Italy raises a number of obvious questions, as does the decision to undertake the comparative analysis of government building programs: why Italy and America, and not other countries such as Britain or Russia? Why community building?

The answers to these questions emerge in the consideration of the material examined in this study. Briefly, however, I would claim that any government architecture has a rhetorical function and, further, that it tells us what the regime wants us to believe about its nature; as we examine the chosen rhetoric itself, it also betrays some things the regime probably did not intend to reveal. This is all the more true of a regime that has embarked on public building projects as a visible and central part of its program, as was emphatically true of both Mussolini's Italy and Roosevelt's United States. In both the public buildings and the new communities the two regimes created, they projected ideal images of sites for human habitation and communal life—ideal cities, in short.

Ideal cities, Helen Rosenau observed, are projections of a perfect image, and they manifest an optimistic faith in a better future through the agency of communal rather than individual effort; further, "the ideal plan refers to the site as a unity and expresses the aspirations rather than the achievements of any particular civilization."[4] Mussolini's Fascist New Towns respond with striking precision to Rosenau's criteria, even though scholars typically choose not to regard them as twentieth-century exemplars of the classic ideal-city tradition.[5] Fascist Italy's close ties to Nazi Germany, its role as aggressor in Ethiopia and in World War II, and its image as a totalitarian state between the wars have led scholars either to dismiss its cultural expressions (including architecture and planning) as avowedly philistine, or to insist that nothing of merit can have had anything to do with the regime.[6]

Art has been assessed as Fascist or anti-Fascist rather than understood as cultural production. To be sure, art—especially architecture—was highly politicized under Fascism, but it should also be recognized that anti-Fascism did not occupy one respectable position on a range of possible responses. On the contrary, in architecture, many different tendencies vied for supremacy not as anti-Fascist vanguards but as the best aesthetic expressions for revolutionary Fascism.[7] In the hands of Italian Rationalists, styles such as Rationalism shed the left-wing associations of northern European Modernism and became instead vehicles for representing Fascism as a forward-looking, modern, and revolutionary agent in Italian society. Instead of categorizing buildings for their stylistic tendencies—and thereby succumbing to the prevailing circumscription of discourse regarding the Fascist period—I propose to assess the public building programs in the New Towns as arms of Fascist cultural and social policy.

To be sure, Italy and the United States had very different social and political traditions in the early 1930s and stood at different stages of economic development. Democracy in the United States was a hundred and fifty years old; and the country had an equally long tradition of prosperity, growth, and high expectations. Except in the South, most farmers owned or rented their land, and as of the 1920 census more people lived in cities than in rural areas. To land-starved immigrants from western and eastern Europe including Italy, the United States offered the promise of independence, upward mobility, and employment. Italy, by contrast, traced its genealogy back to the earliest Etruscan and Latin settlements, but for centuries it had been fragmented under foreign and papal domination. Its unification as a nation dated only from 1870. An agrarian economy supported hundreds of thousands of smallholders, tenants, and sharecroppers in the south and in north-central Italy—comprising families that in some cases had farmed the same land for hundreds of years. Fewer people lived in the cities of northern Italy than on farms, but when restrictive U.S. immigration policies virtually put an end to emigration to the United States during the 1920s, more and more Italians fled to the cities in hopes of finding a better life.

Because of its relatively modest degree of industrialization, Italy escaped some of the worst consequences of the Depression found in America, such as a high incidence of "stranded populations" (entire towns left with no income because of the collapse of a single industry). Problems in international trade generated the first repercussions in Italy, as both imports and exports fell drastically. The need to reduce imports to balance the rate of exports led to reduced demand and finally to reduced prices, as the problem of ensuring a stable balance of payments assumed a crucial role in Italy's political economy.

At first glance, Italy and America during the 1930s hardly seem comparable, and yet the fact that both reacted to the worldwide economic crisis in some remarkably similar ways invites consideration. Britain, France, and Spain, for example, undertook no significant public building programs during the 1930s. Spain was lacerated by civil war, while the governments of Britain and France (which had had substantial public building programs in the nineteenth century) now found no particular need to erect a large number of new public buildings. Germany, Russia, and Italy did, however, and all three merit comparison. Each had undergone a major change in government—all claimed to be revolutionary— and each embarked on a massive public works program in order to resolve current problems and to enhance the new government's prestige.

Unlike Russia, the United States had not suffered a revolutionary seizure of power. But the government did face a general crisis of confidence in the ability of American institutions to cope with the trauma of the

Depression which deepened over time, and it selected public works, especially buildings, as a means of providing employment, increasing demand, and restoring faith in the nation while combating serious economic and social problems. It is worth remembering that the governments of Italy, Germany, and the United States, unlike that of Russia, manifestly favored capitalism. They chose to resolve economic difficulties along traditional lines through cooperation between the public and private sectors, rather than by discarding capitalism altogether.

The existence of Italy's agrarian poor long pre-dated the Depression, as did the plight of southern farmers in the United States, but despite crucial differences in historical and social conditions both Italy and the United States had to deal with poverty, mass unemployment, and crises in industry and agriculture. Capitalism in both countries came under attack as a volatile, disorderly system in which destructive price wars flourished and constant conflict with labor was the rule. Rather than scrap capitalism, however, the two governments sought to eliminate the resultant insecurities through state intervention on an unprecedented scale and scope. During the interwar period, corporatism—which essentially involved a government-sanctioned cartelization—seemed to promise a means of controlling the economy not only in Italy and the United States but also in Germany, Portugal, and to some degree France during the 1930s.[8]

Fascist Italy reacted as the United States, Britain, and France did, by focusing on safeguarding the national economy and, in particular, by making full employment a government objective for the first time. In addition, Italian industrialists encouraged the consolidation of the economy along the lines of corporatism as a way of controlling wages, prices, and costs—not to mention workers—in a time of considerable economic uncertainty. Corporatism promised the stability so desperately desired by industrial, governmental and social elites. Parallel business and labor confederations, organized according to the various sectors of the economy, ensured that labor and small producers could be kept in line by the industrial leadership, concurrently removing much of the uncertainty and unrest that both could generate when left free to operate as they chose.[9] By the mid-thirties, as a result of the establishment of the Institute for Industrial Reconstruction (IRI) in 1933, the public sector in Italy was second only to that of the Soviet Union, for the IRI controlled a wide range of industries. But the IRI was never intended to set up a public enterprise system. Despite the fact that it would have been the ideal vehicle for corporatism, both the industrial-financial bourgeoisie and the political ruling class feared the prospect of an agency which, if allied with the corporations, could wield real economic and hence political power, and both took care to deprive the IRI of that power. Here as elsewhere, the state intervened in order to rationalize the Italian capitalist economy, and the tasks of the IRI were essentially set by the larger private industrial bourgeoisie.[10]

Roosevelt managed to extract from Congress a similar program of government-business cooperation. The Blue Eagle of the short-lived National Recovery Administration (NRA) heralded a new era of price, production, and wage agreements, effectively undercutting the painstaking program of trust-busting that dated back to Theodore Roosevelt's presidency. In fact, much of the criticism of the NRA after 1933 centered precisely on the charge that it promoted monopoly. To organized labor, it meant the abdication of collective bargaining. Neither Italy nor the United States was yet able to embrace the notion of a fully controlled economy, just as neither seemed able to avoid intervention, especially in controlling currency, supply, prices, salaries, agriculture, and foreign trade.[11]

Whatever the particular differences between the corporate state in Italy and the NRA in the United States, clearly both governments undertook strong campaigns to preserve capitalism, and both used techniques that favored bigger rather than smaller businesses, industries, and farms. Objectively, both governments favored monopoly and centralization, a tendency exemplified in America by the NRA and in Italy by the corporate organization. However, neither government could relinquish the traditional claims of the small producers: even though government policies supported the interests of the largest firms and industries, both nations were committed to the interests of "the people," and arguably the most publicized programs were those which directly promoted the interests of small farmers and businessmen and the army of unemployed. Despite Fascist rhetoric, agricultural incomes were redistributed in favor of large landholders rather than small landholders.[12] Programs for the latter probably had less economic importance in the long run, but they tended to generate a good deal of debate, at least in America. Conservatives lamented state intervention in traditionally private arenas, while liberals found most of the programs inadequate. Campaigns to construct public buildings and housing offered a superficial response to the ideological imperatives of the needs of the people in both Italy and America. In the building programs, politics operated at two levels: in the political economics of labor and capital and in the symbolic politics of the architecture itself. By their very nature, the symbolic aspects of the architecture primarily addressed the ideological imperatives, but the significance of construction in the economies is equally important.

One of the barometers of economic health, then as now, was the construction industry. John Maynard Keynes singled out the decline in residential construction in the United States by 1929 as one of two ominous indicators of impending crisis. Moreover, he argued that in order for prosperity to return a steady level of residential construction had to be maintained.[13] In fact, the building industries suffered more after the crash than they had before; although consumer income dropped significantly after 1929, non-farm residential construction declined even more precipitously. The building trades alone accounted for nearly one-third of the unemployed in America, and the reduction in aggregate demand that resulted from the building slump spread out through the economy in waves.

When Keynes visited the United States in 1934, he particularly urged Roosevelt to aid the housing industry. Following the slump of 1937–38, Keynes pressed his case with the President again.

> Housing is by far the best aid to recovery because of the large and continuing scale of potential demand; because of the wide geographical distribution of this demand; and because the sources of its finances are largely independent of the Stock Exchanges. I should advise putting most of your eggs in this basket, *caring* about this more than about anything, and making absolutely sure that they are being hatched without delay. In this country we partly depended for many years on direct subsidies. There are few more proper objects for such than building houses.[14]

In 1933 Marriner Eccles, testifying before the Senate regarding ways to end the Depression, likewise advocated building and construction projects as a prime element of his plan for recovery. He compared the United States unfavorably with Soviet Russia, pointing out that if the Russians had faced a similar crisis they would have put men to work building decent housing for their people. If the government promoted construction projects, Eccles maintained, the social goals of improving and providing housing would dovetail with the economic goal of reviving the economy, and together they would help to accomplish a third goal: preventing revolution.[15]

Revolution, of course, inspired neither Keynes nor Eccles; both wanted to preserve capitalism, with construction programs as the linchpins of their overall programs. Although their prescription might have been just what the country needed, they failed to take into account the longstanding aversion in America to federal involvement in this traditionally private sphere. Unlike other industries that tended to concentrate wealth and power in the hands of fewer and fewer people and firms, during the 1930s the construction industry consisted almost entirely of small businesses. Intervention into this volatile sector demanded acute sensitivity, for virtually any move the government made toward involvement in housing construction aroused storms of protest. Ultimately, the Roosevelt Administration moved as cautiously as did the Mussolini Administration: it rendered aid to the ailing construction industries largely—but not exclusively—through mortgage assistance programs for middle income groups, and threw the weight of direct government building behind the second program recommended by Keynes and Eccles—that is, promoting public works.

As Keynes, Eccles, Simon Kuznets, and others argued, a fundamental condition of prosperity was a steady flow of investment in real capital—particularly in construction of all kinds—which the public sector should augment if private investment flagged. Gross public expenditures on construction were not as important, Keynes insisted, as the expenditures that were met by a net increase in borrowing, and only the state could make such expenditures on the scale necessary to revive the economy.[16] The creation of jobs and the injection of these expenditures into the economy would generate wages, rents, interest, and profits, ultimately putting money back in the hands of consumers, thereby creating higher levels of demand. As a means of reviving the construction industry, public works projects were politically safer than either housing or business construction. The latter would have involved both governments directly in the private sector, perhaps even in competition with it, and was therefore never politically feasible on any significant scale. The sole attempt by the United States government to build and operate a business in direct competition with the private sector (the vacuum cleaner factory in Arthurdale) aroused so much opposition that it was quickly shelved. Building low-cost housing generated equally powerful fears of government competition with private industries. For both governments the safest course involved limited housing construction and a concentration on public buildings and other kinds of public works.

The entire public works program in Italy, as in America, represented an attempt to provide jobs and pump money into the economy through the construction of useful and possibly profitable public works. In neither country did the programs entirely succeed in achieving the goals of economic recovery. Although unemployment fell, the jobless in America still numbered eight million in 1940, tax rates expanded, and fiscal policy was never as expansionary as economists such as Keynes wished. Only after the onset of World War II could politics override objections to excessive government spending. Likewise, in Italy the long-term public debt during the same period increased without significantly increasing private consumption.

In some modest ways, public works programs did alleviate unemployment and increase purchasing power, but the buildings that both nations constructed served more important political and representational objectives. The governments of Italy and the United States faced the 1930s with self-legitimation a major item on their agendas; this was perhaps one of the most important features they had in common. Mussolini's Fascism and Roosevelt's New Deal departed from the practices of previous administrations in a number of ways. With the validity of their programs yet to be proved, they had to reassure their constituencies that they also stood well within indigenous traditions, that they were accomplishing some of their objectives, and that they were in command of the situation [Fig. 1.1]. Statistical compendia lack the immediacy, power, and visibility of a building or a housing project to compel the citizen's awareness of the government. In both countries, buildings were projections of the government's image of itself as well as projections of the populace's beliefs about what the government should represent. However short of the projected goals the building programs may have fallen, in their sheer size and presence, buildings gave the *appearance* of being major and successful achievements and were meant to be seen as emblematic of other dramatic achievements authored by the government; and, as is so often the case, appearance far outweighed reality in the public perception. In Italy and America, the impressive appearance of monumental new buildings masked the failure of both governments to resolve internal crises.

The search for legitimacy by both the New Deal and Fascist administrations led to an emphasis on major public constructions that lent themselves to being photographed and referred to as evidence of an appropriate government response to the Depression. When the Public Works Administration (PWA) or the Works Progress Administration (WPA)

erected a new school, city hall, or armory in a community, it testified in an eminently visible fashion to the involvement of the federal government in the life of the community. The Roosevelt Administration knew what American politicians had long known: patronage helped secure public office by ensuring that people back home felt obliged to the politicians in power for jobs or for purchase orders for equipment and machinery, for contracts, or for new school or recreational facilities. Since the Hoover Administration had been incapable of securing jobs or relief for millions of unemployed people, it is hardly surprising that Americans would feel loyal to the Roosevelt Administration when it made giant strides in supplying jobs and aid to desperate families. New schools, auditoriums, swimming pools, sewage-treatment plants, post offices, and local, state, and federal office buildings all stood as vivid reminders of the Roosevelt Administration's dynamism and, by extension, the sturdiness of the nation. And the public did notice. As one man remarked,

1.1 Poster for the tenth anniversary of the Fascist Revolution, 1932: the poster announces the long-distance flight of Italo Balbo to the 1933 World's Fair ("Crociera aerea del decennale"), and depicts the Duce as a heroic aviator.

Before Roosevelt, the Federal Government hardly touched your life. Outside of the postmaster, there was little local representation. Now people you knew were appointed to government jobs . . . It came right down to Main Street . . . There was the immediacy of its effect on you. [17]

A widespread crisis of confidence about the viability of American institutions and traditions compounded the pressing economic problems of the early 1930s, so this reassurance of the government's ability and strength played no small part in the recovery effort.

Italy's situation differed somewhat; the problems associated with the Depression only complicated the difficulties of an economy still in the early stages of modernization and industrialization. [18] The introduction of corporatism addressed some of the issues, but Mussolini, like Roosevelt, conducted a vigorous campaign on the symbolic level as well. Both leaders invoked a noble past and shared traditions. In the United States, the administration appropriated images of a pioneer past and democratic traditions dating from ancient Greece, while in Italy, the Fascist state appropriated images of imperial Rome and to a lesser degree the medieval commune to fulfill symbolic and rhetorical goals. When Mussolini came to power in 1922, his task was less to restore faith in a discredited state than to inculcate in the citizenry a feeling of national rather than local pride and, specifically, to inspire patriotism in a country which was a unified nation in name only. Not surprisingly, one device which Mussolini used to instill a sense of identification with the state was an appeal to the Roman Empire of two thousand years earlier; the same strengths and virtues that had fashioned Italy's days of glory in the past would promote yet greater splendor in the new empire. When Mussolini remarked to the Senate that "Rome [was] the source of life," he referred to the monuments and symbols and the twenty-five centuries of history to which they bore witness; Rome's vigor would be, in the new Fascist state, the wellspring of an illustrious era to match the best in Italy's past. [19] In this scheme, the state conferred special importance on building. As Marcello Piacentini, a leading architect of the period, commented,

In history there are eras of strength and eras of weakness; a strong people must impose its will in every sphere, including the physiognomy of the city in which it lives and works . . . today we are in an era of strength, and we want to and will leave our long-lasting mark. [20]

If the message about the revitalized Italian state was to be brought home to Italians throughout the peninsula, the Fascist party needed to make its presence felt in every small town and village. New programs and institutions, and new buildings to house them, were highly visible and important elements of the campaign to unite Italy under the banner of Fascism. At the same time, new constructions would join the monuments of the past and testify to another glorious chapter in Italy's history. Minister of Public Works Michele Bianchi declared in 1928 that the public works completed under Fascism "were destined to remain, over the centuries, documents of our [Fascist] faith, our efforts, our labor."[21] Buildings were no less laden with symbolism in the United States. Acting Commissioner of Public Works Col. E. W. Clark closed his address at the cornerstone-laying ceremonies of a hospital in Virginia with the comment that the building would show that "[America] can build, within the framework of democracy, structures emblematic of an effective form of government which will preserve these liberties and ideals which are the most cherished heritage of the American people."[22] One need only look at the frenzied rush to remove Fascist emblems and slogans from buildings after World War II—and in Germany the wholesale destruction of Nazi buildings by conquering armies—to recognize the power with which buildings convey images of government.

It is a noteworthy feature of the creation of new communities in interwar Italy and America that they bestowed on the provision of housing some of the urgency—and the high visibility—that under many regimes are characteristic of monumental public building programs.* The Italian government had subsidized low- and middle-class housing for several decades, but under Mussolini the housing program surged forward with the help of higher state subventions. Expanding industrial enterprises especially in northern urban centers attracted young workers from throughout Italy, but the lack of affordable apartments forced many of these immigrants to live in shanties in degrading squalor on the edges of metropolitan areas. At the same time, local and state programs to widen roads and "sanitize" crowded inner cities only increased an already acute housing shortage. While officially the Fascist government was strongly opposed to urban growth, the needs of industry and the demand for affordable housing induced the government to support low-cost housing projects.

Inadequate and insufficient housing as well as slum clearance projects in the United States also encouraged government sponsorship of low- and moderate-priced housing, even though such enterprises were traditionally

*In this study, I examine building programs in Italy and America with special reference to newly planned communities. Public buildings, including housing projects, are the subject of a second book now in progress.

outside the domain of government activity. Only the emergency of the First World War had induced a reluctant government to construct housing for defense workers, and likewise only the extraordinary economic crisis brought the Hoover Administration to allow partial government aid to the housing industry through the Reconstruction Finance Corporation (RFC). The New Deal saw a significant increase in federal involvement in housing over time, especially after the passage of the Wagner Housing Act of 1937.

The rural-industrial and subsistence homesteads projects of the New Deal involved the government in constructing models for the ideal communities of the future; the way in which these settlements were established yields unexpected information about the character of the new society the government envisioned. Mussolini's New Towns were also models for the future, especially for the corporate or Fascist city—based upon agriculture or one of a few major industries. Although Italy laid claim to a long tradition of new town plantation, the comprehensiveness and ambitiousness of the Fascist enterprises were new to the recently united nation. As was also the case with the New Deal towns, the Italian programs involved the government in the lives of the citizens to an unprecedented degree.

Different historical traditions and social conditions cannot obscure the overwhelming similarities of the agendas in the two countries. The two regimes, entangled in a capitalist crisis of massive dimensions, were nonetheless committed to preserving capitalism. Both governments recognized that earlier policies of non-intervention would not work, and that in order to surmount the problems confronting them the governments would have to intervene directly in the economy. They lavished energy and money on public buildings—without ever spending enough to overcome the crisis—both to alleviate the economic and social crises and because the buildings could also serve a legitimating function. In scope, significance, and purposes, the building programs in Italy and America stood out from those undertaken by other western governments. The impetus for the building campaigns derived from parallel social and economic circumstances and from fears about the loyalty of the public during such a crisis; and both governments engineered the building programs in such a way as to protect and favor existing economic arrangements.

Despite the broad similarities that characterized the building programs of Italy and America and, indeed, their responses to the Depression, any attempt to compare countries with such different political systems is haz-

ardous. Most scholars find Italy and America during the 1930s so different that they venture no comparisons, except those which reflect unfavorably on Italy. "As an authoritarian regime," E. Lipson wrote in 1940,
"Italian Fascism is the antithesis of democracy." Fascism denied and
repressed freedom, while democracy nurtured and protected it.[23] The
war, Italy's alliance with Nazi Germany, and the Italian government's
racist stance in the late 1930s all enhanced the image of a political system completely at variance with that of America [Fig. 1.2]. Such a view
gained ground during World War II, when propaganda in all of the war-
ring nations offered clear and comforting distinctions between friend and
foe, and that habit of mind has persisted in post-war scholarship. One
consequence of this view is that partisans level the charge "apology for
Fascism" at studies which offer anything other than thoroughgoing con-
demnations of Fascism.[24]

As much as scholars dispute what "fascist" means, about one thing

1.2 Unterdenlindenstrasse, Berlin, decorated for Mussolini's visit, 1937.

they are certain: whatever is fascist is bad. But labels can be misleading (as in the case of the "Democratic Republic" of East Germany): labeling invites not considered historical analysis, but a knee-jerk reaction to the name itself. The assumption underlying such a perception of the 1930s is that the political systems of Fascist Italy and New Deal America were poles apart, that they constituted well-defined, discrete, and thoroughly opposed systems. A more accurate perception would recognize political systems as ranging over a continuum in which differences are often less of kind than of degree. In the context of the programs examined here, government activities in Italy and America are more similar than they are different: they constituted comparable responses to similar problems. One virtue of a comparison such as this is the unfamiliar perspective which it affords for viewing each country.

American historians tend to argue about whether the New Deal constituted a radical departure or simply exploited trends that existed well before Roosevelt's inauguration.[25] These arguments and the programs themselves look quite different once historians no longer see developments in America in isolation but instead examine them in the context of similar situations elsewhere in the world.

Several years ago, John A. Garraty examined the New Deal and Nazi Germany and discerned some fundamental similarities between a number of programs in the two countries, which led him to conclude that they responded to the Depression in remarkably similar ways.[26] But Garraty found himself weakly rebutting the argument that therefore either Roosevelt was really a fascist or Hitler was truly a democrat. This is not a particularly useful argument to pursue, any more than it would be with Mussolini replacing Hitler in the equation. By dwelling on the character and ruling style of the head of state, we succumb to the cult of personality which most of these leaders engineered precisely to divert attention from other issues in order to achieve a broad-based consensus. If the character of government and society interests us, then examinations of specific activities—in this case, government building and new town plantation—yield more substantive material.

One final point concerns methodology. Because this study falls between two traditional realms of scholarship, the character of the discourse may seem strange to members of either scholarly community. Historians may feel that too many pages are devoted to the discussion of buildings, while the architectural historian may find the same pages too brief and truncated as analyses of architecture. My purpose here is not to provide exhaustive analyses of architectural styles or of individual buildings, but rather to suggest the political relevance of a large group of buildings which are often relatively undistinguished architecturally. If the buildings and urban arrangements are to support any interpretive weight convincingly, however, the grounds must be established adequately, and this involves descriptions of the buildings. If anything, the structures merit more, not less, detailed consideration than they have received here. The architecture and politics of the two countries have not received the scholarly attention in English that has been lavished on Germany, for example, by Barbara Miller Lane and Robert Taylor.[27] Since most of the Italian towns are celebrating their fiftieth anniversaries during the eighties, they have received scholarly attention and celebratory publications along with their new paint jobs.[28] Much remains to be done, but the following study is a first attempt to set the building programs in Italy and America next to one another and to assess the character of those programs in the context of the political aspirations of the two governments.

2. Italian New Towns

Mussolini is the builder, the Fascist regime is the construction yard, and this is the era of Italian reconstruction. The Duce's mind does not halt at intermediate phases; it goes immediately to the constructive solution. He is the architect.

Paolo Orano, 1937

*Paolo Orano edited a series of books on Mussolini's writings; he extracted comments on issues ranging from public works to agriculture, collected them in twelve small volumes, and wrote extensive, fawning prefaces. One edition of the series was designed especially for Dopolavoro libraries; the volumes which I have studied are part of the library of the Dopolavoro of the Istituto Poligrafico dello Stato, in Rome.

†The twelve New Towns, in order of completion, were: Mussolinia (1928); Littoria (1932); Sabaudia (1934); Pontinia (1935); Guidonia (1935); Fertilia (1936); Aprilia (1936); Arsia (1937); Carbonia (1938); Torviscosa (1938); Pomezia (1938); Pozzo Littorio (1940). Predappio (1925) was not counted as a New Town, in part because it remained under construction for many years, but also because the number twelve had significant historical resonance (see below). In addition to these New Towns, the Fascists also constructed numerous *borghi* in Sicily, and new communities in the African colonies. Probably the most famous African colonization adventure was the one led in 1938 by Italo Balbo, who brought some 1,800 Italian families to settle in new villages in Libya. *Gli Annali dell'Africa Italiana*, I, March 1943.

Mussolini's New Towns in Historical Context

Orano's description of Fascism as a construction yard and Mussolini as builder and architect of an Italian reconstruction is clearly a rhetorical device, but in certain important respects it is not wide of the mark.* Mussolini *was* the chief architect of Fascism as a political system, and he did promote a prodigious amount of building, including the construction of thirteen towns and more than sixty rural settlements *ex novo* in Italy between 1928 and 1940.† Foreign observers watched these massive government building projects closely during the years of the Depression, and within Italy the press turned out a steady stream of documentation and praise.[1] Just as the Fascist state extracted every ounce of propaganda potential from the towns, so historians have been loath to study them and perhaps thereby give credit to a thoroughly discredited regime. Political motives decreed the foundation of the towns, and (different) political motives have decreed their almost total obscurity for nearly forty years. In the last few years, however, scholars have begun to take another look at Mussolini's New Towns.[2] From a distance of several decades, the ambiguities and problematical aspects of Fascism are apparent, and they can also be detected in the buildings and towns commissioned by the Fascist government.

The establishment of New Towns under the auspices of revolutionary Fascism was part of the promise of a presumably forward-looking political program that aimed in part to put Italy on an equal if not superior footing with the rest of the industrialized world. This modernizing trend appears most strongly in the industrial and military New Towns, where the government underwrote the development of industrial resources, but it is also a significant feature of the agricultural settlements, or colonies. With both types of towns, Fascism seemed to be promising a new and bright future with up-to-date, hygienic living conditions and improved agricultural and industrial productivity. The new political system—the Fascist corporate state—in Mussolini's eyes constituted the next and best step after liberal democracy.[3] With fascist movements on the upswing throughout Europe, Italy clearly seemed to stand at the vanguard of a monumental change in the social and political complexion of the world. The establishment of thirteen New Towns in twelve years—largely years of world economic depression at that—offered emphatic proof of the determination and power of the Italian Fascist state.

On the most general level, the New Towns seem to be one feature of a future-oriented Fascist program; but the closer we look at them, the more they appear fraught with the same kind of ambiguity characteristic of Fascism itself. Mussolini's speeches and Fascist propaganda emphasized references to the bond between modern Fascist Italy and ancient imperial Rome: here is one of the first clues to a fundamental ambivalence that surfaces in the New Towns. The architecture and planning are tethered to forms and urban schemes drawn from ancient and medieval types; although not museum-like re-creations (or even reconstructions), they were also not decisively modern. The towns were as much true towns—cultural, political, social, and marketing centers—as they were part of an administrative network to link individual farmers or workers to Fascist organizations and, through them, to national Fascist policies. Despite the declared aim of drawing volunteer colonists for a social experiment, all too often those who answered the call ended up conscripts sent to what amounted to an internal exile.[4] Here too, the precise manner in which the state carried out the enterprise betrayed some of the problematic aspects of the Fascist program itself. Similarly, although the trend in western Europe and the United States for the preceding century had been toward mass participation in politics, and although Mussolini exalted and appealed to the masses, at every point in the physical and social organization of the towns hierarchy emphatically prevailed.

The programs and even the individual buildings have clear—though selective—relationships with Italian history: Mussolini saw most public works not just as enterprises linked with those of imperial and medieval Italy, but as the fulfillment of earlier, unrealized dreams. In a speech about a new aqueduct in Ravenna, for example, Mussolini commented: "Centuries pass, generations pass, governments, the lords, the names change, but the reality is always far from the dream. Only Fascism could do this, since Fascism is at this time above all the verb *to will*."[5] The town programs would not only imitate ancient models, but surpass them; as one commentator noted, "We are now living in a stupendous scene drawn from the Bible and made to live again here, at the gate of immortal Rome. Here is a new sign of eternal Rome, for in her name, in her great shadow, the history of the past millennia is repeated."[6] At the inaugura-tion of Littoria, the first of the Agro Pontino New Towns, Mussolini de-clared: "That which was attempted in vain over the past twenty-five cen-turies today we are translating into living reality."[7]

The relationship to the future seems equally well defined: Italian Fas-cism represented the first realization of a revolutionary political system, and the new agricultural and industrial centers embodied the promise of that future world based upon social order within a hierarchical system. Denis Mack Smith noted that "Fascism lived on dreams of future pros-perity."[8] If past and future seem to be securely in view within these towns and the Fascist system, what about the present? In fact, the uneasy mar-riage of future goals to dreams of past triumphs seemed only to drain the present of its significance. As Mussolini commented, "we are intent upon a great effort, and we want to remove Italians as soon as possible from the constraints and discomforts of the present time."[9] The absence of a consciousness of the moment and an emphasis on deferred gratification is perhaps what laces many of the structures with such profound ambi-guity.

Whether a systematization of an existing site or the foundation of a new community, the operation centered on the urban core. The agricul-tural program consisted of land reclamation and settlement, but social and political aims found their most emphatic expression in the cities. The New Towns were of enormous propaganda significance for the govern-ment, whose ability to produce functioning towns from swamplands in a very short time, almost as if by magic, certainly enhanced the propa-ganda value of the reclamation and industrial projects. Since all were located some distance from any other major centers, local administrative bodies needed quarters, but no less important was the need for towns that would give symbolic expression to the success of the reclamation enter-prise in a highly visible manner.

Settlement and reclamation projects during the interwar period did not always receive such an architectural definition; only three of the many settlements undertaken by the Resettlement Administration in New Deal America had town centers, and even then they consisted of merely a few institutions fitted into a minimal town setting.* Specifically, the recla-mation projects and the rural settlements were not outfitted with towns. Recent town planning ideas had had a distinctly de-institutionalizing em-phasis, in particular Ebenezer Howard's Garden Cities program upon which the U.S. Greenbelt towns were modeled.[10] Not even the bold and

*These included the Greenbelt towns of Greenhills, Ohio; Greenbelt, Maryland, and Greendale, Wisconsin.

decidedly modern plans by Le Corbusier for *la ville radieuse* envisioned separate and distinct administrative organs.[11] An architect who plans an ideal city or who has no patron for his proposal (as was the case with Le Corbusier's *ville radieuse*) need not distinguish the public buildings from the private ones, and is free to avoid setting off the institutional centers from the rest of the town. Certainly these ideas dominated the Modern Movement in architecture. But where the state and a presumably revolutionary party commission the architect, as in Italy, an unspoken necessity to define and make explicit the presence of that state and its institution's traditions intrudes.

Impulses grounded in a perception of Italian history also helped shape the New Towns. With the inauguration of the New Towns during the 1930s in peninsular Italy and Sardinia, the young Fascist state stepped into a long tradition of planned new town settlements. The acquisition and maintenance of conquered territory through town plantation extends back at least as far as the Roman Empire. New Towns coincided with major renovations and urban upgrading in existing towns during the Fascist period as had not systematically occurred before. In the past, concentration on new town plantation had alternated with cycles in which urban renovation dominated. For example, during the communal period a large number of new communities were established, while during the Renaissance princes tended to emphasize major internal renovations in northern and central Italian cities. The reemergence of new towns in significant numbers in the Baroque period preceded a renewed emphasis, in the nineteenth century, on the renovation and expansion of industrial centers.

The particular historical references evident in the Fascist New Towns are to Roman and medieval towns and to the subsequent undertakings of late medieval and Renaissance strongmen, local *signori* who adopted medieval architectural components and configurations in order to legitimize their power and authority. Mussolini saw himself as related to the *condottieri*, and in fact publicity for the projects was replete with battle metaphors. The Fascists built their towns in Italy not to affirm control gained by military action, but to confirm control over land reclaimed for productive use through hydraulic, road, agricultural, and industrial enterprises. Along with increased imperialist rhetoric, the domestic battle for land reclamation in the early 1930s served as a prelude for the military battles for empire beginning in 1935. Before the imperial campaigns of the late 1930s, the Fascists endeavored to bring the same martial energies to bear on vast domestic projects. In this way the aggressiveness and bellicosity which supposedly brought Fascism to power in 1922 were to be kept alive until the next military campaign. Empire, of course, meant colonies abroad, and ample opportunities to establish new settlements of Fascist settlers.

The creation and administration of the Agro Pontino towns fell to the ONC, the veterans' organization, and their chief propaganda organ was the magazine *La Conquista della Terra*. The cover design for this publication merged agricultural implements with the military emblems of Fascism: the *fascio littorio* with the shovel of the farmer.* Those who labored on the reclamation and resettlement projects were a "mass of soldiers in full battle, exposed to the most lethal dangers (malaria), and the conquest of the Agro Pontino took its toll in deaths."[12] The persistent battle imagery no doubt aimed to reinforce the sense of continuity Italians were to perceive between the Great War and the programs of the Fascist state, not to mention the imperial glories of ancient Rome.

The canonic foundation of twelve towns under Mussolini also recalled the political unification treaty that gave rise to the first coherent political body in ancient Italy: the League of Twelve Etruscan Towns.[13] Much later, Cosimo de' Medici also recognized the symbolic significance of twelve towns, and closed his own expansionary campaign at twelve towns precisely in order to strike a parallel between his Grand Duchy of Tuscany and ancient Etruria. As one commentator noted, Mussolini shared a similar concern with the example of ancient Rome, and he also aligned himself with major official patrons of the past: "There is only one privilege recognized, the signs of Rome wherever they are . . . Mussolini realizes the dream of Cola di Rienzo, of pontiffs from the age of Humanism and the Renaissance . . ."[14]

The Predappio Precedent

The Fascist state established its first new community, Predappio, in 1925, and its second, Mussolinia, in 1928. Part of a large plan for the reclamation and colonization of Sardinia, Mussolinia consisted of little more than a loose collection of small buildings to house the essential services required by farm families. Only after the New Towns of the Agro Pontino had established a pattern did Mussolinia receive a civic and market center (between 1935 and 1938).

*In ancient Rome, each magistrate was attended by an officer (the *lictor*) who carried the fasces, the symbol of state authority: a bundle of rods enclosing an ax. Fascism took up the fasces as its most prominent emblem.

The foundation of Predappio is a suitable starting point for this study; for a number of reasons, it is one of the most important of the Fascists' new communities, although it remained under construction for the untypically long period of at least twelve years. In addition to being the first new town, Predappio was entirely Mussolini's idea, from its grand scheme down to its details. And it has been completely ignored by historians, probably because since Fascist propaganda did not advertise it as a New Town but gave it, as Mussolini's hometown, the status of a shrine, a visit to Predappio today seems too much like a pilgrimage rather than an investigation into town planning.

Between 1911 and 1913, the small hilltop town of Predappio (Romagna) began to suffer dangerous landslides.[15] The Ministry of Public Works (Ministero dei Lavori Pubblici) responded with a state-funded program of reinforcement and drainage, but despite the investment of nearly one million *lire* the slides began anew in 1924, leaving twenty-seven families homeless. The Civil Engineer's office in Forlì estimated that an additional two million *lire* would be necessary, but even with further outlays, little hope remained for saving the section of town threatened by slides, nor did the town offer room for replacement housing.[16] These problems with the land were not at all uncommon in the Appennines of Romagna, but once Mussolini came to power, the geological problems coincided with Rome's desire to subdue the predominantly Socialist and Communist administration of Predappio. In February 1925, the Commission recommended the gradual relocation of the village to a new site one kilometer away. Minister of Public Works Giovanni Giuriati thoughtfully notified Mussolini of the problems in his hometown and of the Commission's recommendation.[17] If he expected that this was simply a pro forma gesture, he soon found otherwise.

Mussolini responded a few days later with the firm declaration that "not a penny should be spent to shore up [Predappio]" and that the plan to move the town should be discarded. Instead, Mussolini offered a counter-proposal which, he asserted, was "simpler, safer, more radical, and definitive."[18] The town should be moved into the Rabbi valley below, to the affiliated and much smaller hamlet of Dovia [Fig. 2.1]. The new community would be called "New Predappio" (Predappio Nuova) or simply "Predappio." He noted in a terse series of points that the new site was cheap, open, and landslide-free; furthermore, it sat on the main road between Forlì and Premilcuore, and offered ample building space for new

Localitá in cui esisteva la casa
Eredi Babacci ora demolita.

Palazzo Varano

...a indove nacque il E. Benito Mus

2.1 Center of Dovia, 1925. The road leading from Palazzo Varano to Mussolini's house was straightened out to provide the new Predappio with a decorous axial road appropriate for parades and grand entrances.

public facilities such as a town hall, stadium, school, carabinieri barracks, postal-telegraph office, and private buildings such as banks, insurance agencies, and housing.

Mussolini already envisioned the town: its *comune*, or town hall, would be the former Villa Varano (now Palazzo Varano), Dovia's one moderately significant building, elevated above the road to Forlì; low-income housing could be located in the Puntirola section; and the old town would become the hamlet "Barberino" and would retain only a church and rural school. In short, Mussolini proposed the complete reversal of the towns: not only would the old town lose its name, but also none of its characteristic features would be transferred to the new one. In particular, New Predappio would avoid the steep, narrow streets of Old Predappio, replacing them with a broad new avenue upon which new institutions would stand isolated from one another, on streets which would also allow vehicular traffic. Although geological forces had already condemned the old town to death, in Mussolini's view, demographic pressure and the appeal of the new town would raise the number of inhabitants to between fifteen hundred and two thousand, with ample growing room. With the addition of Fiumana, another nearby *comune*, by 1926 Predappio Nuova numbered 6,742 inhabitants. Mussolini acknowledged that the *predappiesi* would be heartsick about having to transfer to Dovia, but it would not kill them, and in any case, he insisted, the government could not waste money satisfying *sentimenti campanilistici* (hometown loyalties)—although his own feelings were arguably the most *campanilistici*. The Duce urged the minister to have the engineer in charge get the proposal under way as he had spelled it out as expeditiously as possible; in fact, so clear was Mussolini's idea of the new town that he included in his letter a sketch (now lost) of the proposal.*

It is worth noting that there had been a recent example of an urban building campaign similar to that proposed for Predappio: Marcello Piacentini's program for the new city of Bergamo (1914–29) preserved intact the medieval town of Bergamo on the hill and replaced the old fairgrounds below† with a monumental new town disposed around an enormous town square.[19] Piacentini's architectural language of stripped classicism and powerful massing probably also set the pattern for the modern architecture Mussolini sought for Predappio Nuova.‡

One other serious problem in Predappio promised to be resolved by the construction of the new town: unemployment.[20] Long before the decision to build the new town, officials had written about the alarming unemployment rate in both the public and the private sectors. Many public projects such as roads, public housing, and school building had been halted for lack of funds.[21] Although Predappio was a silk-producing area, textiles remained the province of female workers, and providing jobs for men was a constant problem.[22] Agricultural work alone failed to assure full employment, so eventually an airplane parts factory, Stabilimento Caproni, was established on the road midway between the two towns. Throughout the 1930s, however, only substantial public works programs kept the town afloat; land reclamation alone employed over a hundred people annually, and building programs were hastened even in the late 1930s to help reduce unemployment.[23]

No one was more aware of the enduring unemployment problems throughout Italy than Mussolini. As new Fascist agencies were formed—the Gioventù Italiana del Littorio (GIL), the Opera Nazionale Dopolavoro (OND), and the Partito Nazionale Fascista (PNF)—they distributed aid of various kinds to the indigent and the poor, generally in return for mem-

*Mussolini had been premier for just over two years; however, he had only recently survived the Matteotti crisis and confirmed his control in January 1925. The plan for Predappio was one of the first major building campaigns of his rule.

†The two-hundred-year-old Fair of Bergamo had been one of the most important in Europe. See Roberto Papini, *Bergamo Rinnovata* (Bergamo, 1929).

‡Piacentini later became the premier architect of the Fascist state; his significance extended far beyond his actual buildings, though they were numerous and influential. As editor of *Architettura*, member of countless juries, and respected cultural figure, his role in shaping the architectural physiognomy of the regime was unparalleled. Unlike Albert Speer in Germany, Piacentini was no Fascist ideologue; rather he made a pragmatic accommodation with the regime, as did many other intellectuals. See my entry on Piacentini in *The Macmillan Encyclopedia of Architects* (London, 1982) for a more complete discussion and bibliography.

bership in the organization. At the same time, the agencies themselves employed many people, which also alleviated unemployment. But the benefits offered beyond simple aid advanced the PNF's aims in significant ways. Through the new agencies Fascism made the amenities of modern life available to many people for the first time.[24] Though few could afford even the discounted radios on sale through the OND, for the price of membership anyone could go to the OND's recreation rooms and listen to one there. Better yet, members could enjoy the novel experience of watching the movies presented in the OND theater. Indeed, when *predappiesi* failed to join the OND, the director shrewdly introduced movies in town—available only to members of OND, of course—and membership rolls promptly swelled.[25] (Another device for seducing *predappiesi* to join the Dopolavoro was the formation of a soccer team.) Most of the organizations also arranged trips to take adults and youngsters out of their rural backwaters for the first time. On the monumental plane, spatial relationships between new and traditional seats of power—as well as new buildings, exhibitions, and mass parades and demonstrations—brought the people to the party and the party to the people in dramatic and powerful fashion, and as the tools for fashioning a united and Fascist policy their importance in domestic politics must be recognized.

In Mussolini's long list of reasons in support of his plan he touched only briefly on one of the most important, when he remarked that the transfer would end the ridiculous friction between Predappio and Dovia. The stone house where he was born sat not in Predappio but in Dovia, which occupied a distinctly inferior role with respect to the village of Predappio [Fig. 2.2]—creating a tension that Mussolini fully recognized. Sitting on a narrow, tortuous, rocky road to Forlì, Dovia consisted of little more than a few stone houses and a ruined eighteenth-century palazzo, while Predappio was a hilltop town. Mussolini long resented having come from what was in effect Predappio's wrong-side-of-the-tracks. His plan would resolve the dispute—which seems to have emanated from Dovia—in favor of Dovia, much to the hostility of the *predappiesi*. During the years of the First World War after Mussolini abandoned Socialism his wife, Donna Rachele, had suffered insults and worse from the Socialists of Predappio, and by some accounts her determined but underground actions stood behind the decision to upgrade Dovia and downgrade Predappio.[26]

Mussolini could also find indigenous models for the task of re-creating his hometown. The most famous such example is the work of Aeneas

Silvius Piccolomini (Pope Pius II) and his architect Bernardo Rossellino in transforming the Pope's hometown of Corsignano into the episcopal seat of Pienza (1459–62).[27] En route to Mantua to launch a new crusade against the Turks, Pius II stopped for a few days in February 1459 at Corsignano, where he was appalled by the poverty of the town and by the age and infirmity of his boyhood companions. Motivated perhaps by devotion to his hometown, perhaps by the specter of decay, but also by the example of illustrious and architecturally distinguished humanistic courts such as those of Mantua and Ferrara, Pius decided to raise the status of Corsignano to that of a city, an episcopal seat for which he would provide a monumental new center. Pius followed the progress of construction with loving care, and wrote about it extensively in his *Commentaries*.[28] Although he hoped to revitalize the city not only architecturally but intellectually and economically, his death halted any prospect of improving Pienza's status, and his edict forbidding any alterations to his handiwork effectively doomed it to stasis. Rossellino's monumental center and a single block of housing remained the only signs of activity after the town fell

2.2 Mussolini's birthplace, Dovia, 1925. The two-story stone building just to the right of the access road was the Mussolini home. Leaving the house unrestored made it a more appropriate cult site because it emphasized Mussolini's humble origins.

back into slumber following the brief burst of activity in the mid-fifteenth century.

There are intriguing parallels between the two ventures. Pius II's family had been transferred to Corsignano—impoverished and humiliated socially and politically—in the late fourteenth century by the Sienese nobility. The Italian historian Sara Rossi has suggested that Pius II sought to recoup his family's prestige in Sienese territory through the revitalization of his hometown—much as Mussolini sought to ennoble his birthplace nearly five centuries later in response to slights suffered in childhood. Pius II stopped short of trying to outdo Siena, however, whereas Mussolini planned to vacate the original Predappio and, in the ultimate act of destruction, to rob it of its very name.* Pius II had persuaded members of the ecclesiastical hierarchy to build family palazzi in Corsignano; Mussolini induced their twentieth-century equivalents—banks and insurance companies—to open branches in Predappio Nuova. Predappio Nuova received Mussolini's personal attention throughout the fifteen years of its construction, just as Pienza had been personally overseen by Pius II. Even Mussolini's family was involved: Donna Rachele inaugurated many of the new public buildings, donated money and food to local charities, and even intervened to ensure that the new Casa del Fascio† made prime office space available for the local Dopolavoro.[29] There are, however, limits to the parallels: although Mussolini interested himself even in matters as small as deciding whether to use Latin or Italian for the inscription on the cornerstone of the new Casa del Fascio,‡ his attention was sometimes less kind.[30] He frequently turned down requests from Predappio for aid, new buildings, and special favors, and when invited to the traditional open-air dance in the summer of 1935 he responded with a remark more reminiscent of Marie Antoinette than of Pius II: "Let them dance—I won't go."[31] It is worth noting that on the whole Mussolini lavished less attention on his hometown—perhaps because of residual resentments—than many of his leading henchmen bestowed on their own hometowns. Edmondo Rossini, for example, very nearly built his own new town in Tresigallo (Ferrara); Italo Balbo created an industrial zone in Ferrara; and Araldo di Crollolanza built up many parts of Bari.

The construction program in Pienza had marked one of the high points in Pius II's papacy; but for Mussolini, Predappio represented only the first in a series of such enterprises [Fig. 2.3]. Urbanistically and architecturally, Predappio lacks distinction, but Mussolini's ideas about new

*Despite Mussolini's orders, people resisted and procrastinated, and Predappio Vecchia remained a flourishing community. By 1936, in fact, the townspeople voted to change the name from Predappio Vecchia (Old Predappio) to Predappio Alta (Upper Predappio), a name which allowed it to be recognized as a still vital town. "La Voce d'Italia," 8 March 1936.

†A new Casa del Fascio, headquarters for the Fascist party, was erected in nearly every Italian town.

‡He opted for Latin.

town construction nonetheless took shape here. With Predappio he artic-
ulated for the first time his ideas about the image of public buildings and
the construction of new towns as a fundamental expression of Fascist aspirations, forging early in his career a link between modernity and Fascism. In a telegram to the Mayor of Predappio on 12 June 1925, Mussolini offered the following arguments to urge him to cooperate:

> Today Chief Engineer Province of Forlì showed me projects construction
> Predappio Nuova. Severe lines public buildings will make Predappio Nuova
> a little town with a secure future. Pray see projects to be convinced that to
> build a new town is as I have said one of the most noble enterprises Fascist
> spirit.[32]

Most of the features typical of subsequent Fascist town planning make
their appearance, albeit in somewhat crude form, in Predappio: long,

2.3 View of Predappio (photo by author). The tower of the Casa del Fascio
to the right of center obstructs the view
of the church and dominates the town.

2.4 Opera Nazionale Balilla, Predappio; Cesare Valle, architect (from *Architettura*, 1938). Except for its streamlined styling, this building is highly traditional in plan and spatial organization. Nonetheless, it is significant that such an apparently modern building could appear in Predappio as late as 1938.

2.5 Corso Mussolini, Predappio, 1985 (photo by author). The axial road terminates at St. Anthony's church, with its free-standing tower; the Casa del Fascio is to the right.

broad avenues; an overscaled piazza for mass demonstrations; new building types isolated in monumentalizing fashion [Fig. 2.4]; major institutions fronting on the central piazza [Fig. 2.5]; fixed spatial and axial relationships [Fig. 2.6]; and the prominence, both in plan and elevation, given to the new Fascist institutions with respect to the older organs of the commune.* None of the 1930s New Towns slavishly followed the model adopted at Predappio of aligning public buildings along a main throughfare—in fact, the linear plan of Predappio resembled the layout of Pienza more than of the later Fascist New Towns. But the strategic placement of the most important civic buildings on thoroughfares and major piazze characterized the earliest New Towns of Littoria and Sabaudia as well as the later ones of Guidonia and Pontinia. Because construction in Predappio continued over a period of twelve years, the architectural style underwent alterations as new institutions were inserted into the urban fabric. In subsequent New Towns, by contrast, designers sought to achieve a unified stylistic language in all the buildings. The Predappio Casa del Fascio, for example, completed in 1937, contained

*In most respects the planning programs of the New Towns followed the general guidelines set out by Leon Battista Alberti nearly five hundred years earlier, especially his prescription that long, straight avenues be used to express dignity and grandeur. Alberti would have disapproved of the monumental piazze in Predappio and elsewhere, however—piazze were indeed necessary, but Alberti stressed moderation and disliked ostentatious displays. L. B. Alberti, *De Re Aedificatoria, libri decem* (1546), IV, 5.

2.6 Predappio, market, ca. 1938 (contemporary postcard, "Le grandi opere del Regime"). The curved portico still shelters demountable fruit and vegetable stalls. Behind the market sits Mussolini's childhood home. The architect, Florestano Di Fausto, subsequently directed many of the rural and urban architectural settlements in Libya.

all of the typological and heraldic elements by then typical of Case del Fascio—the town hall configuration rendered in a modern idiom and placed on the town square with the town hall and the church; but its style differed radically from that of Palazzo Varano and the church.

Another element of Fascist urban policy that also made an early appearance in Predappio was the "liberation" of monuments from the accretions of centuries in order to privilege one particular historical period or moment in the life of a structure.* The tomb of Augustus and the Roman Forum itself were two of the prime examples in Rome, but many antique buildings received similar treatment.[33] Dovia lacked structures of comparable historical significance, but it did boast one villa of modest historical merit, and of course the stone house of Mussolini's boyhood. Both were stripped of adjacent buildings; Villa Varano became the new town hall, and Mussolini's house became a pilgrimage site for Fascists to visit in subsequent years [Fig. 2.7].† But in Predappio, as elsewhere in Italy, such decisions to "monumentalize" a building of propaganda value

*Isolamento—freeing buildings of their accretions of centuries to monumentalize them and thereby endow them with greater significance—was already an accepted strategy in Italian historic preservation, but it reached its zenith under the Fascists.
†Even at this early stage in his career, the character of the future cult hero was already taking shape.

2.7 Demolition of old buildings around Palazzo Varano, Dovia, December 1925.

Lavori di demolizione dei vecchi fabbricati retrostanti il Palazzo Varano.
Domenica, 6 dicembre 1925

required that it be freed from a jumble of surrounding structures, an action which depleted the local housing stock and led to the displacement of many families. Wooden multi-family barracks were constructed as temporary quarters for the families in Predappio, with more permanent housing still years away; the temporary discomfort of the inhabitants was apparently a matter of indifference.[34]

Background and Goals

By the beginning of the 1930s, Fascist ideas about cities had taken more definite shape. It became increasingly apparent to anxious Fascist officials that crowded urban areas could promote revolutionary unrest. Early anti-urban sentiments in the Fascist state began to harden into policies directed toward reducing the size and power of cities and inducing people to return to the countryside.[35] The New Town program never fit comfortably into this anti-urban scheme, however; when so much rhetoric extolled rural over urban life, justifying the foundation of new conurbations involved delicate maneuvering. As a result, propaganda about the New Towns lauded their qualities as small towns—that is, as centers of rural rather than urban life. Indeed, as anti-urban rhetoric waxed, the New Towns of 1935 and later (after Sabaudia and Littoria) shrank in size precisely because of the growing emphasis on ruralism.

Similar rhetoric surrounded the grand *sventramenti** in Italian cities. Such clearing operations in Rome led to the establishment of twelve rural *borgate*. Isolating monuments from antiquity normally involved displacing numerous poor inhabitants, but apart from the supposed gain for the worlds of art and architectural history, officials rationalized the massive displacements on the grounds that the residents would be moved from the crowded urban core to healthy country air outside—well outside—the city. At first, rapidly assembling cheap single-story, two-room houses without sanitary facilities (supposedly only temporary quarters), the government eventually began to produce more substantial two- and three-story buildings. The only thing rural about them was the total absence of urban amenities, including streets and transit connections to the city. Eventually the residents took matters into their own hands. At the *borgata* in Primavalle to the northwest of the city, on the long, daily walk home from the last bus stop, each resident carried one stone to place in the dirt, eventually creating a stone road. In this and other matters, since

Sventramenti literally means "disemboweling," razing entire sections of the city. The story of the *borgata* of Primavalle was told to me by one of the earliest inhabitants, Vittoria Bertuccioli, in October 1988.

they were not showpieces for the regime, the *borgate* never received even a fraction of the attention lavished on the New Towns.

The first sustained program for New Towns unfolded as part of a major reclamation enterprise in the Agro Pontino and parts of the Agro Romano—a region roughly south of Rome, bounded by the Mediterranean coast to the west and by the Alban hills to the east. For centuries it had been a malarial, unhealthy, largely uninhabitable area. Reclamation of these marshes, as well as similar ones elsewhere in Italy, had been attempted several times in the past, most notably under Pope Sixtus V, but none had succeeded in draining and working the land.* The marshes remained and so did malaria. Between 1868 and 1921 the new Italian state issued over fifty laws aimed at reclaiming the marshes, but on the eve of the Fascist takeover nothing had been accomplished.[36]

The Fascists also knew that the New Towns were being constructed in a territory that had been abandoned by the ancient Volsci tribe after the Romans conquered them and destroyed their settlements in 328 B.C. The name of one of the Fascist New Towns, Pomezia, was that of a Volscian settlement destroyed by the Romans during the long war.[37] The choice of the name of an ancient site for Pomezia was consistent with the programmatic latinization of place names under Fascism (the most notable example of which was the renaming of Borgo San Donnino as Fidenza). For the New Towns, the Fascists also followed the ancient example of naming towns after conquerors (Mussolinia, Sabaudia, Guidonia) or giving them names suggesting what towns were supposed to do—to flower (Fiorenza) in the ancient example, and to be fertile (Fertilia) or to produce coal (Carbonia) in the recent example.

Constantino Andruzzi recounted his version of the history of the Agro Pontino in the organ of the ONC in April 1932; he identified the gradual decline of the Agro Pontino into a malarial swampland as a casualty of Roman expansion:

> as Rome expanded and, to the cadence of its marching legions, brought the victorious eagle to the edges of the known world, the Pontine marshes were depopulated. This phenomenon can only be explained by the fact that the future dominator of the world, distracted and preoccupied by the many wars she provoked, of necessity had to ignore that rich region, whose conquest had absorbed much energy at the dawn of her history.[38]

In the new Fascist mythology, while it was the fault of the ancient Romans that the Agro Pontino became unhealthy marshland, the ONC and

*Even Leonardo da Vinci got into the act. Drawings by Leonardo commissioned by Leo X and dated after 1513 (now in the Queen's Collection, Windsor Castle) include one of the Mediterranean coast from Terracina north, as part of a study for the reclamation of the marshes. In a commentary to Vitruvius (Como, 1520, fol. 20), Cesarino prematurely noted that the Palus Pontina "sono sta purgate et evacuate, cosa che mai romani il poteva fare." The project was abandoned after the death of Giuliano de' Medici in 1516.

the Fascist state were capable of a breakthrough that would redeem this region as no state or pontifical regime since Julius Caesar had been able to do. Presenting the reclamation of the Agro Pontino as mopping up what the Romans had left undone enabled the Fascist state to trumpet domestic programs when no imperial adventures comparable to those of antiquity were as yet on the horizon. Earlier efforts to reclaim the region

> failed because they were not preceded and prepared by a persistent policy to bring man back to the land, to fix him there, to root him with every available means; to create those environmental conditions which would make life possible there; and to follow up, step by step, with all social and hygienic defenses . . . but above all because they lacked a program to regulate and discipline immigration in the Agro.[39]

The ONC's plans were quite different: "not only a reclamation project, but also a civilizing enterprise: houses, aqueducts, will be . . . the milestones . . ."[40]

By implication, then, the Fascist reclamation efforts took up where the Romans left off, but the triumph of Fascism would be the conversion of the Agro Pontino into a productive agrarian region while the new Italian empire would first flourish and then expand abroad. To make the connection between the New Towns and the Roman settlements even more explicit, Mussolini mounted a tractor and traced a perimeter around the projected communities, mimicking the Roman ritual in which the founding commissioner of a new *colonia* plowed a symbolic furrow for the placement of perimeter walls and gates.[41]

The fledgling Fascist regime soon recognized that it was possible to harness the clearing of the marshes to other Fascist programs. After the close of the First World War, Mussolini and the Fascists gained the support of many of the demobilized soldiers by promising to give land to those who actually worked it.[42] Once in power, Mussolini propagandized against the phenomenon of urbanism, the spectacular growth of the cities, and the depopulation of the countryside. Political reasons underlay this position, for the crowded urban areas held a potentially radical working class, dangerous if unified. In consequence, Fascist propaganda extolled the virtues of rural living, healthy physical labor on the land, and a renewed morality, and ultimately set in motion an unsuccessful campaign to stem the flow of population from the country to the city.[43]

The anti-urban sentiment eventually touched Predappio Nuova as well. By 1938 new landslides endangered houses in the old city, but even though Mussolini's original intention had been to evacuate Predappio Alta, officials elected not to transfer the stubborn *predappiesi* to the new town in the valley precisely because the authorities wanted to avoid urbanizing it. The Prefect of Forlì outlined the reasons for leaving the old city intact:

> Perhaps today it is appropriate not to insist on the transfer [from Old to New Predappio] in order not to urbanize New Predappio too much. To leave the inhabitants of the old rural village attached to Old Predappio—and therefore to the land—is preferable for [this reason] and for many other economic and social reasons.[44]

In fact, some two hundred families emigrated from the area—many to the Agro Pontino New Towns.[45]

Beyond the demographic shift from country to city, Mussolini mourned the general decline of Italy's population. Emigration had taken its toll, and so had a steadily declining birthrate. In 1927 he alerted the nation to the need for a growing population to keep Italy strong. He found a correlation between the declining birthrate and unhealthy industrial centers; in fact, he proclaimed that industrial urbanism "sterilized the populace." The province of Basilicata—one of the poorest provinces in Italy, entirely rural and painfully pre-industrial—earned praise for having the highest birthrate in the nation;* "virile and strong, [it was] evidently not yet sufficiently infected with the pernicious currents of contemporary civilization."[46] Mussolini's campaign for a fecund population enabled the Fascists to line up on the side of motherhood, at that time a virtually unassailable position.†

The campaign against urbanization, like that in support of fecundity, took up considerable space in Fascist rhetoric. Anti-urban impulses had been at work during the pre-Fascist period for similar reasons—fears that resources in the cities were insufficient to cope with a dramatically increased population, fear of a potentially radical and disruptive urban working class, and a desire to retain traditional and stable relations in the countryside—but only under Fascism did the government institute laws to impede migration to the cities.[47] The first major effort provided for a permanent committee to regulate internal migration, which later became a Commission reporting directly to Mussolini. In 1928 the state charged prefects with controlling the influx of new residents, but the law lacked provisions for enforcement. A second attempt in 1931 to give the Commission power to enforce migration regulations ended up with the

*Like the rest of the industrialized world, Italy was experiencing a slight fall in the birthrate, but it still had 27 births per 1,000 people, a rate slightly higher than that of the post-World War II "baby boom" in the United States.

†As part of the exaltation of the cult of woman-as-mother, Fascism forbade nude or semi-nude photographs of women, and even fashion layouts could not include women who were unusually thin, for they represented the "sterile" women of the western world. Cannistraro, *La fabbrica del consenso*, 89.

Commission supervising seasonal migration and temporary employment on public works. Only in 1939 did the state institute a law which stood any chance of being effective.[48] Tying employment to residency and residency to employment seemed a promising means of interrupting migration, but the outbreak of war curtailed its effective enforcement.

Weak as the early juridical provisions were, the press waged a vigorous campaign to keep Italians on the farm, and the Fascists found a dramatic and easily exploitable point of convergent interests in the reclamation and settlement of the Agro Pontino: in addition to the obvious aim of clearing the marshes, the project would also help reduce unemployment and make more land available for subsequent cultivation, as well as serving as a model for the Fascist town. In actuality, the reclamation projects only modestly reduced unemployment; in 1933, for example, with 679,279 unemployed in building and agriculture, only 51,258 people—approximately one-thirteenth of the unemployed—worked on reclamation projects. Indeed, of all the land subject to reclamation, only a small part actually reached the point of being tilled.[49]

Land reform was an old rallying cry in Italy, dating back to government promises of change after unification, although the promised reforms were never implemented. In the ensuing decades, millions of Italians emigrated to North and South America for the express purpose of earning enough money to return to Italy and purchase land in their home provinces. Some managed to do so, but many more did not.[50] During World War I, the absurdity of fighting only to return as sharecroppers or day laborers encouraged among the soldiers an increasingly relaxed attitude toward fighting—or so the government believed. The government and Socialist organizations quickly exploited the idea of redistributing the land. The reform-minded Senator Leonida Bissolati promoted a plan that would have made each soldier a small-scale capitalist landowner, while the Socialists argued for a "socialist socialization" of the land, with cultivation by farmers in associations.[51] The liveliest demand for land reform came from the provinces of Venice, Tuscany, and Romagna, but farmers and veterans throughout the peninsula and in Sicily restlessly awaited the promised redistribution.[52]

Much of the credit for the success of Fascism in rural northern Italy goes to the Fascist land program, for the Fascists, unlike the Socialists, promised to place individuals on their own plots of land. Even in heavily Socialist areas such as Ferrara, once the outlines of Mussolini's agrarian policy became known sharecroppers and day laborers abandoned the Socialists and joined the Fascist party in 1920 and 1921.[53] This shrewd maneuver, engineered in large measure by Fascist party members who were also large landholders, took account of the fact that the fiercest opposition to Socialism came precisely from landowners, even those with only tiny plots; by the same reasoning, the more small landholders there were, the less likely became any kind of Red revolution. Farmers had supported the Socialists only when there appeared to be no other alternative for combating the power of large landowners, but what they really wanted was exactly what Fascism promised to give them: their own land. Once they had a stake in society, the Fascists reasoned, they would be likely to offer strong opposition to any attempt to turn back their gains. But as in America, the Fascist government chose to do more than redistribute land: both the American and the Italian programs envisioned establishing new communities with social and political goals well beyond pragmatic economic concerns.

The agency chosen to be responsible for the undertaking in the Agro Pontino was the ONC, a creature of the war years established in order to assist demobilized soldiers.[54] At its foundation in 1917, it had received an unclear mandate to "help veterans." After lengthy parliamentary battles over whether the ONC should be concerned with all veterans or with farmers only, in 1918 its role received more precise definition when Minister of the Treasury F. Saverio Nitti convened a commission to elaborate the precise responsibilities of the ONC. It was to give specific aid to veterans wishing to farm, assisting them with finances and instruction in cultivation; along with the government, it was to see to the distribution of the land "a chi la lavora" (to the one who works it).[55]

Despite what appeared to be very broad powers, when the former soldiers began returning home after the war the ONC had made no concrete moves in the direction of land distribution. Subsequent Fascist accounts claimed that veterans simply requisitioned land where they could, and spontaneously organized themselves into agricultural cooperatives. The ONC encouraged these groups at first, but soon shifted to a more conservative approach and tried to evaluate the veterans' "sincerity," since the ONC aimed primarily to ensure land distribution to small farmers rather than to the politically suspect cooperatives. Even before it became a Fascist agency, then, the ONC was promoting policies congenial to Fascism, policies which the party later exploited more emphatically: anti-urbanism and anti-cooperativism.

The ONC floundered along for several years until under the aegis of the Fascist party in 1926 it changed from an agency that gave modest assistance to the immediate claims of the demobilized soldiers to the first large state structure for the agrarian transformation undertaken by the Fascist regime. Only a few months after the March on Rome, the event that inaugurated Fascist rule in Italy, Mussolini ordered the removal of all of the ONC officials and a complete inquiry into the activities of the organization. The results of this inquiry indicated that for all practical purposes the ONC had become totally removed from the veterans; it did not serve their interests and in some instances actually hindered them.[56] These conclusions may well have been self-serving claims in order to gain the tactical advantage of control over the veterans; the record is not clear, but such a move would certainly have been a wise one if Mussolini wanted to ensure that his party remained in power.

As finally spelled out in 1926, the task of the ONC was to

> promote the growth of agricultural colonies and new living centers, bringing veterans there—especially those who were farmers. The importance of this task is obvious: only with the formation of new living centers will it be possible to resolve a grave problem of hygiene and morale: to clear out overcrowded areas, especially in the south [the Mezzogiorno], and to give veterans sanitary houses; and at the same time, to eliminate the damage done to agriculture by urbanization, which does not permit farmers to dedicate themselves to the land fully and to extract from the earth all that it can yield.[57]

Obviously, in choosing to invest enormous sums of money and manpower in reclaiming the Agro Pontino, constructing towns, and provisioning farms, the Fascists managed to avoid what would have been the far more nettlesome problem of seizing Church and private land. In the contemporary mythology, only bandits lived in the *palude*; therefore any expropriations by the state would only bring a better class of people to live in the area. In reality, large tracts of largely uncultivated land were owned by the Torlonia family, by the Borghese family, and by one Felice Trossi; another 30,000 hectares were owned by as many as 121 proprietors, most with only a couple of hundred hectares each. The state either expropriated or purchased this land, or else received it as a donation made, most likely, in the hope of a future quid pro quo from Mussolini. Most of the land for the various reclamation programs was expropriated, although the owners received reimbursement supposedly at the going market rate.[58]

The ONC confronted an enormous task in the Agro Pontino. Settlement demanded a complex program of reclamation and regional planning, for the swampy land had several soil types and no effective road or irrigation systems.* The activities the ONC undertook included draining the marshes, planting thousands of fruit trees and vines for individual farm plots, planting windbreaks to protect soil and farm from the murderous scirocco, conducting experiments on the different soil types with chemical fertilizers, setting up lines for electricity and telephones, conducting a campaign against malaria, preparing miles of roads, and establishing a complete irrigation network. After the massive preparatory works, the ONC also saw to building the towns and farmhouses, dividing farm plots, providing seed, animals, and mechanical equipment, and bringing in the colonists. The massive cost of these works was covered by loans to the ONC from the private bank Monte dei Paschi di Siena—at, of course, favorably low interest rates—as well as by sums from the Consorzio delle Opere Pubbliche, a state agency, which also helped repay the loans from Monte dei Paschi until crop returns allowed the ONC to take over the payments. The ONC subcontracted the construction work and the furnishing of materials to private enterprises, also at discounted rates.[59] This vast regional planning effort was only one aspect of the reclamation project in the Agro Pontino, however, for in addition to redeeming the land the ONC aimed to redeem the people—that is, to take unemployed wage-earners and artisans from the north and turn them first into share-croppers and then into small landholders.[60]

Originally the Agro Pontino colonization scheme envisioned selecting volunteer veteran families from the most crowded provinces, in what was called "disciplining" internal migration—that is to say, stemming the flood of immigrants to the industrial centers. On 15 November 1930, Mussolini presented a new law to the Chamber of Deputies; among other things, it provided for awards to colonists who settled in the new zones for at least three years.[61] Despite promises of land and prizes, many appear to have been reluctant to move to the new colonies. One Italian recalls that his father, a successful Vicentine farmer and father of seven at the time, refused the offer to move to Littoria, and although he had difficulties with local authorities he did not have to make the move.[62] This farmer apparently was one of many, as occasional reports from prefects indicate.[63] Although theoretically the law aimed at transferring

*The reclamation in the Agro Pontino is comparable to the much larger reclamation and electrification program by the Tennessee Valley Authority in Muscle Shoals, Tennessee, which extended to another five states; or even to the reclamation program in Holland to add land for cultivation to its relatively small patrimony.

workers from overpopulated areas, a memo from the Commissioner for Migration, Luigi Razza, to the PNF Federal Secretaries in 1932 indicated that all too often men transferred only individually and temporarily for construction work, and instead of migrating to the New Towns they were traveling from Varese to Milan, Vicenza to Rome, and similar short-term migrations, while the steady flow of people from the countryside to the city continued unabated.[64]

When it became clear that quotas could not be filled by eager volunteers, the promises became more alluring and the PNF Secretaries entered the process, taking recommendations from local unions and forwarding them to Rome for approval. The ONC later protested that provincial officials found this an altogether irresistible temptation to expel from the province families thought undesirable or troublesome—socially as well as politically. Cencelli charged in 1935 that by and large the provincial selection committees either had taken anyone who knocked at their doors or had responded to local political needs, rather than selecting able and industrious families.[65] Even though the Commission on Internal Migrations supposedly conducted a rigorous application procedure for selecting families—which included giving health examinations and seeking reports from local unions as to a family's agricultural capacity and previous history—unquestionably the colonization program offered a perfect opportunity to clear from the province individuals and families with problems. As one commentator noted, it was not always possible even to choose "naturally constituted" families for migration to the Agro; "many families were constituted artificially just for the occasion."[66]

Additionally, while the law provided that farmers should be sent to the Agro, in one typical *borgo* in the Agro over 90 percent of the families were not farmers—they were drivers, fishermen, shoemakers, barbers, millers, beggars, and so forth. It is not clear whether these individuals and families even wanted to become farmers, whatever the case, this made the situation for the ONC much more difficult. Cencelli's report commented that the colonists were resistant toward "rural education," which hardly implies that they were eager agrarians. Not only did the ONC have to teach the men to farm; it even had to instruct the women in baking bread and other household arts.

Riccardo Mariani has argued that the recruitment policies favored bringing people from politically troubled provinces. Discerning a positive correlation between recruitment from the Veneto and Emilia and a high rate of indictments, convictions, and imprisonments in those provinces in 1927 and 1928 (see the adjoining table),* Mariani attributed the high percentage of Venetians and Emiliani in the New Towns to the political troubles in the two provinces; but others have disputed this. Pino Riva has pointed out that in fact Lombardy and Tuscany were underrepresented in the colonization program, though they had higher proportional

Home Provinces of Colonists in the Agro Pontino (1934)

Province	Number of families	Percentage
Ferrara	467	18.1
Treviso	316	12.3
Udine	311	12.1
Padua	273	10.6
Littoria	245	9.5
Rovigo	233	9.0
Vicenza	227	8.8
Verona	215	8.4
Veneto	107	4.2
Rome	66	2.6
Reggio Emilia	34	1.3
Modena	29	1.1
Belluno	25	1.0
Other provinces	26	1.0
	2,574	100.0

Population of the Agro Pontino 1932–37[a]

Year	Population
1932	5,200
1933	15,700
1934	19,300
1935	23,200
1936	24,700
1937	25,850

*See Mariani, *Fascismo e città nuove*, 122. The term "Veneto" is used here to embrace Friuli, Venezia-Giulia, and Venezia (often referred to as "the three Venetos").

[a]Colonists and families only; does not include town residents, administrators, or day laborers working on reclamation and building projects.
[Source: Alemanni, "La conquista rurale," in ONC, *L'Agro Pontino*, 821]

rates of indictments per capita than the Veneto and Emilia.[67] He argues instead that what led the ONC to favor colonists from the latter regions was the high unemployment rates there, coupled with the belief that Venetians had a "natural immunity" to the malaria* endemic to the Pontine marshes. Logic alone also suggests that the state and the ONC would not want anything but enthusiastic settlers in the new communities.

So the colonists came to the Agro, some under duress or threat of punishment, some drawn simply by the prospect of owning their own land and being set up as farmers. In September and October of each year, families with their belongings loaded into trains destined for the Agro Pontino. Immediately upon arrival they received food for the first day's meal and set off for their assigned houses. The new dwellings were one- or two-story single-family residences whose indoor floor areas ranged from 128 to 213 square meters, with four or five bedrooms upstairs, and kitchen, storeroom, and stables for cows and horses downstairs; they were constructed of brick and local calcareous and tufaceous rock, with lime and pozzuolana for mortar, and with chestnut framing and fixtures. Since all materials with the exception of some fixtures were local—including the tile roofing—the farmhouses followed local vernacular traditions in appearance and size [Fig. 2.8]. All told, the ONC built eighteen types of houses (since each type could have either pitched roof or terrace, there were actually thirty-six possible varieties) with variations in materials, in color, or in placement of the staircase (external or internal) so as to avoid tedious uniformity. Since the houses were well spaced and separated by fields and trees, there was little danger of monotony in any case, except from one feature: each house had the words "Opera Nazionale Combattenti" and "Podere [Plot] No. ———" emblazoned over the doorway in large and eminently visible letters. Even though they were someday to become the property of the colonists, the overwhelming impression they gave was that of being government property. The letters are still visible today—nearly fifty years later—on many of the houses.

Although spacious, the houses were hardly the last word in modern living. All had outdoor toilets but no running water, and most lacked sinks and other sanitation facilities. Wood-burning stoves served for cooking. There is also some question about the quality of construction. Mussolini wrote to Serpieri in March 1933 to indicate his displeasure at the news from a group of northern Italian engineers that the colonists' houses were far from solid; the wood in particular was poorly seasoned

*Cencelli commented (in his report: cf. note 65) that the fundamental notion underlying the colonization of the Agro Pontino was to bring a large nucleus of colonists from the Veneto and Emilia. Settlers came exclusively from the north, although during the same years southerners were fleeing the depressed south to seek industrial employment in the north.

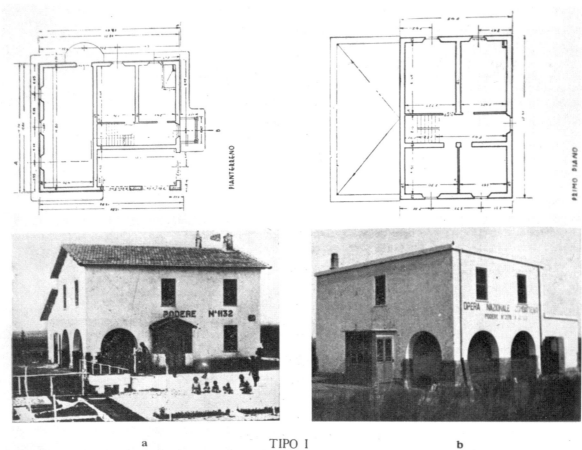

a TIPO I b

Numero vani 5 – Numero « poste » della stalla 10 – Superficie coperta mq. 200 – Cubatura mc. 1132.

2.8 Agro Pontino, Housing Type I (from *L'Agro Pontino*, 1938). This two-story, 200-square-meter farmhouse included five rooms and came with either a pitched tile roof or a flat roof.

and even unsound. Serpieri agreed that the engineers' observations were correct, but argued that these were niggling concerns, given the high value of other aspects of the project.[68]

In addition to the chicken coop and shed, newcomers also received whatever farm implements they had not brought with them on their trip. To Cencelli's dismay, more often than not they had nothing; but since 90 percent had not been farmers before arriving, this should have come as no surprise. At a minimum, the ONC provided each colonist family with a cart, two animal-drawn plows, and a scraper, a fodder-cutter, and two harrows. The colonists could also borrow (with proper supervision) some of the ONC's equipment, including 165 tractors and 1,452 farm implements of various types. The settlers did not receive their tools gratis, however: each colonist had a *libretto* (account book) in which all credits and debits were entered. The first debits began to mount even before they arrived: the cost of the train trip, the first day's meal, each item meticulously entered in the *libretto*. Since the colonist also received animals upon arrival—chickens, pigs, and rabbits especially—these too were charged to his account. Cows and mules, although stabled with the colonists, remained the property of the ONC, and the colonist and the ONC shared equally the interest and losses. Colonists bore charges for their tools through government loans because, in the logic of the ONC, "it was thought appropriate that through his own work and productive capacity the colonist would begin to develop the first nucleus of property which would at least be represented by his work implements."[69]

Since they had to wait several months before new crops could be harvested, the settlers received a twice-monthly allotment of flour and cornmeal, based on family size, as well as a minimal cash advance for those necessities which they could not produce. In effect, the settlers lived as *mezzadrie* (sharecroppers), except that now the landlord was the ONC. What the reclamation effort would need most was manpower, it was argued, so the colonists—who had no capital but their own labor—ought to bear the burden of starting up the operation. Since the land would be theirs someday, it seemed obvious to the ONC that the only reasonable contractual relationship was that of sharecropping.[70] Apparently the settlers did not like these arrangements, because Mussolini asked Cencelli to see to it that rather than having the colonists receive their seed and meal allotments in small portions they should receive their full quota for the year. Cencelli responded that he had already attempted something similar, only to find that as well as selling the flour and cornmeal colonists were even selling the seeds. Cencelli proposed a compromise whereby settlers would receive a six-month ration (which would also relieve the chronic storage problem), and those who did not sell it would receive a new allotment at the appointed time; those who had not been so thrifty would return to the semi-monthly system.[71]

Especially in the early years, administrators were not particularly happy with the people they received in the Agro; Cencelli observed that as soon as they had a little money they spent it on drink and other wasteful pastimes. They did not have the mentality of true farmers, let alone sharecroppers, Cencelli believed, and they did not realize the virtue of saving scrupulously for the future. Characterizing them as indolent and incapable, Cencelli remarked that even monetary awards failed to spur many of the families to tend their gardens, keep their animals well, and care for their land. Although the vegetable garden should have supplied many of the colonists' nutritional requirements, of 1,900 families in 1934 only two or three hundred cultivated their gardens, despite the provision of free seeds from a Venetian firm.[72]

The ONC quite openly declared that it sought to develop a sharecropper mentality in the colonists. Had they been sharecroppers previously, there would have been no problem. Instead, most colonists had been wage-earners accustomed to having money to spend, and therefore cash remained a problem on the farms. Each family received a total cash allowance of 50 *lire* weekly, regardless of family size, so the desire to acquire funds is not surprising.* In Cencelli's survey of early 1933, only 60 families said they were satisfied with the sum; the remaining 395 families requested increases of from 10 to 100 *lire* per week.[73] Except for such items as shoes, household utensils, oil, wine, and cigarettes, the economy in the Agro was to be essentially a barter economy with as little cash as possible. Vegetable gardens on the plot as well as the animals would provide the essential foodstuffs, and the small cash allotment the balance. But the families were unhappy with this arrangement, and within a few months after the first settlements Cencelli reported that he had forbidden the colonists to leave their farms because they persisted in going out to work as day laborers elsewhere in the Agro, "running after today's wages rather than being concerned with tomorrow, which is and will be on the land readied by the ONC."[74] Eventually each colonist and workman received a *lasciapassare per l'interno*, or internal pass, and failure to carry it or to abide by the provisions of remaining in the area constituted grounds for eviction or repatriation to their former homes.[75]

But even these controls failed to quell the discontent, so finally in 1935 the ONC developed a new contract with the colonists. It called for a guaranteed minimum annual cash income of 1,500 *lire* per family in addition to earnings from poultry, milk cows, garden and fruit trees, and prizes for farm production. Since under the earlier arrangement the weekly payment by the ONC had been reduced by whatever each colonist earned from his agricultural work, the new regulations promised a significant increase in family income.[76] Without revealing the magnitude of the discontent, the ONC granted the new pact with great fanfare, referring to the insufficiency of cash earnings on the farms yet expressing the authorities' reluctance to provide "subventions prejudicial to the healthy spirit of parsimony in the colonist and to the consolidation of the family-farmstead relationship."[77] At the same time, the ONC took pains to affirm

*In 1933, a day laborer in agriculture might earn an average of 100 *lire* per week for six days' work; on the other hand, a typesetter would earn 40 *lire* per day, a mason 29 *lire* per day, and a bus driver 29 *lire* per day. See ISTAT (Istituto Centrale di Statistica del Regno d'Italia), *Annuario Statistico Italiano 1934—XII*, Series 4, 1 (Rome, 1935), 148–49.

that such arrangements would be neither necessary nor desirable in areas where there was a longstanding tradition of sharecropping—no doubt to forestall possible requests for cash allowances by sharecroppers elsewhere. Indeed, Alemanni warned of the dire consequences which would surely befall any efforts to implement the Agro system elsewhere.[78]

Not unexpectedly, the earliest years were also the most difficult. Despite a good harvest in the summer of 1933, the ONC claimed that colonists seemed uninterested in becoming good farmers. The only available assessments are those prepared by the ONC, and while they can hardly be called impartial, even these records suggest a high level of discontent in the Agro. Strikes were unheard of—and illegal—in Fascist Italy; nonetheless colonists in the Agro several times refused to work, in protest against irregular payments and deductions from their wages.[79] Far more common than strikes, which carried the risk of imprisonment, were thefts, sabotage, slowdowns, and absenteeism. Within the first few months of the settlement of Littoria, twenty-six families left; most of these families chose to go because they disliked the program, but five were evicted for being "troublemakers."[80] The eviction process accelerated over the next three years, with more than a hundred families being repatriated for failing to comply with ONC regulations. By October 1938, discontent had grown so acute that 26,000 colonists and laborers reportedly threatened a total shutdown if their demands for cash paid promptly and in full were not met. Their leader was a *sindicalista* named Baraldi, an official representative of the Confederazione Fascista di Agricoltori, whom the ONC described as a demagogue highly popular among the colonists and laborers.[81]

The affair was hushed up and some demands were temporarily met, but the incident unveiled widespread discontent. Mussolini saw the dismal state into which many farms and even the canals and infrastructures had fallen by 1938.[82] The Prefect of Rome could not hide his dismay at what he found during a visit to Pomezia in 1940. He noted a heavy feeling of misery everywhere; some houses lacked furniture, including beds, and everywhere colonists complained that they lacked shoes, clothes, or linens. An expenditure of 1,700 *lire* per family, he calculated, could obtain the necessities and overcome the most severe problems. Some of the colonists, brought back to the motherland from France and Yugoslavia, had arrived with no provisions; but the ONC insisted, in response to these charges, that the requisite items were already in place when the colonists arrived.[83]

Several agencies notified the Presidenza del Consiglio Ministeri that the colonists lived in a state of abject misery; they charged that the ONC and the agricultural experts had extracted taxes, duties, and fees, leaving the families with nothing to eat.[84] Moreover, Luigi Razza charged that the ONC treated colonists without understanding and with excessive attention to formal discipline (and claimed that only the attentive care of the Commission for Migration—which he headed—kept them docile).[85]

It is difficult to sort out the truth in these accounts, for tension certainly existed between the ONC and the Commission for Migration: the ONC accused the Commission of sending the worst-equipped and least-prepared families to the Agro, while the Commission insisted that the ONC treated them poorly once they arrived. There was probably a good deal of truth in both sets of charges; even the ONC's own publications remarked on the need to be patient with the colonists and not to burden them with debts from which they could free themselves only with difficulty.[86] But the ONC also repeatedly made it clear that the colonist was not in charge of the farm—the ONC was. Just as the owner had to be the boss in the traditional landlord-sharecropper relationship, so too should the sharecropping colonist yield to the greater experience and authority of the ONC. The ONC specifically renounced the idea that the colonists should be left free to tend to the farms themselves; it might be true that the worst problems historically befell owners who left the initiative to the sharecropper, but in any case that the owner should be in charge was a "question of hierarchy, a question of principle."[87] Given this attitude on the part of the ONC, it is not difficult to imagine both the reluctance of the colonists to comply with orders and their hostility toward the ONC agents.

Frequently colonists insisted on repatriation to their former provinces, and the ONC compiled narratives about the way such malcontents had maintained their plots and cared for their materials and animals. Normally the evaluation did not flatter the colonist, stressing their laziness, lax morality, marital discord, and lack of cooperation. The reports must be read with caution, however, for they never reflected poorly on the ONC; nonetheless, they suggest the degree to which some colonists attempted to evade the agrarian life into which they were thrust.[88] Some men refused to work because farming was not their occupation, and others seemed to have little desire to work so hard for so little reward. No independent verification of the ONC's evaluations is possible, but some colonists did work hard and cared about their land,* while still

*An increase in agricultural productivity during the pre-war years does indicate that some people were working.

protesting their treatment and the failure of the ONC to make good on earlier promises. In an articulate and well-conceived letter, the colonists of Borgo Hermada protested the treatment which they had received since their arrival in February 1935. They compared their condition to that of other colonists in the Agro: as far as they could tell from reports coming from members of one family that had transferred to another *borgo*, conditions were better elsewhere. They declared their willingness to work, their willingness to leave good conditions in the north, and their complete loyalty to Mussolini; but they could not continue to live with insufficient foodstuffs and inhumane treatment by the agency.[89]

Both the ONC and the Commission for Migration were responsible for putting severe constraints on the free movement of colonists and of day laborers in the reclamation program. In addition to requiring passes for movement within the Agro, the ONC forbade laborers to enter farm houses. There were no women in the Agro except among farm families, and after a thirteen-year-old girl attempted a self-induced abortion the ONC insisted that it was important to safeguard colonists from the laborers. Whatever the reason for the restriction, it obviously also kept the farmers and their families isolated from laborers and another potential source of unrest.[90] The Commission also limited the movement of laborers by keeping them under the armed guard of the Milizia Volontaria della Sicurezza Nazionale (MVSN) from dusk to dawn (ostensibly to control them during the hours of greatest malaria risk), and the MVSN was also responsible for ensuring that workers maintained discipline and kept domitories and kitchens clean.[91]

Although the tactics employed by the Mussolini administration may appear to be uniquely characteristic of twentieth-century governments, a longer historical perspective affords a different picture. In many cases throughout history, when the community agreed to provide shelter for indigents, the quid pro quo was that the recipients had to abide by certain rules. In fifteenth-century Venice, widows and children housed in La Marinarezza di Corte Colonna (welfare housing for widows of sailors) had to stay indoors from dusk to dawn.[92] City-operated shelters for the poor elsewhere in Europe enforced the same kinds of rules.

Nor should the popular image of Fascism permit the assumption that the curtailment of individual liberty and authoritarian control have been, even in the twentieth century, a special feature of totalitarian states. The Resettlement Administration in the United States also exercised controls and posted guards on occasion. At Jersey Homesteads, one of the early

New Deal communities, guards were posted and journalists and visitors excluded after several expensive and widely publicized failures in experimental housing. Embarrassed by the cost and by the unresolved problems with construction methods for prefabricated housing, the Resettlement Administration did not want to provide fuel for more controversy.[93] Through home visits and elaborate reporting procedures, the Resettlement Administration also controlled the behavior of its clients on the subsistence homesteads. Those who sought aid at New Deal transient camps found their movements restricted by numerous regulations and by guards, some of them armed with billy-clubs.[94] The notion in New Deal America that recipients of government largess should at least be required to work is (as we shall see) an extension of the same principle: when the community agreed to provide for its poor, it generally exacted a price.

Despite unrest and periodic repatriations, it appears that after the first difficult years in the Agro Pontino farm production did increase. Initially the ONC emphasized cereal cultivation for use on the farm; in the first year 480 farm plots produced only 2,714 quintals* of grains (wheat, corn, and other cereals), and in 1933 only 200 quintals of sugar beets. By 1937, however, grain production on 2,574 farms soared to 118,000 quintals, and sugar beets to 191,000 (sugar beets were planted on only about 4 percent of the land).[95] Other crops included hemp and flax, as well as fodder for farm animals in the Agro. On paper the "social experiment" in farming seemed successful, but the social costs of this increase in production may have been considerable. Certainly the colonists knew that they had to produce to survive, and if the ONC repatriated them they lost their entire investment in labor and anything they had earned toward the purchase of their farms. Wherever the problems were most severe, the ONC regularly blamed it on the colonists' lack of industry and the fact they lacked the proper sharecropper mentality. This may well have been true of some of the families; but fully half of the newly reclaimed marshland was of average or below-average quality, so farmers accustomed to the rich land of northern Italy and those unfamiliar with farming at all found themselves facing an extraordinarily difficult and no doubt discouraging task.[96]

The programs in Italy and America for farm families were strikingly similar—even to the submarginal quality of the land distributed to colonists—but one distinctive feature of the Italian New Towns was that the ONC so emphasized ruralism that it would not permit farmers to work off the farm except on communal enterprises such as reinforcing irrigation

*One quintal = 100 kilograms or about 220.46 lbs.

canals. The ONC believed this was important both to ensure that the new farmers would tend their land and to promote their families' attachment to the land. If farmers were working elsewhere in the Agro, it meant either that they did not earn enough on the land or that they disliked it; either admission would have put a severe crimp in Fascist propaganda extolling agrarian life. Americans, by contrast, were encouraged to seek employment off of the farm and to look on their homesteads as places where they could provide part but not all of their annual food requirements.

Since the ONC's goals involved the redemption of both the land and the people, the colonists could not simply be left alone to farm their land. The PNF recruited zealously among the colonists (11,150 members were enrolled by 1937), good membership statistics being an important index of the New Towns' Fascist character. And, since the state exercised virtually complete control in these new communities, unencumbered by the longstanding associational and community traditions found in older towns, the imperatives of the Fascist image required demonstrations that people were involved with the party. The control the state exercised through the ONC extended to the colonists' cash allowances, and although concrete evidence is lacking one may suspect that some of the payroll deductions colonists complained about were party dues and other special contributions. If the ONC automatically deducted such fees, this would account for the exceptionally high membership statistics it claimed in these areas.

The Opera Nazionale Balilla (ONB) also enrolled 100 percent of the children in the Agro; this, like the suspiciously high PNF figures, suggests that membership may have been obligatory, even automatic. In return for their support, the PNF provided the farmers with mass demonstrations for Fascist holidays, summer colonies for the children, financial and other types of assistance, ceremonies in honor of the thirty colonists who died in Ethiopia, and a variety of exhibits and conferences. Membership in the OND was also suspiciously high (9,200 in 1937), but understandable in light of the rewards: enrollees had access to libraries (one in each *borgo* and sometimes several in the cities), courses in agriculture and auto mechanics, trips to Rome for special Saturday theatrical performances, musical groups, and—for forty-five lucky families—radios.

Even while the colonists were settling into their new houses, day laborers from throughout Italy continued the process of land reclamation that underlay the entire community building program in the Agro Pontino. All major public building projects in Italy provided employment to similarly large groups of men, both single and married, although married men had to leave their families in order to work in the government enterprises. In the Agro Pontino, metal and wood dormitories for five hundred inhabitants, demountable and fireproof, housed groups of up to four thousand workers in each of the reclamation areas. Electric lights and running water served all of the dormitories, where the workers slept behind closed doors under the watchful eyes of guards. Even in the hottest weather, the guards made sure that (for health reasons that were never entirely clear) the workers did not commit the error of trying to sleep outside. Those found out of the dormitories were quickly conducted back inside. A barbed-wire fence usually encircled the entire complex.

The operation of the dormitories, including preparing meals and cleaning, was contracted out to a private company. Each unit was disinfected every day. For meals, workers received coffee and bread in the morning; a hot soup or pasta, meat, wine, and bread at lunch; and soup or pasta, wine, and bread in the evening—a diet notably short on fruits and fresh vegetables.

Models for Town Planning

Despite the party's frequent denunciations of modern trends toward urbanization, the New Towns which the Fascist state built in the Agro were in fact full-fledged cities. Officials were alert to the implied contradictions, but hastened to assure observers that in fact they were more apparent than real. In defense of the cities, Ugo Todaro argued that in the first place they served the colonists themselves, who would have memories of the little shops and assistance agencies of their old homes.[97] Furthermore, these towns were not examples of urban centers in the traditional sense—poles of attraction which drew the farmer away from the country—nor was the ONC simply indulging the farmers' desire to flee to the cities by providing their equivalent in the Agro. On the contrary, Todaro insisted, the New Towns, with their ample green spaces and openness, exemplified a new "rural town planning" which contrasted dramatically with the closed, cramped, oppressive cities of old. In these new centers, colonists would have access to modern comforts without having to abandon the rural environment.[98]

"Rural town planning" in the Agro came in two sizes: tiny hamlets and larger towns. The hamlets (*borghi*) initially were merely supply centers and command posts for one hundred farms each, consisting of a pharmacy, chapel, perhaps a school, an ONC office and storage for supplies and equipment. In Todaro's opinion, the conception of the *borghi* changed over time from that of a service center (Borgo Piave) to a center of life (Borgo Pasubio) equipped with a church, sports field, post office, and Casa del Fascio; the only gatherings, in effect, were those for physical exercise, prayer, or Fascist party functions, so it would seem that Todaro's was an impoverished view of a "center of life."[99]

Although some of the *borghi* were associated with the Agro Pontino reclamation, many others were not (see the Appendix); like the Resettlement Administration in the United States, the ONC oversaw an extensive resettlement program which also looked forward to the "redemption" of the new inhabitants.

Typical of such *borghi* was the hamlet of San Cesareo, about 27 km. from Rome on the via Casilina. In the ONC's view, the inhabitants had failed to exploit the rich, fertile land they occupied, so the ONC expropriated large tracts of land and distributed them in units of about one hectare each to new colonists. For 100 *lire* rent, colonists were given four years to establish a vineyard, plant olive trees, and fix up the property; if they proved industrious, they then received a sale contract with a low-interest mortgage, much as Resettlement tenants did in the U.S. The ONC saw to the construction of the little hamlet, initially building sixty houses for 115 families but ultimately distributing land to 700 families. The four- to six-room houses enjoyed running water and electricity in addition to service structures such as chicken coops. The hamlet's center, comparable to the minimal centers of the United States Greenbelt towns, included an elementary school and a nursery school, carabinieri barracks, post office, church, and some housing for the personnel of the various institutions. Since the Case del Fascio were to take on typological form only after 1932, they did not appear in the ONC *borghi* until well into the 1930s.

Although the issue here was not land reclamation, the ONC did identify the most "urgent and serious problem" as that of the "social redemption and reclamation" of the inhabitants.[100] Labor on the land carried with it associations with a purer, more loyal populace. Although most of the *borghi* were constructed during Mussolini's rule, the ONC began establishing San Cesareo in 1920 with "redemption" of the colonists high on the agenda. These early ONC activities, though still modest in scope, were amplified in San Cesareo over the next two decades and in subsequent *borghi* and New Towns throughout the Fascist regime, but the later Fascist programs were not inconsistent with the ONC activities launched under the premierships of Francesco Nitti (June 1919 to June 1920) and Giovanni Giolitti (June 1920 to July 1921).

The town, on the other hand, while still essentially only an administrative and service center, had to be larger and distinct from the *borghi*. All of the major government agencies had headquarters in the towns, along with banks and stores, and the people living in town had "cultural and practical needs different from those of the farmers." Apart from being service centers, towns also fulfilled a second role, a representative one; thus they had to accomplish "certain scenographic effects" and appropriately set off and enhance the public buildings. [101]

Designed to embellish the Fascist image and to weld the country together as a nation, the New Towns offer evidence of two distinct impulses at work which were also fundamental elements of Fascist ideology: they were to conserve the traditional (but appropriately purified) agrarian society and at the same time to serve as models for the future political and physical shape of Fascism, to be emulated elsewhere in Italy. The architecture and urban planning of the New Towns reveal these often conflicting aims in concrete terms.

The subsequent twelve New Towns surpassed Predappio in almost every way—size, prestige, publicity, and importance—but the programs and aims that underwent elaboration in the later towns had existed in embryonic form in Predappio. Most of the later towns were rural centers in areas where the regime was funding land-reclamation programs; of the twelve, the five in the Agro Pontino were lavishly publicized at the time and have received the bulk of the scholarly attention since then. Unlike all of the others, the New Towns of the Agro Pontino were coordinated within a larger network, with Littoria (now Latina) as the provincial capital and Sabaudia, Pontinia, Aprilia, and Pomezia its satellite centers. [102]

Although Predappio's urban plan was drawn up in 1925, building continued over the next twelve years or more, and at the hands of several different architects. Predappio's plan, apparently established by Mussolini, is crude, almost a child's image of town, with the large piazza framed by new and traditional institutions and the grand promenade from his birthplace at one end to the center of institutional power at the other. Mussolini was fully aware of such spatial relationships. In his own vast office in the Palazzo Venezia in Rome, his desk was placed on a diagonal axis from the corner door, so that the visitor both traversed the maxi-

mum distance to the seat of power and experienced the forced perspective which centered on the Duce at his desk in the cavernous room.

Ideas about buildings and institutions changed and matured throughout the two decades of Fascist rule, changes which are evident in the different buildings in Predappio.* Compare for example the massive Casa del Fascio (1937) with its flat roof, monumental stripped columns, bold streamlined curves and banding, which clearly dates from the late 1930s, with the much earlier carabinieri barracks, market, or apartment buildings with their pitched tile roofs, cornices, protruding corner balconies and *novecento* detailing [Fig. 2.9]. In the 1930s New Towns, however, planners scrapped the idea of incremental building programs in favor of coordinated schemes carried out by one architect or group of architects in a brief period, usually one year. Part of the mystique of Mussolini's Fascist state was its ability to accomplish massive projects in record-breaking time; so once the plans had been drawn up the towns had to be inaugurated one year after groundbreaking, even if workers

2.9 Corso Mussolini, Predappio, n.d. Looking from the piazza in front of the church, the Casa del Fascio is on the left and the militia barracks are to the right.

*Several designers worked on the buildings in Predappio, including Geometro Adolfo Costa (the Dopolavoro, 1935–36); Arch. Bazzani (Chiesa Sant'Antonio, 1932); Ing. Elio Danesi and Ing. Adolfo Volpi (Casa del Fascio, 1937); Arch. Cesare Valle, Balilla. Until 1928, Arch. Florestano Di Fausto was in charge of the entire building program; he designed the kindergarten, market, and slaughterhouse, and the renovation of Palazzo Varano.

*Postwar Italian scholarship attempted to dissociate modern architecture and Rationalist architects from Fascism. The exercise was ultimately futile, as I have argued elsewhere (see Ghirardo, "Italian Architects and Fascist Politics"); there is simply no gainsaying the fact that most of the best architects were dedicated Fascists. One litmus test is the date of enrollment in the PNF. Membership became obligatory (if one wanted to work) only in October 1932, and many joined then (Mario Ridolfi, Gio. Ponti, Eugenio Montuori, Antonio Carminati, Marcello Nizzoli, and Luigi Piccinato). Others had joined long before: Gino Pollini (26 March 1928), Enrico del Debbio (10 July 1923), Adalberto Libera (1 August 1926), Pietro Lingeri (4 April 1923), Lodovico Belgioioso (28 February 1928), Ettore Rossi (23 September 1922), and Giuseppe Terragni (26 April 1928). The closest contemporary parallel is the mass shift of Italian academics and intellectuals to Communism after 1968. Dedication to Fascism led many of the Rationalists to direct their energies toward convincing the state that Rationalist architecture was an ideal style to represent modern and revolutionary Fascism. No decision was ever made among the competing stylistic tendencies (this too was an aspect of Mussolini's political strategy), but the Rationalists made more impressive gains than any of their counterparts in the United States, Germany, Russia, or England. ACS PNF 572, Servizi Amministrativi, Busta 334, Fasc. 5.1, and Busta 335, Fasc. 5.1.2.

struggled round the clock and only managed to complete exteriors. Although additional housing and some minor administrative buildings usually followed, the institutional and representational core presented a spatially and architecturally unified self-contained whole. Modernists viewed such stylistic unity as a positive feature, while they frowned on the stylistic diversity of towns like Predappio; the coordinated planning of the New Towns in the 1930s can therefore be seen as a victory for the Rationalists' point of view.*

On the other hand, Rationalist stylistic idiom characterized only one New Town, the aeronautical town of Guidonia, on the outskirts of Rome near Tivoli. No doubt this was possible because Guidonia made no pretense at ruralism—the town housed the Italian Air Force, for which a sharply modern rendering of traditional motifs was appropriate. Again, Mussolini was highly conscious of these issues. Carlo Belli tells a story about seeking an audience with Mussolini for Le Corbusier about his urban proposals for Rome in the mid-1930s. But despite Belli's friendship with a highly placed member of Mussolini's staff, Mussolini rebuffed the Swiss architect and refused to see him. When Belli later sought an explanation from his friend, the staff member apologetically reported that Mussolini had asserted that Italy would be built by Italians, not foreigners.[103]

As the capital of the new province, Littoria was completely outfitted with the national and local institutions necessary for the administration of the town and the province—town hall and municipal offices, or *comune*; Casa del Fascio; post office; carabinieri headquarters; ONC headquarters; Dopolavoro; GIL; militia barracks; as well as churches, schools, hospital, cinema, and sport facilities [Fig. 2.10]. All the towns included these facilities, but on a less generous scale than at Littoria and Sabaudia.

Building locations and spatial relationships in the New Towns reveal the PNF's political and social strategies. In Predappio, for example, the church, town hall, and Casa del Fascio all shared the same monumental piazza, but this pattern changed in subsequent towns as the church was shifted to a secondary piazza, a telling indication of the PNF's expectations about the role the church could play in Italy's future: its presence was accepted, but as a decidedly subordinate element, although this is perhaps less evident in plan than in reality. From a bird's-eye view, the church usually sits at the terminus of the second or third significant street in town, and is often monumentalized by means of isolation. In Guidonia,

for example, the church sits atop a low hill and occupies the highest spot in town; in Sabaudia, the church with its elaborate mosaics and high bell tower terminates the important axis which passes the town hall and the Casa del Fascio. But the designers frequently emphasized the secondary character of this institution through subtle design strategies. Its placement on a hill in Guidonia away from all commercial and civic activity only marginalizes the church, as does the urbanistically dead space in Sabaudia. The axial approach to the church in Sabaudia is organized so that the tower of the town hall and that of the Casa del Fascio frame one's vista, but the church itself is blocked from sight by a row of trees which runs down the dead center of the axis from the Casa del Fascio to the entrance of the church's piazza.

Of the three major centers in the towns (civic, market, and church), only the piazza on which the church sits tends to be vacant. The market square is usually near but not continuous with the civic center, although hotels and some shops of various kinds usually front on the main civic

2.10 Town Hall, Littoria; Oriolo Frezzotti, architect (photo by author). The town hall initially doubled as a Casa del Fascio, so that Mussolini made his ritual appearances on this balcony.

square. The separate market square accommodates Italy's traditional open-air markets for vendors who set up demountable stands one or more days each week: these squares tend to be crowded and messy, and no doubt planners wanted to keep the urban civic core free of such undignified encumbrances.

The town hall at Sabaudia stood at the terminus of a spur on the main Rome-Littoria axial road, and at the precise center was Mussolini's balcony and the tower; across the street the Casa del Fascio, occupying the block at which the four main roads converged, sat between the *comune* and the rest of the town. Predappio, on the other hand, offered a blurred message about the respective roles of Italian institutions: the grandiose church dominated the square, and in scale and position the Casa del Fascio—far too large for the town—was clearly an attempt twelve years later to achieve the appropriate balance. In the smallest New Towns, such as Pontinia, the same structure did double duty as a *comune* and a Casa del Fascio, visual testimony to the absence of local control in towns whose fates were decided in Rome rather than in communal assemblies.

Of the towns discussed here, Littoria has the most grandiose character, appropriate to its status as provincial capital. The *mundus* at the precise point where the cross-axes intersect before the Palazzo del Comune is an immediate and highly visible reference to the Roman Empire. The other New Towns drew more self-consciously on northern and central Italian models, particularly in the arrangement of the central piazze and the variations in tower placement. To some extent, this reliance on northern typologies derived from the fact that the intended population came from the Veneto, the Romagna, Lombardy, and Ferrara. A closer connection, however, was with the medieval communes and, through them, with Roman settlements in northern and central Italy. Building *ex novo* allowed the Fascists to clean up the inevitable irregularities found in the earlier examples, but the configurational elements are clearly the same.

Two of the most notable instances of planned settlement of new towns in the Italian past are the Roman military colonies and those of the late medieval period, such as the Terrenuove of Tuscany during the late thirteenth and fourteenth centuries. The Romans began to establish their military colonies from the mid-third century B.C. onward, in the north of Italy. These military colonies—Rimini, Cesena, Faenza, Bologna, Pavia, Como, Verona, Padua—secured the northern provinces under Roman control and served as models for subsequent town planning in the western provinces of the Empire. After Caesar conquered the three Gauls (58–51

B.C.), the Romans began to build systematically in the European provinces, often establishing colonies for veterans just as the Fascists were to do two thousand years later. Such colonies included those in Provence, Lyon, and Augst, near Basel.[104]

The Roman town, like the Roman military camp, was laid out on an orthogonal grid, usually in equal quadrants divided by two axial streets and consisting of square blocks. One of the chief advantages of such a format was that it allowed for orderly future expansion and could, in addition, be readily adapted to most locations. The difference between this pattern and that which followed emerges in the layout of Piacenza and Bologna, among others, where the original Roman grid pattern is still visible, as are the wandering and far less orderly streets deflecting from the grid. Once a new colony was laid out, the Romans immediately set to work not only on the walls, gates, and water supply and drainage system, but also on the nucleus of the civic center, the forum-basilica complex. This consisted of a rectangular, porticoed piazza, with a basilica at one end and the temple at the other, an urban type evolved in northern Italy in the late republican period. Originally the forum included market activities, but as its civic and political importance grew the markets moved out to secondary locations.

Although the Romans developed a standard planning layout for their colonies, this did not confine them to a monotonous repetition of the same pattern. Roman engineers considered topography and existing structures and, especially in religious and domestic architecture, local materials and building traditions. This permitted considerable variety within the same basic plan, and reinforced Roman attempts to assimilate the locals into the Empire rather than merely to subjugate them.

The Fascists followed the pattern established by the Romans in their planning and use of local materials. The cities were laid out on modified orthogonal grids, normally with four quadrants, with a central piazza, rectangular and usually at least partially porticoed, serving as the civic center. Occasionally a project re-created the Roman military encampment to a startling degree, as in a project by Adalberto Libera for Aprilia. After the sanctions enacted by the League of Nations following the Ethiopian adventure in 1935, with the policy of autarky the Fascists relied increasingly on local materials and local building traditions, particularly in the party buildings constructed in the smaller centers. By 1940, this adherence to traditional local types had become party policy: the 1940 competition rules for typical Case del Fascio for small and medium-sized centers urged architects to consider the local traditions in their designs.[105]

From a bird's-eye view, then, the planning of the Fascist New Towns corresponded to that of the Roman military and provincial colonies; their layout and purpose mirrored that of imperial programs to a striking degree. These concepts ran counter to the regnant tendencies in European town planning, such as the Garden City concept popularized in England and even adapted to some Italian projects during the 1920s, including the Garbatella and Aniene quarters in Rome.[106] For the skyline, however, the Fascists chose not the Roman model but that of the medieval commune. There was no particular reason, especially within the vocabulary of modern architecture, to endow the Palazzi del Comune and the Case del Fascio with towers, for example, save for symbolic purposes. They rejected the form of the typical medieval city with its narrow, wandering streets; to adopt it would have made the New Towns picturesque but less functional. In effect, the Fascists erected a medieval skyline on a Roman ground plan.

The late medieval period had known two distinct planning traditions, both of which the Fascists recovered in their building programs. Medieval communes had taken up the first—laying out new towns explicitly based on the *castrum romanum*—following the practice of the Romans.[107] The towns thus established were colonial or military outposts, much as settlements had been for the Romans, although medieval examples were far closer geographically to the mother city. The placement and design of public buildings in these medieval new town plantations, as with the Terrenuove of the Tuscan communes in the late thirteenth century, repeated the configurational elements found in the communes, which engineered them into an existing city fabric.

The second element the Fascist regime recovered from the medieval past was the public buildings of the twelfth- and thirteenth-century city-republics. New political and social institutions evolved during this period, which required the construction of fixed representative structures.[108] The enlarged role of the citizenry, or the commune, gradually replaced episcopal and other authority during the eleventh and twelfth centuries. Usually a *podestà* (mayor) recruited from outside the commune acted as executive administrator on behalf of the assembly of the citizens.[109] The form of the assembly hall, Palazzo del Comune, and Palazzo del Popolo all gradually received typological definition over the twelfth to the fourteenth centuries. Although considerable variety characterized the architectural arrangements, all included a rusticated, unfenestrated tower, sometimes placed eccentrically with respect to the building, sometimes centered, and sometimes detached. The body of the building, generally of ashlar construction, often contained a loggia, a ceremonial staircase, and an assembly hall. The building itself usually stood isolated from surrounding structures.[110]

The street layout and design of piazze in the New Towns, as well as the isolation of monumental public buildings, recalled the imperial grandeur of ancient Roman prototypes. The view above ground recalled the independent communes of the late medieval period, where the local citizenry participated more or less directly in the decision-making process and a tradition evolved of autonomy and vigorous civic life.

Fascist planners reconciled these two traditions—the regularity of the *castrum romanum* and the focal position of various public buildings—by introducing various functional elements from the modern or other traditions, such as the stellar avenues in Littoria. This solution derived in part from ideal city plans of the fifteenth century, such as Filarete's design for the city of Sforzinda, adopted for military outposts only later in the sixteenth century.[111] In Pontinia, some of the institutional buildings are disposed around the central piazza, but others line the two cross-axes leading to the piazza. This placement derives from seventeenth- and eighteenth-century traditions, where the increasing number of public institutions required solutions different from the customary disposition around central piazze.

Renaissance architects had taken the basic components of medieval institutional structures and rendered them architecturally more coherent, as in Michaelangelo's reconstruction of the Campidoglio in Rome. The Fascists did much the same thing, in taking a non-hierarchical layout— the Roman *castrum* system—and superimposing upon it a medieval skyline that brought with it a markedly hierarchical order. When the project for Sabaudia was selected, a dispute erupted because the tower of the Palazzo del Comune in Sabaudia was scheduled to be higher than that of Littoria, the capital city of the province—not that anyone would notice, since they were several miles apart. But a long debate ensued until Mussolini himself had to intervene, decreeing that Sabaudia's tower should be (as originally designed) taller than that of Littoria. The fact that such a debate—echoing the medieval concern with tower heights—could arise at all only confirms the hierarchical ordering of institutional placement in New Towns.[112] Building arrangements, the division of living quarters according to social class, and the external relationship of *podere* to *borgo*, *borgo* to city, and city to Rome all expressed the Fascist policy of *gerarchia* (hierarchy).

The patterning of architectural and urban schemes after Roman models involved more than a theoretical re-creation of Roman monumentalism or the *castrum* system; Rome itself saw the superimposition of three Fascist forums onto the urban fabric as a continuation of the tradition of the imperial forums established by Julius Caesar, Augustus, Trajan, and other Roman emperors. The Foro Mussolini (now Foro Italico) celebrated physical prowess and martial arts (with, as in Littoria, the Roman *mundus* prominently gracing the central piazza); the University of Rome became the cultural and intellectual forum, its layout based upon that of the basilica; and E'42 (EUR, Esposizione Universale di Roma) would be a new governmental and administrative center for the city and the nation. Each of these urban arrangements sought to bridge the gap between the ancient empire and the modern Fascist one, primarily through the use of a revamped—but nonetheless ancient—vocabulary.

Architecture and Urban Planning in the New Towns

Mussolini announced his plan to build the first New Town in the Agro Pontino during a visit to the land reclamation project in April 1932.[113] By the end of the month, the project had been entrusted to the Roman architect Oriolo Frezzotti, and by December 1932 the first nucleus of buildings and the road network had been inaugurated. Littoria (now called Latina) was to be both the first of the Agro Pontino New Towns and the capital of the newly reclaimed province; the urban design expresses this distinction from the subsequent towns [Fig. 2.11]. The central rectangular piazza, with the Municipio and the offices of the ONC prominently lining it, gives onto four stellar avenues at the corners, with the religious center at the terminus of the north-south axis. Two orthogonal thoroughfares, broken by the central green piazza, serve as implied cross-axes in this modified radial plan, and a set of secondary roads are laid out on a grid further traversed by a series of encircling roads (*annulari*), the largest one terminating to the west with a sports facility and a low-income housing district. In a pattern repeated in all but one of the Agro Pontino New Towns, the final *annulare* closes off the city both visually and physically from the countryside. In Littoria as in Sabaudia, Pontina, Pomezia, and other new towns, the road which marks the

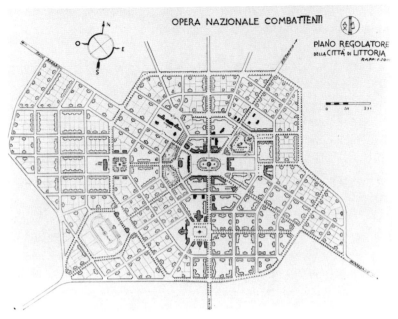

2.11 Early plan for Littoria; Oriolo Frezzotti, architect (from *Architettura*, 1933). In this plan, Frezzotti placed the town hall centered on the open piazza; subsequently it was shifted to one side, off center of the main square.

boundaries of the town also identifies the ideal size of the town; in theory it would not grow beyond this road in order to retain its character as a rural center.

To the extent that some of these features emulate traditional patterns in Italian city planning, a contemporary critic correctly pointed out that the planners of Littoria had ignored some issues addressed in congresses and conventions on town planning.[114] But just because it failed to meet the urban planning criteria established in these congresses does not mean that the planning did not refer to highly specific historical models with equally specific political intentions or, indeed, that it was unsuccessful. One of the earliest examples of such a plan is that of Filarete for the ideal city of Sforzinda, itself in turn a model after the plan of medieval Milan.[115]

Urban renewal schemes and selective renovations were undertaken by newly powerful lords in cities throughout northern and central Italy in the sixteenth century. Filarete's ideal city and his designs for the city of Milan aimed to convey the eminence and power of the city and its rulers. Sforzinda and medieval Milan, both circular in form with continuous radial axes (approximate in the case of Milan) leading to a final ring of fortifications, have centers marked by a rectilinear core surrounded by institutional buildings. In his text accompanying the design for Sforzinda, Filarete describes the construction of this imaginary city, noting the unearthing during construction of the remains of an ancient town and its legal codex; in this way Filarete metaphorically united the new site with the best of the ancient world. A later example is Giulio Savorgnan's plan for Palmanova, constructed between 1593 and 1600, with a central hexagonal piazza and radial axes leading out to the bastioned, nine-sided walls.[116] Littoria did not pretend to the grandeur of Milan, but within its own province it occupied a position of eminence and in turn conveyed the power and status of a new lord—Mussolini. The name alone underlined its significance: it derived from the Latin *lictor*, the officer in ancient Rome who carried the fasces before a magistrate. The Fascists in turn adopted the lictoral fasces as one of the chief symbols of Fascism.

The urban scheme proposed and executed by Frezzotti for Littoria embodied the medieval vision of cosmological unity based upon the circle, but in this case within a modern idiom. It also appeals to the ancient notion of planning a town within a circle with the *cardo-decumanus* (two main perpendicular streets, based on the ancient Roman N/S–E/W cross-axes) radiating out from the center to the rest of the world in the cardinal directions, although the axial roads in Littoria do not fully bisect the square. The contemporary objection that Littoria's urban plan took no account of recent developments in town planning was not entirely accurate. The best-known recent examples of a similar plan are those of the early-twentieth-century design of the town of Canberra, Australia, and indeed Raymond Unwin's New Town plans for England.[117] To be sure, in the planning stages Canberra already exceeded Littoria in size, and the designers intended to have several hexagonal centers connected by broad avenues and traversed by stellar avenues. L'Enfant's plan for Washington, DC, was another such example, although it was polycentric like Canberra. Both Canberra and Washington were national capitals, while Littoria's status as a provincial capital accounts for its more modest dimensions.

In Littoria as in several of the other New Towns, planners incorporated both an axial entrance and entrances from the flanks—the latter a typical feature of medieval Italian piazze. Andres Duany has called to my attention the fact that the general plan—orthogonal thoroughfares serving as implied cross-axes and a set of secondary roads laid out on a grid further traversed by a series of encircling roads (*annulari*)—may well derive from Unwin's *Town Planning in Practice* (1909), certainly well known in Italy by the 1930s. The proposal adopted in Littoria avoids the monotony of the endless grid and follows, in Unwin's explanation, a traditional irregularly radiating system of streets and cross streets.

The town hall, a two-story structure with trabeated *loggie* on the lower level and a centrally placed tower, still dominates the central piazza of Littoria [cf. Fig. 2.10]. The body of the building could be any office block, accommodating a variety of services and demands;* but with the massive portal and arched opening for the *arengario*, or balcony, we are reminded that the tower is to serve a unique function.[118] It is at once a symbol of power and a stage for the theatrical presentation of the Duce. The tower is emblematic of the Duce's figure standing above and isolated on the *arengario*, either in reality or symbolically through his appointed representative. The gesture of the Fascist salute—the right arm thrust out and slightly up—corresponds to the gestural function of the tower.† Such symbolism affirmed the unity of the populace and their allegiance to the Duce. The tower not only represents the ritual salute: it becomes itself the locus of memory, power, and order, an ever-present, starkly compelling backdrop for the virtual presence of the Duce. Ritual is tied to visual and collective memory in a formula so ancient that it needs no explanation. The oversized fasces that sometimes lined the Duce's speaking platform became like secondary towers, broadcasting the same message.

The tower in Littoria also boasted one of the two public clocks in town (the second was on the smaller tower of the post office one block off the main square). The medieval feat of harnessing and measuring time was often celebrated by placing the sole—and expensive—timepiece in the Torre del Comune. By the twentieth century, the clock was no longer the rarity it had been in medieval cities, but in the tower here, set above the *arengario*, it at once recalls its medieval prototype and visibly unites the passage of time with the forward march of Fascism: directly beneath it and above the *arengario* was a stylized metal fasces.[119]

Perhaps because it had been designated provincial capital, Littoria has a more urban character than the smaller centers in the Agro Pontino: in fact, the rural and agrarian themes so prominent elsewhere are absent here, in contrast to the emphatic presence of administrative and service functions (tertiary activities). On the whole, the buildings are treated as free-standing monuments in a sensitively organized urban scheme.‡

Since the entire reclamation project was consigned to the ONC so as to "promote the solution of the demographic problem, diminish unem-

*The Municipio ultimately doubled as a Casa del Fascio.

†In many towns the *arengario* was in fact cantilevered out from the building: in such cases the gestural analogy was particularly vivid.

‡The administrative buildings designed by Frezzotti for Littoria form a notably coherent group. For the offices of the ONB, Frezzotti clearly modeled his design on Aschieri's well-known Casa per i Ciechi di Guerra of 1930, in Rome.

ployment, and return to the land," the rural dwellings also warrant attention.[120] The stated aim of settling each farmer in a house on his own plot of land, clearly a more expensive venture than multi-family complexes would have been, was to ensure "a greater attachment of the farmer to the land."[121] One presumes that this specifically marked a rejection of the multi-family *fattoria* type of housing common to most sharecropper quarters. The houses are one- and two-story dwellings constructed of local pozzuolana, tufo, limestone, and brick. A *porticato* normally separated the house from the adjacent stable. The provision of three to five bedrooms for each house vividly reflects Mussolini's aspiration for a fecund population: "Mussolini wants the people to be prolific and the nation to be enlarged, because numbers are power, and where a population's birthrate is falling the people are fatally condemned to be defeated and to perish."[122] By contrast, most urban low-income housing units had only one or two bedrooms, rarely three, in infinitely more cramped quarters; the Agro Pontino homes were deliberately made more attractive than urban low-cost housing so as to tempt settlers to transfer to the Agro and raise larger families there.

Among the most interesting projects in Littoria—perhaps in all of the Agro Pontino New Towns—are the urban low-cost housing units (*case popolari*) built between 1934 and 1936 by the Istituto Autonomo per le Case Popolari of Rome and designed by Giuseppe Nicolosi [Fig. 2.12]. Initially as an employee of the IACP and later as a consultant, Nicolosi designed three phases of low-income housing for Littoria, for a total of 542 units. Low-income housing had begun to change in Rome during this

2.12 Low-income housing, Littoria; Giuseppe Nicolosi, architect (photo by author). The central courtyard is surrounded by single-loaded access corridors. These buildings, still in use as low-income housing, have been in extremely poor condition until the last few years, when some efforts have been made to improve them.

period from the large urban block to lower-density, lower-scale housing on the urban periphery, and Nicolosi's apartment buildings reflect this change. Nicolosi projected three different groups of apartment units with a total of 542 units. The first group of 190 dwellings was reserved for the lowest classes, and the second two for middle-level bureaucrats. Such neat divisions of social classes in the apartment blocks extended to apartment sizes, equipment, and construction costs (6000 *lire* per room for the first unit, 6500 per room for the other two), and correspond to the hierarchical ordering of housing and services that we find in other new towns, particularly Carbonia.

Just as Frezzotti's design for the city successfully fulfilled the compelling demand to wed modern functional needs to traditional motifs by making the urban plan grandiose, with a spacious central piazza and broad avenues, so Nicolosi wedded traditional Italian housing types to modern prototypes. As he explained in an article in *Architettura*, the Modern Movement critique of housing constantly guided him in his designs, but he also had to heed certain traditions. Consequently, telling appeals to traditional housing motifs surface occasionally, particularly the *galleria* type around a central courtyard, recalling the *fattorie* (farm complexes) of northern and central Italy.[123] Here as in his buildings in Guidonia, Nicolosi was especially effective in handling the detailing but was also successful in his planning of the ensemble. The apartments are still inhabited, and although in 1979 and 1986 they showed the effects of decades of inadequate maintenance and no attempt at landscaping, their debt to the Modern Movement and to Bauhaus prototypes is still evident.

Nonetheless, to measure the presumed historicist dimensions in Littoria or in the other New Towns solely with the yardstick of Modern Movement aesthetics would be to miss the significance of the venture. For one thing, the Modern Movement critique focused almost exclusively on housing and tended to neglect other architectural and urban issues. Littoria, however far from the tenets of the Modern Movement in many of its buildings, reveals a true planning effort within a comprehensive program, much like the comprehensiveness of Ernst May's program for Frankfurt. Quite clearly, the Fascists attempted to establish a provincial capital that could accommodate a number of functions, a center from which the agricultural efforts of the colonists could be supervised and controlled. To this end, every one hundred farm units also had a small service center with eight officials, and health and sanitation centers close

2.13 Plan of Sabaudia; Gruppo Urbanisti Romani (Gino Cancellotti, Eugenio Montuori, Luigi Piccinato, Alfredo Scalpelli), architects (from *Architettura*, 1934). The town hall sits isolated in the main square, with the church and school complex to the west and the Casa del Fascio between them.

2.14 Town Hall, Sabaudia (from *Architettura*, 1934).

by. Frezzotti's design for the city successfully fulfilled the less explicit but equally compelling demand to unite modern functional needs and traditional motifs; he accomplished this by making the urban plan grandiose, with a spacious central piazza and broad avenues, and by making the architecture sober and beautifully detailed if unadventurous. Nicolosi's low-cost housing reveals the influence of the attention accorded to the pressing problem of housing throughout Europe after World War I.[124] It is something of an irony that these rural types were used not in the countryside—where they were associated with sharecropping—but for urban low-cost housing. More coherently than the other New Towns, Littoria negotiated the difficult conjunction of the modern with the traditional in housing and urban planning.

Sabaudia is the best known of the New Towns, its urban plan widely praised by Modern Movement aficionados at the time and hotly debated even in the halls of the Italian Parliament [Fig. 2.13].[125] Visiting the town now, it is difficult to see why it was so controversial at the time, and why subsequent scholars have lavished such praise on it and not on the other towns. Sabaudia has a distinctly rural character, although it is now also a flourishing summer resort. In urban arrangement, the subsequent New Towns are patterned more after Sabaudia than after Littoria, so its urban arrangements warrant a closer look.

Sabaudia is surrounded on three sides by Lake Paola and cut off from the Mediterranean by a narrow strip of land. Two orthogonal arteries bisect the town, one connecting with two spurs of the Rome-Littoria highway, the other with a road to Terracina, and just south of the point where these two roads intersect is the Piazza della Rivoluzione, the political center of the town. The axial approach of the spur of the Rome-Littoria highway terminates precisely at the tower of the Palazzo del Comune, which stands isolated at the angle of the L-shaped piazza [Fig. 2.14]. The major political and civic institutions flanking the Piazza della Rivoluzione, moving clockwise from the Comune, are the Associazioni Combattentistiche, the Casa del Fascio-Dopolavoro-Sindacato complex, the cinema-theater, and the hotel-public office space [Fig. 2.15]. The army barracks are at the far end of the piazza, while the carabinieri headquarters are situated on the secondary axis behind the Casa del Fascio. From the town hall, one could look out either on the cross street leading to the religious center or to the Rome-Littoria spur road, or on the piazza fronting on Lake Paola.

The designers of Sabaudia's urban plan, the Gruppo Urbanisti Romani

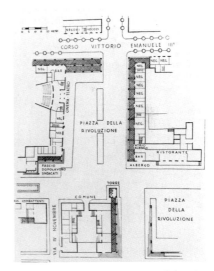

2.15 Detail plan of center, Sabaudia (from *Architettura*, 1934). The fact that the two piazze to the east and south of the town hall bear the same name reveals that the L-shaped area was conceived as a unified space incorporating the town hall as a free-standing block within it, although on site it is not perceived as such.

(GUR), artfully combined axial approaches with approaches from the flanks of piazze, the four quadrants of the center rotating around the block which housed the Casa del Fascio. The axial approach heightened the perspective and emphasized the structure at the end of the axis (in this case the town hall and Mussolini's balcony), while the approach from the flanks afforded a controlled vista whereby a particular building, such as the Casa del Fascio, could be perceived as a free-standing object without separating the buildings as awkwardly as in the piazza at Predappio. Alternatively, each building could be perceived as part of the urban ensemble from the axial thoroughfares. There are weak spots, however; urbanistically, for example, the area around the church, baptistry, convent, and school is simply dead space.

Church, convent, and nursery school constitute the religious center of town, located on a secondary axis to the west of the Casa del Fascio and Comune, with the market center to the east of the roads to Rome and Littoria. Secondary institutions such as hospitals, stadium, post office, schools, and slaughterhouse are disposed outside the central area [Fig. 2.16]. Although the road that circles the town curves gently at the northern and southern quadrants, the town is laid out on an orthogonal grid. The Casa del Fascio complex and the Palazzo del Comune are both isolated from the surrounding buildings, and although the tower of the Comune is centered on the Rome-Littoria axis, the Casa del Fascio complex occupies the symbolically significant block that results from the intersection of the four main streets in town connecting the religious and civic centers. One enters the Piazza della Rivoluzione from the flanks, but entry to the secondary Piazza Regina Margherita, the religious center, is on an axial approach.

The Piazza della Rivoluzione, with its low, porticoed buildings, constitutes the center of life in Sabaudia, but it opens on one full side to the panorama of Lake Paola and the Mediterranean, so that political gatherings could be conducted not in a closed piazza but in a spacious one facing the sea. Most of the buildings in Sabaudia are of a modest height, as one commentator noted, "recalling the line of the horizon and the tranquillity of the surrounding plains, with rare vertical elements signaling the points of major interest." The same writer, Marcello Piacentini, described the architecture as "*italianissima* . . . The form of the buildings, their mass, the prevalence of horizontal lines, the light colors, the long porticoes, the little windows well spaced in the full walls, give it a clear

Mediterranean flavor."[126] Most of the buildings have reinforced-concrete frames, and all have reinforced-concrete foundations.

Sabaudia and Guidonia afford two of the best examples of some design strategies which tend to characterize all of the New Towns. For example, within a general conception of buildings as containers and definers of space rather than as isolated objects in the landscape, the buildings hold the lines of the streets in these towns. A particularly felicitous example of this is in Guidonia, where the main street leading to, and on axis with, the Casa del Fascio is lined with housing on either side of the street. The unified blocks of housing step up the low rise to the civic center, but at either end arcaded extrusions visually and conceptually close off and define the street: it could never become an endless baroque street precisely because of this one simple maneuver. Streets in the New Towns also tend to terminate either at major buildings or in piazze, again resisting both the notion of streets which seem infinite and the modern notion of streets as thoroughfares with buildings as free-standing objects in the green

2.16 Post Office, Sabaudia, 1934; Angiolo Mazzoni, architect (photo by author). Mazzoni designed post offices throughout Italy, with a craftsmanship, imagination, and attention to detail that hold up well today. This building has a midnight-blue revetment.

space lining the streets. In most of the New Towns, the streets also help set up picturesque vistas: for example, the view in Sabaudia along the axial road leading to the church, with its three towers of different sizes and its row of trees; or the view in Guidonia from the market, centering on the tower of the Casa del Fascio with the *comune* beyond, seen through the portico to one side of the piazza. Such controlled vistas recur regularly in the New Towns and testify to a design philosophy which still favored the perception of the town and its buildings from the standpoint of the pedestrian rather than the automobile.

The town of Sabaudia is the center of an agricultural community, as are most of the other New Towns. With the exception of five hundred hectares left as woods, the entire region was divided into individual holdings of between fifteen and thirty hectares each. Radiating out from Sabaudia are little *borghi*—small centers with school, church, ONC office, post office, and pharmacy—satellite centers for the convenience of the farmers for their day-to-day needs. Most striking is the absence in the satellite centers of one of the most cherished institutions of Italian community life—the *osteria*, or bar. The omission of a place for casual group gatherings could only be deliberate. In fact, it is clear that in all respects these were closed communities: geometrically closed in the urban layout, and closed to visitors as well as new inhabitants. The layout of the cities with respect to the farmholdings kept the farmers at a safe remove from one another and from the white-collar workers in town. By creating a deliberate power vacuum, and by physically and institutionally hampering the formation of grassroots social (not to mention political) organizations, national agencies could freely exercise a greater degree of control than was possible in older communities with entrenched elites and assorted vested interests.

Building locations and spatial relationships in the New Towns reveal the PNF's political and social strategies. In Sabaudia, for example, it is the Casa del Fascio that sits at the intersection of the four main roads, even though the town hall terminates the main road. Perhaps it is to emphasize the separation of the commune from local control that the tower of the town hall stands detached from the building—something we find repeated in the Casa del Fascio at Guidonia. In Predappio, the church, town hall, and Casa del Fascio all shared the same monumental piazza, a scheme not at all untypical of Italian towns (although the Casa del Fascio was a newcomer on the block); but in other New Towns this pattern changed. The church was often shifted to a secondary piazza, a telling indication of the PNF's expectations about the role the church should play in Italy's future. In Guidonia the church is approached on a secondary axis, but the monumental civic center sits, as in Sabaudia, around the block framed by the four main streets. When Predappio was initiated in 1925, the Casa del Fascio had not yet been adopted by the PNF as its headquarters building, and it received typological definition only in 1932; but once established it edged the church out to a secondary setting except in the smallest of New Towns, such as Fertilia or Aprilia.[128]

The third of the Agro Pontino New Towns, Pontinia, is also the smallest and the most modest in plan and architecture [Fig. 2.17].[127] Its boundaries are formed by roads leading to the other Agro Pontino towns,

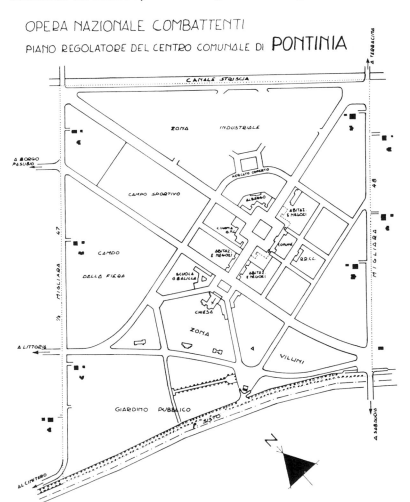

2.17 Plan for Pontinia; Alfredo Pappalardo, architect (from *Rassegna d'Architettura*, 1934). The smallest of the Agro Pontino New Towns remains the least developed today. All pretense of a distinction between the town hall and the Casa del Fascio is dropped here, as the same building does double duty.

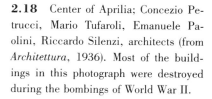

2.18 Center of Aprilia; Concezio Petrucci, Mario Tufaroli, Emanuele Paolini, Riccardo Silenzi, architects (from *Architettura*, 1936). Most of the buildings in this photograph were destroyed during the bombings of World War II.

and within the square only three major thoroughfares traverse the city. The civic and administrative center, Piazza 28 Ottobre, sits at the right angle formed by the intersection of Viale del Re and Viale del Duce; this latter road in turn continues and terminates at the religious and educational center to the west, also traversed by the third major road. All of the essential institutional buildings are present as two-story trabeated structures, but the avowed aim of the town was for "everything to breathe . . . a simple rustic air."[129] In fact, the plan is very nearly as simple as that of Predappio; the approach to both piazze is axial, the one terminating at the church and the other at the centrally placed tower of the town hall, which also served as the Casa del Fascio.

For the construction of Aprilia, the ONC announced another competition, again giving participants the charge of minimizing urban features in favor of rural ambience.[130] The winning entry was that of a group of Roman architects, Petrucci, Tufaroli, Paolini, and Silenzi, who also later won the commission for Pomezia [Fig. 2.18]. Once again the town is conceived as a closed corporate entity, roughly rectangular with curving roads at the corners. The institutional center, slightly displaced to the west, places the Casa del Fascio and the church in direct confrontation with one another, perhaps in ironic acknowledgment of their historical confrontation and their parallel hierarchical structures. The Palazzo del Comune, with its full complement of heraldic elements, is at a double remove from its historic predecessor; it received a Fascist gloss not so as to serve as a Casa del Fascio, but because it represented the last vestiges of popular rule.

The difficulty of transportation to town seems to have been designed to discourage farmers and their families from using the towns as social and cultural centers. The rural *borghi* also offered no convenient place for socializing—although they did provide offices for the local arm of the ONC as a ready resource for farmers and as a convenient supervision post. In the conventional Fascist view, cities and their gathering places had deleterious effects on people, and only rural and isolated settings promoted healthy individuals and families [Fig. 2.19]. As one architect remarked, "Only a living and regenerated countryside is capable of regulating urbanism and containing it within the limits demanded by healthy necessities . . . this is a natural law."[131] In this respect, the planning for the New Towns shared some of the basic conceptions of Ebenezer Howard's Garden Cities which, despite their de-institutionalizing emphasis, nonetheless acknowledged industrialism as a condition that was here to stay; but in the cities of the Agro Pontino the Fascist state demonstrated its distrust of urbanization and its belief in the agrarian life by failing to provide for industrial development in the plans. Ironically, several of the communities have nevertheless become centers of small manufacturing and light industry; Pomezia and Aprilia in particular, directly in the path of the industrial sprawl south of Rome, have become such centers.

Despite the distrust of industrialism, the Fascist state was solidly aligned with modern industry in Italy and needed modern industry in order to create an empire. In the realm of town planning, this led to the founding of two "coal towns," one in Arsia (Istria) in 1937, and the other, Carbonia, in Sardinia in 1938 [Fig. 2.20]; and also to the establishment of a town designed to serve as Italy's principal aviation training center, Guidonia [Figs. 2.21 and 2.22]. With the exception of Pomezia, all of the agricultural towns were under way before 1936, and the industrial towns were all founded during or after 1936; but despite this apparent shift in policy, Mussolini sought to unite the newer industrial ventures with the old agrarian policies. In his address at the inauguration of Guidonia, he remarked that "so the workers in the field can make the land increasingly fertile, vigilance and protection must be in the skies of the homeland. Italian aviators have provided this in the past and will do so in the future."[132]

The impetus to encourage industrial enterprises coincided with Italy's imperial adventures in Africa and the enactment of economic sanctions by the League of Nations; and coal was in any case one of the most important ingredients for industrial growth in Italy. In February 1935, Mus-

2.19 Cover illustration, *L'Agro Pontino*, 1938. The magazine reported on events and progress in the Agro Pontino; the line at the top proudly draws a parallel between the founding of Aprilia ("25 April, year XIV of the Fascist Era") and that of ancient Rome ("Rome, 753 B.C.").

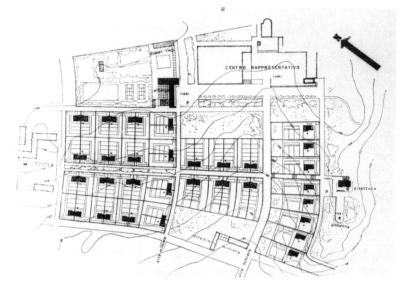

2.20 Plan of town center, Carbonia; Giorgio Calza-Bini, Gino Cancellotti, Giuseppe Nicolosi, architects (from *Architettura*, 1940). The director's quarters sit to the far right, close to the town center but well separated from the apartments for miners.

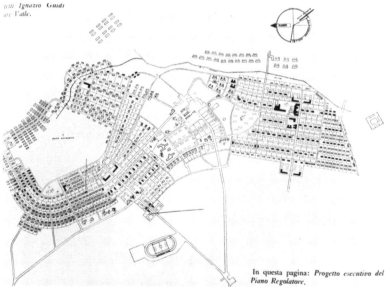

2.21 General plan of Carbonia (from *Architettura*, 1940). The plan is profoundly hierarchical, with housing for officials separated into zones quite distinct from the zones of working-class housing; note also the three separate access roads to the mines.

*The low-grade coal that the New Towns were to produce proved in the end inadequate to support Fascist military ambitions, and Italy's coal imports grew steadily during the 1930s despite foreign sanctions. See the figures in ISTAT, *Annuario . . . 1935*, Series 4, 2 (1936), 87*, and *Annuario . . . 1939*, Series 4, 6 (1940), 119*.

solini announced that although the country would need to import coal during peacetime, it could gain self-sufficiency (autarky) in supplies of low-grade coal for wartime activities.* This statement (whose obvious inconsistency does not seem to have caused concern) was part of a larger propaganda campaign to assure Italians that Italy's low economic position with respect to the rest of the industrial world was now a thing of the past.[133]

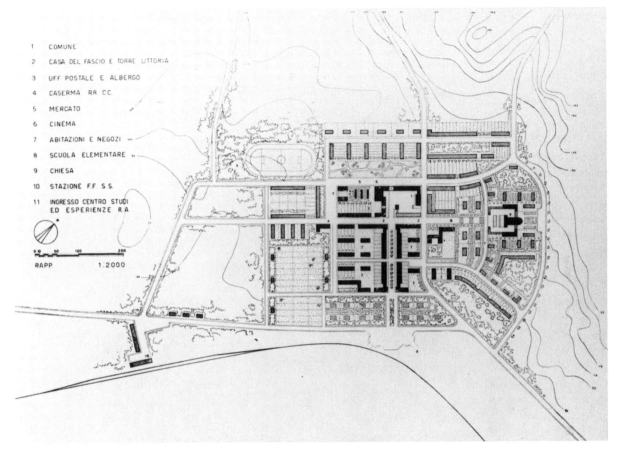

1   COMUNE

2   CASA DEL FASCIO E TORRE LITTORIA

3   UFF POSTALE E ALBERGO

4   CASERMA RR CC.

5   MERCATO

6   CINEMA

7   ABITAZIONI E NEGOZI

8   SCUOLA ELEMENTARE

9   CHIESA

10 STAZIONE F.F. S.S.

11 INGRESSO CENTRO STUDI
    ED ESPERIENZE R.A

RAPP   1:2000

Like the agricultural towns, the industrial towns played a double role: on the one hand, they had to produce the requisite commodity and help Italy gain self-sufficiency; on the other, they were major instruments of propaganda for the increasingly bellicose Fascist foreign and domestic policy. At the same time, imperatives of Fascist domestic policy demanded the retention of the agrarian air of the Agro Pontino towns, and, indeed, both Guidonia and Carbonia relate typologically to the earlier towns [Figs. 2.23 and 2.24]. From the institutional arrangements on the central piazze to the hierarchical ordering of housing for the various classes, the model appeared with only trivial variations. Guidonia differed from Carbonia in that the primary and secondary roads, the piazze, and indeed, the entire urban ensemble are carefully ordered in relation to the volumetric disposition of the buildings—that is, not primarily according to the abstract, almost indifferent geometries and volumetric placements of the Modern Movement, but rather on the basis of visual

2.22 Plan of Guidonia; Giorgio Calza-Bini, Gino Cancellotti, Giuseppe Nicolosi, architects (from *Architettura*, 1938). This team also designed Carbonia, and individual members had been involved in Sabaudia and Littoria. The main cross-axis leads to the church, which sits atop a small hill. The main square appears closed at all but one corner in the plan, but in fact the portico of the Casa del Fascio is fully open to one side, and there are exits by the town hall and across from the tower of the Casa del Fascio.

2.23 Urban center of Carbonia (contemporary postcard). Housing for the miners is at the upper left. Note how the church and free-standing bell tower are raised on a podium and isolated from the other structures surrounding the piazza—an ambiguous gesture of both isolation and monumentalization.

2.24 Casa del Fascio, Guidonia (from *Architettura*, 1938). After decades of neglect, this and other buildings in Guidonia are now being cleaned and restored. Note the open portico underneath the two-story Casa del Fascio, which both opens to the town beyond and serves as a viewing platform for the ubiquitous parades sponsored by the Fascist state.

relationships calibrated to take into account changing perspectives and foreshortenings [Figs. 2.25 and 2.26]. Sabaudia and Guidonia offer the two best examples of this urban and architectural design strategy. The enduring power of both communities derives from the ways in which the designers informed traditional strategies with insights derived from Rationalism, and rendered traditional building types in a modern idiom.

Proximity to the mines was important in Carbonia, and accounted for the longitudinal and extensive rather than intensive development, but even here rigid planning criteria separated each group from the others down to the provision of separate access roads to the mines for miners,

2.25 Housing in Pomezia; Concezio Petrucci, Mario Tufaroli, Emanuele Paolini, Riccardo Silenzi, architects (photo by author). These apartment buildings are directly adjacent to the town center.

white-collar workers, and directors.[134] These New Towns addressed certain themes related to the urban center, the spacing of buildings and the grouping of activities—but these objectives could have been fulfilled in many ways. In Guidonia and Carbonia, as in the other New Towns, the planning criteria facilitated administrative control, mirrored and solidified existing social divisions, and emphasized the centralizing power of the Fascist party.

Like Carbonia, Arsia, and Pozzo Littorio, Torviscosa was designed as a one-industry town, except that the product was not coal but cellulose. The Italian synthetic textile industry, by contrast with the fragmented coal industry, was basically a monopoly by the late 1920s. While the coal towns represented the state's attempt to dominate an industry characterized by many small producers through the introduction of a single large agency, in Torviscosa the state simply aided an already powerful monopoly. Franco Marinotti, President of the Società di Navigazione Italo-Americana (SNIA, later becoming the Società Agricola Industriale Cellulosa Italiana, or SAICI), selected the site in Friuli in consultation with Mussolini on the grounds that the locale met the following criteria: it was not a strong agricultural area, hence no local farm production would be damaged; it was in an area of high unemployment; its site was accessible to various forms of transport. In practice, this third condition had eliminated southern Italy as a possible location, although the south suffered from an acute agricultural malaise and high unemployment. Once the site (between Venice and Trieste) had been chosen and the state

2.26 Town hall and tower of Pomezia (photo by author). A free-standing arcade unites the tower with the rest of the arcaded piazza. Pomezia is now at the heart of Italy's "Silicon Valley."

had expropriated land from the property owners and granted it to Saici, a cellulose plant quickly appeared, followed by a plant to produce soda and a hydroelectric plant. The company, which received massive infusions of funds from the state to fund research in synthetics, also constructed the town and the housing. Just as the PNF preempted the role of the traditional autonomous *comune* in the Agro Pontino New Towns, so

did Saici control the town of Torviscosa, even more than did the Fascist party. Even today, the town is dominated by the adjacent industrial plant.

Torviscosa's first building phase, planned for five thousand inhabitants, was completed in 1938, and the second and final one in 1940. The enormous cellulose plant, with high towers and grandiose entrance, dominates the town, but the rest of Torviscosa is modest in scale and generously spaced, in marked contrast with the tightly organized towns of the Agro Pontino. Several of the institutional buildings and much of the working-class housing frame a large, open, grassy field or park lined with trees, which separates the civic center from the industrial section. The very modest public buildings consist of a combination town hall and Fascist party building; church; Dopolavoro, with a movie theater; hotel with restaurant and tavern; school and nursery school; and playing field and swimming pool. Torviscosa boasts some of the most generous working-class housing in all of the New Towns; while unmarried workers lived in dormitories here as in the Agro Pontino, families received spacious two-story units with small yards [Fig. 2.27]. The single largest error in plan-

2.27 Workers' housing, Torviscosa (photo by author). Each of these spacious units, constructed around 1940 near the town's public square, enjoys a garden in the back.

L'ILLUSTRAZIONE

Anno LXII - N. 44   **ITALIANA**   3 novembre 1935 - Anno XIV

Per tutti gli articoli, fotografie e disegni pubblicati è riservata la proprietà artistica e letteraria, secondo le leggi e i trattati internazionali.

2.28 Cover illustration, *L'Illustrazione Italiana*, 1935. Italian encampments in Ethiopia, with an overscaled image of the Duce to remind friend and foe alike of the power behind the war.

ning here is found not in the disposition of the private civic structures, but in the proximity of the plant to the town. The dangers of the chemicals used at the plant were certainly not fully understood at the time, especially the danger of the pollution of underground aquifers and of the air, even though there were numerous health problems among workers in the plant who came into contact with the dangerous chemicals.[135]

Imperial Building in Italian East Africa

The third major colonizing program between the two wars took place in Italy's colonies in Africa:* Libya, Somalia, Mogadisciù, and Ethiopia [Fig. 2.28].[136] But Italy's imperial aims in Africa had precedents far older than Fascism itself.

In 1896, Italy suffered a humiliating defeat at Adowa, a defeat which subsequently gave rise to exhortations to recover Italy's lost honor. During the peace negotiations after World War I, Italy advanced its claims to Ethiopia but was rebuffed by the Great Powers here as it was in its claims to Fiume.† As early as 1925 Mussolini planned to take over Ethiopia, but he was unable to mount the campaign until 3 October 1935. Mussolini's prestige played a crucial role here: he wanted to avenge Adowa as well as to recover an Italian empire, a feat which had eluded Italian leaders since the fall of the Roman Empire.[137] Indeed, of all the European powers only Italy and Germany lacked experience both in mercantile imperialism, since the sixteenth century, and in the impe-

*The African colonies had no direct parallel in America, just as the American transient camps discussed in Chapter 3 had no direct parallel in Italy. However, although modest in scope, they constituted significant aspects of the community-building programs in their respective countries and therefore are included in this study.

†Fiume, with its large Italian-speaking population, was the border area between Italy and the Austro-Hungarian Empire. Gabriele D'Annunzio led a celebrated assault on Fiume in 1919 in an attempt to annex the area and thereby settle Italy's claims after World War I.

rialism of the industrial era. In part, Mussolini's task in the formation of empire demanded that he make up for the lead held by the other great powers. Since Italy was a newly formed nation, Mussolini was able to capitalize on ideas of national mission and racial supremacy which began to take hold, however tenuously, during the drive for nationhood. In fact, even during the nineteenth century the fate of modern Italy was seen as linked with the recovery of the grandeur of ancient Rome. The defeat at Adowa had ended these aspirations, but they were revived by the conquest of Libya in 1911.

While pacification campaigns against rebellious natives continued for more than twenty years, settlement programs were part of the Italian agenda from the outset. Initially, private rather than public enterprises accomplished the settlements, although always with favorable subventions and assistance from the state. Eventually it became obvious that the private colonies tended to be large, almost industrial farms which neither settled many colonists nor absorbed the unemployed from the mainland. In 1928, the state began to be directly involved in colonization, in the so-called *colonizzazione demografica* program—basically, moving entire families to the colonies. The operation was managed by a state agency, the Ente per la Colonizzazione della Libia (ECL); after 1934 land was no longer granted to private initiatives. Initially the ECL tended to grant farmland to colonists in widely dispersed settlements, without building towns; at most the ECL would occasionally construct a minimal complex of church, dispensary, cistern, and store strung out along some main road.

All of this changed in the late 1930s, when colonization entered a new phase of even greater state control, and greater efforts were under way to absorb excess labor and to encourage colonists from the mainland to move to Africa—Ethiopia belonged to Italy by 1936, so colonization proceeded both there and, at an accelerated rhythm, in Libya. Farm plots in Libya were strung out more or less linearly along the road, usually a road joining major cities. One would pass through several such rural centers on the road between Bengasi and Derna or Barce and Derna. Although still very small, the post-1936 hamlets contained full-fledged civic centers, with school, church, Casa del Fascio, post office, carabinieri barracks, first-aid clinic, and housing for various officials. The towns tended either to be an enlargement of an existing road with the central piazza therefore traversed by a thoroughfare, or to have a fully enclosed piazza entered at the corners and almost invariably porticoed.

If the villages seem extremely similar, it is probably because the ECL hired three architects to design them, architects who also worked on urban expansions in existing Libyan cities: Florestano Di Fausto (originally the planner and architect for New Predappio), Giovanni Pellegrini, and Umberto Di Segni. Di Fausto worked for a number of years in Libya and was responsible for setting out the norms for the farm houses as well as designing many of them himself. For these very simple colonial houses for Italian farmers transplanted to new soil, Di Fausto recommended wide verandas, walls at least 40 cm. thick, small windows, raised floors, large kitchens, and white stucco finishes—obviously, norms designed to cope with the heat.

In the late 1930s, the regime decided to initiate an agrarian colonization program for the indigenous population. The largely nomadic and pastoral culture of the natives had been seriously damaged by the Italian expropriations, and the ECL program can be seen as an attempt to control potential opponents without undertaking any real reforms. In place of the campanile of the Italian settlements these towns put a Muslim minaret, and provided market and school in complexes with arcuated porticoes, along with stables and enclosed lots for animals. Housing was dispersed in the countryside. Several such villages were initiated in 1938–39, but they were not notably successful: the nomads, unsurprisingly, resisted such settlements, although a few families had transferred to some of the settlements by the time the Second World War interrupted the entire program.

Public and private agencies also undertook colonization in Somalia. For example, in 1920 a private agency, the Società Agricola Italo-Somala (SAIS), established colonies in Italian Somalia, of which the largest was Villabruzzi (Villaggio Duca degli Abruzzi), a colony promoted for its business potential by Luigi of Savoy, Duke of the Abruzzi. Throughout the Fascist period, SAIS undertook the mechanized cultivation of land around Villabruzzi after preparing hundreds of miles of irrigation canals and channels. With a population of around 9,000 by the late 1930s, Villabruzzi produced hemp, sunflowers, eucalyptus, legumes, sugar cane, cotton, and bananas. Tropical-style housing for natives and Italians alike provided by SAIS utilized local materials and customs. Although not planned or administered by the government, this and other towns run by SAIS survived through state subsidies, but the absence of the traditional Italian institutions testifies to these towns' genesis in the private rather than the public sector. The institutional core of Villabruzzi consisted of church, school, treasury department, SAIS offices, and carabinieri quarters. Even in the late 1930s, no plans were afoot to introduce traditional institutions, let alone new Fascist ones, to this or other company towns.[138]

Italy pinned many hopes on Italian East Africa (Africa Orientale Italiana, or AOI), quite apart from the obvious gains in international prestige that accrued in the face of half-hearted sanctions from the League of Nations. From this imperial beachhead Fascism planned to launch a new era for Italy. Officials believed that ultimately AOI would serve as a breadbasket for the homeland if it could achieve agricultural autonomy, thus reducing Italy's dependence on foreign sources. They dreamed about rich imports of grain, meat, vegetable oils, cotton, coffee, wood, wool, rubber and minerals. This followed a fairly traditional and rapacious imperialist strategy of milking the new territory of its riches [Fig. 2.29]. At the same time, they also hoped that AOI would become a market for Italian goods, and that it would siphon off excess population from among the chronically underemployed in Italy [Fig. 2.30].[139] The presence of Italian settlers tended to temper some of the rapaciousness of Italy's imperial policies.

In common with other instances of European and American imperialism, a healthy dose of cultural chauvinism and paternalism shored up

2.29 Albergo Croce del Sud in Mogadisciù, 1935. Insufficient and inadequate local housing made hotel-building a necessary enterprise.

2.30 Casa del Fascio, Mogadisciù, ca. 1935.

Italy's imperial policies. Not only would the indigenous population reap the advantages of advanced civilization and culture, it would also see actual living conditions lifted above the subsistence level and would receive the benefits of Italian citizenship—always remaining below the level of the whites, however. Not surprisingly, the native population (with the exception of Islamic groups, who united with the Italians against a common enemy) remained unenthusiastic about Italy's grand programs for them.[140]

The government planned a program of agricultural colonization consistent with Mussolini's preference for ruralism, but as part of a grand scheme which entailed massive public works (roads, irrigation, airports, and military installations) and ultimately thousands of Italians who would

be settled on their own plots of land [Figs. 2.31 and 2.32]. The reality did not quite match up to the plan.

As early as November 1935 the Italian government planned to have the ONC organize and supervise settlement programs in the new African colonies.[141] Only in October 1936 did the program get under way; Minister of the Colonies Alessandro Lessona informed Araldo Crollalanza, the President of the ONC, of his new charge, and he identified two sites upon which farm colonies could be established on behalf of demobilized veterans of the Ethiopian campaign. Lessona's intention was to undertake minimal infrastructural work and to set up something he vaguely described as "collective colonization."[142] He reckoned without the ONC, however, whose long experience with land reclamation and colonization programs made it an unlikely vehicle for a minimal program that was to be both rapid and cheap. In fact, the ONC officials who were sent to

2.31 Triumphal arch in Bengasi. Roman generals celebrated triumphs by erecting arches on the periphery of Rome; Fascist generals emulated them with arches in Africa.

2.32 Sketch for the Africa Orientale Italiana pavilion at the Eleventh Fair of Tripoli, 1937; Pietro Lombari, architect. Whatever else such displays accomplished, they did call attention to the role of the Duce, Mussolini.

*Dr. Giuseppe Taticchi, the director of the AOI colonization program, had formerly headed the ONC Agrarian Agency in Sabaudia; Dr. Angelo Ponzetti, director of the ONC colony at Olettà, had directed an agency in Altura; and Dr. Benigno Fagotti, director of the ONC colony at Biscioftù, had worked for the Inspectorate in the Agro Pontino. Five of the agrarian agents and draftsmen who also came to AOI in November 1936 had formerly lived and worked in ONC *bonifiche*. See the personnel information in ASC, ONC AOI, b.2.

†At one point the Governor General's office in AOI even proposed building defensive fortifications around the settlements, but the ONC resisted on the grounds that photographs of such settlements would make powerful statements not only in Italy but elsewhere in the world. Crollalanza to the Governor General's office, 8 December 1937, 4. ACS, ONC AOI b.1, f.c.

‡The Governor General's office even encouraged the ONC to move its future activities to Galla and Sidoma, where presumably more and better land would be available. Governor General's office to ONC headquarters, 17 November 1939. ACS, ONC AOI b.5.

Africa in November 1936 (many of whom remained until shortly after Italy entered World War II) all had experience in ONC colonization programs in Italy.*

Within days of their arrival, the ONC officials realized that colonization and land improvement programs would not be simple tasks. Although in theory colonists would take only land confiscated from the Ethiopian royal family or from rebels, in practice this proved insufficient. For one thing, in an uncertain political climate and with regular guerilla activity the ONC found it advisable to group the farm plots together, which often meant acquiring land from friendly or at least neutral natives.† ONC funds covered the expenses of infrastructural work (roads, sanitation, hydraulic work) and the building of houses and related farm structures, as well as office management, but no provisions were made for land purchase: in practice this meant that the ONC had to rely on the colonial viceroy to confiscate and distribute land. Understandably, colonial officials had more on their minds than the ONC colonization program, and they were reluctant to upset friendly natives or to give rebels yet further grounds for opposition. The difficulty of assembling plots of land to divide into individual farm plots characterized the program from beginning to end, and led to a whole constellation of complications.‡ Eventually colonial officials and the ONC worked out a system whereby native landowners received new pieces of former imperial land in exchange for land taken over by the ONC; native landowners moved to their new farms, but the ONC wanted their hired laborers or tenants to remain at the ONC villages as hired hands or sharecroppers.* Although the ONC program began in late 1936, land acquisition problems so slowed progress that the first group of colonial families, originally scheduled to come in 1937, did not actually arrive until nearly two and a half years later.

But land acquisition was only one problem ONC officials faced in November 1936. Taticchi, the director of the program, despaired of being able to initiate any operations at all because of inadequate transportation, the absence of offices and equipment, and the difficulty of even visiting the proposed site at Biscioftù, where rebels had burned all existing buildings and appeared to be in some control.[143] Grim as the conditions were that Taticchi encountered at the new sites, he found the situation of the expected budget even worse. Although the colonies were expected to be profitable both within Africa and for Italy in general, Taticchi found the estimate of 1,250,000 *lire* for setting up the colonies to be far too low, and he did not anticipate returning a profit for some time to come. He wanted to avoid the huge outlays which the ONC had expended on the mainland in part by taking profits from crops cultivated by native tenants but on land which now belonged to the ONC.[144] He also proposed to begin planting crops which could profitably be marketed in Addis Ababa, a plan which eventually led to the establishment of "agrarian industries" such as commercial fishing (from Lake Biscioftù), a sawmill and a coal plant (from forests on ONC land), and a flour mill (for pasta), all to produce goods for markets in Addis Ababa so as to help underwrite ONC expenses in the colonies.[145]

For security reasons as well as in order to ease the cost of transportation of goods and materials and, eventually, of crops to markets, the two ONC colonies were established on the central Ethiopian plateau near the capital in Addis Ababa: Biscioftù, about 45 km. southwest of the capital on the road to Moggio, and Olettà, about 40 km. to the west of the capital. Relative to other places in East Africa, the climate here was reasonably mild although still tropical, with heavy rains between May and October. The soil, either loose and sandy or largely clay, had always been only modestly productive, but ONC officials hoped that irrigation, fertilizers, and other advanced cultivation technologies would render marginal land productive.[146]

Discharged veterans helped prepare the land once the war ended, and some of them were even scheduled to receive farms. But preparing the

*The system, called *permute*, involved sending natives and their belongings to former imperial holdings elsewhere in Ethiopia. The ONC had to cover the expenses of such activities. Governor General's office to ONC headquarters, 17 November 1939. ACS, ONC AOI b.5.

2.33 Italian colonists in Olettà, Ethiopia, ca. 1939. Because rebel activity was considerably less severe in the region of Olettà than elsewhere, the ONC could set the houses out in rows rather than in the circular formation found at Biscioftù.

land was only one aspect of the ONC's activity: communication, roads, storehouses, and a full range of agrarian facilities had to be constructed, in addition to houses for the colonists and, eventually, a small rural "center" for each of the communities. Since land transfers proceeded at a maddeningly slow pace, the ONC found itself continuing to pay wages to colonists who needed to be supported until they received their farms. The problems of providing work, materials, transportation, and funds constantly bedeviled the two ONC colonies, so much so that construction on the first hundred houses did not begin until December 1937, and by June of 1939 only sixteen farms were operating in Biscioftù and eighty-two in Olettà.[147]

Although much of the publicity surrounding the Italian adventure in Africa took as its point of departure the alleged inferiority of the native population and the consequent need for the superior talents of the Italian conquerors, the ONC agrarian experts knew better. In a November 1938 report, Dr. Benigno Fagotti acknowledged that for the most part the best agricultural land had been well cultivated by Ethiopians prior to the arrival of Italians, and only the poor lands had been left as pasture. Most of the land the ONC acquired in the first year and a half fell into the second category and required significant irrigation or other preparation. Through the *permute* system, the ONC expected instead to acquire good land which could be promptly cultivated and settled.[148]

In any case, the ONC hoped to exploit the land far more thoroughly than the Ethiopians had, in part through the use of modern technologies but also by introducing new crops which would bring good prices in African markets. The ONC conducted extensive experiments with a whole range of vegetables and legumes, finding for example that cabbage brought low prices because of extensive native competition, while fennel brought excellent prices and could be grown without much difficulty.[149] Grains presented much greater problems. Fagotti believed that they did not grow well in Ethiopia, and only Italian dietary habits forced AOI to

2.34 ONC house, Ethiopia, ca. 1939. The plan of these houses roughly corresponded to the guidelines set out by Florestano Di Fausto for houses in Libya: few and small windows, porch, thick walls, cross-ventilation.

grow or import grain. Importing grain was expensive, since anywhere between 800,000 and 1,250,000 quintals per year was needed. Most Italian grains were susceptible to devastating blight, so the ONC eventually imported grains from Kenya which resisted Ethiopian pests, but some colonists ignored ONC advice and used other grains—with predictably disastrous results.[150]

Fagotti also pointed out a second problem with the cultivation of grains: it was a relatively labor-intensive crop, but native laborers were becoming increasingly difficult to find. In the earliest days 3 *lire* had been sufficient for one day's wages, but because of competition from public works projects wages had more than doubled—if day laborers could even be found. While an Italian needed a daily wage of 70 *lire* in Ethiopia, a native could be paid 15 to 20 *lire* per day, so the construction companies employed many natives, and the ONC, as Fagotti complained, could not begin to match even the low native wage scale. Fagotti believed that the natives should grow grain, which still would turn only a small profit, while Italian colonists should grow the more profitable legumes and vegetables.[151] More than anything else, of course, the figures only point out the difficulty of trying to build agricultural economies in an industrializing world—the same problem that surfaced with the New Deal communities.

As vexing as the agricultural problems were those of construction. Ethiopians built their tuculs (round huts with conical roofs) out of eucalyptus fibers and a sort of eucalyptus paste. Although a few stone quarries functioned, and lumber and lime could also be found in the new colony, the absence of roads, the inadequacy of the frail one-track railroad, and the limited number of vehicles at the ONC's disposal made the movement of goods and materials intolerably slow and expensive. ONC officials used a tucul for their office in Addis Ababa, and most had to live either at a hotel or in a tucul.[152] Although transportation problems eventually eased up they never disappeared, and they added significantly to the cost of construction. Taticchi urged his superiors to cut housing construction costs by allowing colonists to build their own houses. He reasoned that some would build tuculs, which were cheap and quick, while those with more ample resources might build something more substantial. In any case, the ONC would save significant sums of money on labor and materials, and no doubt the homes would go up more quickly, since the colonists would have a vested interest in finishing them so that they could be joined by their families.[153] Despite Taticchi's frequent assertions to

ONC headquarters that this would be the best way to build the houses, President Crollalanza's answer was a firm No from the outset. Not only would such a policy reveal the ONC to be inept in organizing an appropriately organic and economical building program, it would also leave the new communities without a minimum of "decorous and unified housing types." Crollalanza deplored the disorder which would be inherent in Taticchi's proposed house building policy. This was not to say, however, that colonists should not help build their own homes, Crollalanza assured Taticchi; rather, construction should proceed according to designs which he would personally approve.[154] The ONC engaged private construction firms to build the houses, frequently with very poor results; within one year many structures revealed serious cracking and had to be repaired.[155]

The decision to group the houses into settlements of eight, largely dictated by security considerations, also helped limit transportation and road building costs. The typical configuration grouped the eight houses in a circle, with the individual farm plots radiating out from the center in pie-shaped wedges.[156] Ethiopian laborers were required to place their tuculs at the extreme periphery of the property in order to avoid a "promiscuous mixing" of the races, a policy which continued throughout the ONC's tenure in Ethiopia.[157]

Although the ONC continued to stress the preeminently rural character of the settlements, the farms were sufficiently distant from Addis Ababa to require a small-scale urban center. For every 200 farms the ONC planned a small center consisting of church, school, Casa del Fascio, ONC office, police department, and medical dispensary: in effect, much like the *borghi* of the Agro Pontino. As Alemanni noted in a 1938 report, the small community centers would help provide the necessities of life for the dispersed rural population, but they would not become urban centers for the farmers, even though they were also to help provide security in the area.[158] ONC colonists paid for their houses and for the improvements on their land, as well as for commonly shared improvements such as roads and sanitary facilities, but the centers were constructed at state expense. An independent architect designed the buildings, with complete sections and plans, but the ONC engineering office took care of explaining the projects, making cost estimates and working drawings, and overseeing construction. Most of the centers had been constructed by the time Italy entered World War II.

ONC officials demanded that the colonists themselves be worthy of the assistance the agency provided, so they wanted to be sure of the merits

2.35 Colonial house, Olettà, ca. 1939. As in the Agro Pontino, the ONC in Africa proudly displayed its name on the houses along with the number of the farm and the year of construction (counted in years of the *era fascista*).

2.36 House building at Biscioftù, Ethiopia, ca. 1938. Italian laborers build masonry walls for colonists' houses. Note the circular disposition of the houses to enhance security, and the untilled, unirrigated land behind the still empty houses.

of each colonist before they allowed his family to join him. "The concession of a farm is a reward for the best rather than a right," asserted Taticchi in 1940, and this explained the occasional need to remove a colonist from the land. Some colonists tended to pay attention neither to advice nor to orders, Taticchi lamented, and they needed to be brought up sharply. Personal family disputes, the colonists' eagerness to conduct separate businesses (everything from a bakery to the sale of perfumes!) instead of tending to their farms, and even leaving the farm to open a store in Addis Ababa all emerged as problems which the ONC had to deal with in the two agencies. Although the Governor General's office opposed repatriating colonists, the ONC found it necessary to do just this in a few cases.[159]

The entire enterprise drew to a close in late 1940, when most able-bodied men were called to arms, and Allied forces took control soon afterwards.

The schemes for the African colonies mirrored those of the Agro Pon-

2.37 Casa del Fascio, Olettà, ca. 1940. The flat-roofed masonry structure with its deep entrance looked modern (except for the base) without adopting the typology of the Casa del Fascio common on the Italian peninsula. The three fasces and the motto "Believe Obey Fight" flank the entrance as a visible reminder of the source of authority even in this little rural hamlet.

2.38 Officers' housing, Libya, ca. 1934.

tino, since small villages serviced groups of farms, just as the little *borghi* did in Italy. Church, Casa del Fascio, stores, school, post office, and market usually clustered around a central square in the villages, presenting the familiar physiognomy of the civic or public core of an Italian New Town—except that those in Libya seem to have been unimaginatively mass-produced [Fig. 2.38]. Even if colonists did not find them reminiscent of their homes in Italy, the villages certainly evoked images of Fascism and its public works program [Fig. 2.39].

Although colonization moved at a snail's pace, Fascist officials attached increasing importance to *colonizzazione demografica*, a concept implying that it was in the combined dedication of husband, wife, children, house and land that the old traditions of the homeland would flourish [Fig. 2.40]. Indeed, by 1939 Alberto Lombardi saw the *casa coloniale*, or colonial house, as the key to the entire colonization program.[160] However sturdy and industrious the settler, Lombardi argued, he would have no success without an appropriate house. Simple good sense dictated that the house respond to the site, altitude, and climatic conditions, to local materials and technologies, and to the social class of its inhabitants. Although it should be hygienic and rational, it had to serve the human needs of the residents; and, Lombardi warned, in a direct swipe at the claims of Rationalist and modern architecture, it could not be "a house that [is] *a machine for living in.*"*

*Le Corbusier's celebrated characterization of the house as a *machine à habiter* drew the ire of opponents of modern architecture, including (as we see here) petty bureaucrats.

2.39 Kitchen at Villaggio Savoia near Addis Ababa, 1937. The design of this building owes more to local Ethiopian traditions than it does to Italian ones.

Fascist control over AOI was relatively short-lived, too brief for the ambitious urban schemes Italian architects drew up for the colony to be realized. Ingegnere Guido Ferrazza drew up detailed plans for the expansion of Dire Dàua and Harar. For Dire Dàua, Ferrazza planned a new district based on a system of streets radiating from a semicircular piazza to the southwest of the existing town. It would include areas for upper-class villas and for working-class housing, and the full complement of public buildings would be inserted into the existing town: town hall, Bank of Italy, new hospital, sport facilities, and so forth. Harar, with a population of 45,000, was more than twice the size of Dire Dàua. Some public buildings were inserted into the old walled city (church, Bank of Italy, post offices. police station), but most of the new ones (Casa del Fascio, hospital, insurance institute, schools, sporting facilities, cinema) flanked the thoroughfare leading to Dire Dàua, with the piazza of the government office building connecting the new and old cities. But the program for African towns unambiguously embodied the principles of the Italian New Towns, particularly those of hierarchy and "scenographic effect," calling for representative public buildings which had to "command the respect of the natives . . . [they had to] speak a very clear language to the subject population" [Figs. 2.41 and 2.42]. That language was not the native vernacular but the "Roman classicism" of Fascist Italy, which would undergo "cordial" adaptation to the environment; this seems to

2.40 Sign at Villaggio Savoia near Addis Ababa, 1937. "Believe Obey Fight," a key Fascist motto emblazoned on buildings and posters throughout the Italian peninsula, here reminds the residents of the presence of the Fascist state as well as of their duties as its citizens.

2.41 New arcade, Libya, ca. 1935. The arcade not only appealed to Italian traditions but also served to provide shade in the hot months.

have meant in practice flat roofs and many arches.[161] Most important for the urban plans, however, was the separation of the natives from the white population; in Addis Ababa, a greenbelt, a river, and the urban core of the city divided the two races. The contemporary guidebook of the Italian Touring Club (TCI) explained the program for Addis Ababa as being inspired by the

> concept of creating a new Italian city, totally separate from the indigenous one and constructed according to criteria of monumentality and grandeur.[162]

The old town, in turn, would be disencumbered of indigenous buildings and become a site for villas and parks. In effect, this meant that anything which would remind Ethiopians of the previous government or institutions would disappear, an architectural strategy which served two goals:

2.42 Town Hall for Addis Ababa; Plinio Marconi, architect (from *Architettura*, 1937). Even highly traditional local Italian institutions such as the town hall were to be transported to the colonies, and with the same configurational and typological elements.

it reminded Italians of institutions in the homeland, and it reminded the native population that indigenous institutions had been supplanted by more powerful ones. Italy's budding racism found full expression in the new urban arrangements for Ethiopia; and, indeed, the opportunity to settle in a place where Italians would automatically be the privileged class surely accounts for the appeal of the African colonization program. Conquest itself, as well as the building and architectural program, only returned to Africa the civilization it had lost when the Roman Empire declined—or so ran the argument [Figs. 2.43 and 2.44]. That the expenses of empire bled Italy almost dry in the crucial years before World War II illustrates the high cost of image-building.

The practice of racial segregation adopted in Africa was hardly unusual, nor was it a particularly "fascist" political policy. It had long been customary in the United States to separate races, especially blacks from

2.43 Triumphal arch for Marshal Rodolfo Graziani, ca. 1937. Graziani commanded the Ethiopian campaign and was subsequently Viceroy of AOI. Once again the title of the Duce is extravagantly prominent (cf. Fig. 2.32).

whites. When the Roosevelt administration entered the business of low-cost housing, community planning, and the operation of transient camps, the government did not lead the way toward integration. Separate housing developments for the races were the rule, the declared goal being to create homogeneous communities. While the PNF had to work to stir up racism in the Italian populace, the New Deal had no such problems: racism was already deeply engrained in American life.

The calculated reformulation of tradition and the manipulation of historical models in the Italian New Towns dovetailed with the broader aims of the Fascist state. Despite the pressing need to build up Italian indus-

2.44 Construction of the Opera Nazionale Balilla, Libya, ca. 1936. The acquisition of Ethiopia and the proclamation of empire speeded up the pace of building, particularly institutional building, throughout the colonies.

try, the Fascists also invested energy in promoting the virtues associated with rural life. In the statement for a proposed urban project in Pavia, the architecture group BBPR acknowledged that the corporate state sought to create an ideal balance between the liberty of the individual and the needs of the collective. Neither the individual nor the community could have unlimited freedom, they believed, and it was the task of the Fascist state and Fascist urbanism to fulfill the needs of the people who, they claimed, "[sought] not only their own material elevation but, even more, their own spiritual elevation."[163]

In choosing to mine only two urban and architectural traditions from Italy's rich past, the Fascists tried to conflate the autonomy of the medieval commune and the authority of the Roman Empire, a strategy already under way in Italy during the nineteenth century.[164] In the last analysis, this artful collage of institutional and architectural traditions in Italy and the new African colonies merely bent them to the purposes of the new state. The Fascists by no means held a monopoly on the cooption of tradition; it had long been the practice of Italian princes, who even deployed the same images and buildings that the Fascists drew upon. The choice of certain symbolically charged motifs, especially for that most representative of Fascist buildings, the Casa del Fascio, was more than a Mussolinian show of bravado to link Fascism with two venerable Italian traditions. It also recalled the Renaissance model of a strongman who, while consolidating power under his personal rule, left the architectural and institutional shells of the preceding government intact as a way of acquiring instant legitimacy.

The architectural, urban, and social arrangements of the Italian New Towns brought into clear focus the conflicting aims of the search for traditional rural stability and the need to build a modern industrial society, without fulfilling the claims of either imperative. Rather than being organized to promote either a dynamic industrial hub or a tranquil nexus of agrarian life, the towns were simply planned as centers of administration and control, hierarchical solidifications of Fascist notions about social classes, nationhood, the Italian past, and the organization of daily life.

With an architecture and urban planning which manipulated traditional formulas, Fascist programs sought to promote stable cultural images to reassure the populace of the continuity of the new regime with its distant precursors. The precursors had to be distant to be effective: when a *condottiere* seized control of a medieval commune, the Torre del Comune represented an immediate threat to his authority, for the memory of the vanquished social order it stood for remained vivid to the townspeople; he had to coopt the emblem of the earlier power and transform it to serve his needs and legitimize his new status. At a safe remove of several hundred years, the imagery had stabilized; cleansed and rendered an object of nostalgia, it no longer threatened.

What is most remarkable, however, looking back across five decades, is how successfully these towns have fitted into Italian traditions, how easily their citizens have carried on their lives with the same rhythms found in older towns: how very Italian, in the end, the towns are. They are unique as modern examples of town planning which do not subject the sites to abstract geometries; instead, they adapt and modify traditional elements. We can attribute their long-term success precisely to this design strategy. At the same time, they are utter failures as small rural centers: urbanization has caught up with most of them, and Mussolini's desperate attempt to stem the tide of change clearly failed.

The limitations of such a program are all too obvious, but it is worth noting that the Fascists were in step with some dominant early-twentieth-century notions. From the Communist plans in Russia to the city plans of Le Corbusier to the Resettlement Administration plans in the United States, programmatic efforts by governments to mold society into some ideal of streamlined, mechanical perfection abounded. In each case, the notion of modernity seemed to be expressed in a society that would be orderly, rational, efficient, and cooperative, a society where choices were not necessary because the government had preempted them. When the United States involved itself in the building of new communities, government administrators burdened them with the same kinds of objectives and ideals.

3. American New Towns

My idea was to go just outside centers of population, pick up cheap land, build a whole community, and entice people into them. Then go back into the cities and tear down whole slums and make parks of them.

Rexford G. Tugwell

Resettling the Poor

One of the local initiatives with which the Hoover Administration sought to mitigate the effects of the Depression was subsistence gardens for the poor, often simply continuations of World War I "war gardens."[1] Under the auspices of local industry, charitable organizations, or the community as a whole, the gardens were meant to provide food supplies for the families who worked the plots. The President's Organization on Unemployment Relief set forth the following objectives for subsistence gardens:

1. To enable families to supplement their income by providing an adequate supply of such foods as they can produce at home.
2. To supply these foods not only during the growing season, but, if possible, for the winter months as well.
3. To encourage thrift and to help maintain the morale of families suffering from unemployment.[2]

Many families with no income to supplement needed no encouragement to be "thrifty"; in failing to recognize this and in relying on local volunteer efforts, the subsistence gardens program could hope for only the most minimal impact. The efforts of the International Harvester Company in Chicago, for example, extended only to employees—people who obviously had a salary.[3] Elsewhere, however, the gardens proved to be a major source of subsistence for a few lucky families. The United States Coal and Coke Company supplemented part-time work with employee gardens at many of its plants, in a program that dated back to 1910. Policies varied from location to location, company to company; sometimes gardeners received free seeds, elsewhere it was free equipment. In some cases the company prepared the land, in others the gardeners used hand labor.[4] But with twelve million unemployed, these projects for at most a few hundred families barely scratched the surface of the need. Even the largest project, the Detroit Thrift Gardens, supplied food to only 4,369 families. In all cases, the projects depended on the willingness of an industry or a community to initiate the program, secure the land, and supply seed, equipment, or paid supervision.

With the passage of the National Industrial Recovery Act (NIRA), the Roosevelt Administration transformed such voluntary programs into a federally subsidized program for subsistence homesteads that tied the idea of home gardening to the establishment of new communities.[5] Section 208 of the NIRA provided for "aiding the redistribution of the over-balance of population in industrial centers . . . making loans for or otherwise aiding in the purchase of subsistence homesteads." In July 1933, Roosevelt charged Harold L. Ickes, Secretary of the Interior, with the responsibility of overseeing the Subsistence Homesteads project, while Harry Hopkins hired Col. Lawrence Westbrook to ready his own communities under the Federal Emergency Relief Administration (FERA).*

The Roosevelt Administration distinguished three major groups in need of assistance because of unemployment: distressed families in rural areas; those composing "stranded populations," that is, people who had lost their jobs in single-industry communities where the industry had failed; the unemployed in large cities.[6] Subsistence homesteads aimed particularly at assisting "stranded populations" and the urban unemployed by transferring them to a site developed by the government and providing them with a house and assistance in starting their gardens. As first set forth, the program also proposed to foster "supplemental industrial opportunities to provide for a normal standard of living."[7] Administrators geared the resettlement projects (which later were united institutionally with subsistence projects) to meet the needs of people who had traditionally made their living in agriculture by settling them either on individually operated farm projects or in cooperatives. Westbrook described the purpose of rural rehabilitation programs in general as that of placing

> destitute persons on land where they may ultimately work out their self-maintenance . . . The general plan takes two forms: 1) The establishment of organized rural communities which are designed as instruments in the hands of the Government for rehabilitation of destitute families 2) The placement of farmers on individual non-community farmsteads where self-maintenance can ultimately be established.[8]

The American programs paralleled those of Fascist Italy in certain key respects. Both shared the goal of relieving overcrowding in urban cen-

*Under the laws of Delaware, Ickes set up the Federal Subsistence Homesteads Corporation as the fiscal entity to administer the program. Two of the projects which this chapter discusses in detail—El Monte Homesteads and San Fernando Homesteads in California—originated in the Division of Subsistence Homesteads on 3 March 1934. Paul K. Conkin's book *Tomorrow a New World* remains the best on the subject of the Subsistence Homesteads.

American New Towns

111

ters, and both viewed rural farm communities and individual farms as the most promising means of achieving that end. In each instance, the government initiated and directed the programs. But key differences also distinguished them. First and foremost, government resettlement farms and subsistence homesteads in America grew out of relief programs; the initial impulse behind them was to alleviate the problems of the unemployed in industrial and agricultural sectors, and thus to restore a lost prosperity.[9] Most discussions of the New Deal emphasize the difficulty in resolving the competing demands of reform and recovery, but recent studies suggest the primacy of recovery, at least on the highest levels of administration, even while tenacious mid-level reformist bureaucrats tried to press for reform.[10] Although unemployment was no less a problem in Italy, other factors played a greater role in shaping the Fascist New Towns: the prosperity that had eluded Italy for centuries had to be acquired, not regained.

In America, the virtual collapse of many industries left most "stranded" families unable to support themselves; they took to the road in search of work, or relied exclusively on the government—the dole—for their maintenance.[11] With over four million people on relief in July of 1934, the expenses were staggering. Haunted by the specter of families, middle-class men, women, and youngsters joining traditional groups of homeless, and by strident objections to the "dole" from those fortunate enough to have escaped the worst consequences of the Depression, the Roosevelt Administration cast about for effective means of providing both work and relief.

In the early months of 1934, the potential of the subsistence homesteads idea as outlined in the NIRA was still unclear. In a letter to Secretary of Agriculture Henry Wallace, Harry Hopkins suggested that under the NIRA he could settle stranded farmers then living in cities on farms currently held by insurance and mortgage companies. As well as providing food for the farmers and reducing the relief rolls, such a program would eventually allow the farmers to purchase the farms.[12] Wallace took issue with Hopkins's program in a well-thought-out response a few days later.[13] Not only would such families be unable to provide for their full food subsistence from the farms; without cash crops they would neither be able to purchase the farms nor to pay for such things as clothing, furniture, and health services. Cash-crop farming did not provide a decent living for most farmers at the time, and if the cash income were to be spread over yet a greater population each family would earn a propor-

tionately smaller sum. Wallace instead proposed an alternative to dispersed individual farms. He suggested restricting

> these subsistence settlements to concentrated areas picked for their adapt-
> ability for the development of new industries. In these areas the stranded
> workers might be settled on relatively small tracts, say not over 5 acres,
> reasonably close to some existing industrial center or some area which had
> good natural advantages for development of new small-scale industries.
> They should be settled with the understanding that they would grow only
> crops for home consumption or consumption of their neighbors in the com-
> munity and that they would continue to receive relief payments until such
> time as part-time labor was developed for them from industrial sources.[14]

Wallace envisioned such a program as particularly beneficial in the
South, where it would expand the production of manufactured goods and,
ultimately, significantly raise the standard of living. Perhaps more
acutely than other administrators, Wallace realized that returning masses
of people to the farms from which they had fled during the preceding fifty
years would not resolve the problems of depression in an advanced industrial society. At this time Wallace was contending with disputes over
how to resolve the problem of low prices in agriculture and enormous
surpluses at the same time that many were near starvation. One school
of opinion held that surplus commodities should be dumped on overseas
markets, while another held that production should be controlled by payments to farmers not to grow more than a certain allotment. Ultimately
the latter strategy, favored by Wallace, prevailed; the longstanding characterization of this policy is that the New Deal resolved the problem of
plenty in the midst of vast poverty by doing away with the plenty. To be
sure, a program "to spread [people] around where they will have more
elbow room and raise a large part of their own food supply"[15] was one of
Roosevelt's "pet children." But as Wallace noted, agriculture was no less
troubled than industry during the Depression.

The New Deal addressed farm problems through a wide range of agencies: the Agricultural Adjustment Administration (AAA); the Federal
Emergency Relief Administration (FERA); the Resettlement Administration (RA) and its successor, the Farm Security Administration (FSA); the
Rural Electrification Administration (REA); the Farm Credit Administration (FCA); and the Tennessee Valley Authority (TVA), an initiative for
one hard-pressed area with national implications.[16] The proliferation of
agencies signals one of the chief problems: consensus on an agricultural

policy or policies eluded the New Deal. Soil conservation, resettlement, reforestation, retirement of submarginal lands, tenant purchase programs, the "ever-normal granary," credit, electrification, allotments, distribution of surpluses to relief clients, and subsistence homesteads programs all targeted different problems and groups, and sometimes competed with one another. The AAA took its cue from industry and reasoned, in effect, that restricting production would keep prices high and reduce farm distress—and although in the last analysis it was not very successful in accomplishing its goals, it remained the primary program throughout the Depression. This particular AAA policy combined with technological change to favor commercial farms, tenants, and sharecroppers.

The Resettlement Administration, under the Department of Agriculture, encountered significant resistance to its program of assistance for those low-income groups which fell outside of the compass of the AAA programs. As Rexford Tugwell noted later, poor farmers, tenants, and sharecroppers were inadequately represented in farm organizations such as the Grange and the Farm Bureau, and carried little weight with Congress. Many activists and agricultural theorists believed that little help should go to poor farmers on the grounds that they would never be successful anyway, and if the lot of tenants and sharecroppers were to improve too much they might become difficult to deal with.[17] Particularly in the South, strong opposition to government assistance for tenants helped limit the effectiveness of many programs. The Bankhead-Jones Act of 1937 enabled only about 47,000 tenants to purchase their farms over a ten-year period—leaving another two million to remain as tenants.[18] As Director, Tugwell earned few points for tact, since he was often outspoken about the shortcomings of the AAA and about the problems of the poorest farmers. Tugwell lasted little more than a year, and eventually the RA became the FSA, an agency more dedicated to long-term rehabilitation and one which tried to maintain a low profile.

To supplement simple relief programs with something which might promise long-term assistance and rehabilitation, Hopkins and Westbrook in the FERA and Ickes in the Department of the Interior set out to join forces with the Department of Agriculture in developing several programs over the years.[19] Some of these aimed at the farmer who already had a plot of land but who could not make ends meet: he received loans and guidance geared toward making him self-supporting again.[20]

For the landless, the Roosevelt Administration proposed cooperative farms* and the Subsistence Homesteads program. Section 4, subsection (c) of the Federal Emergency Relief Act of 1933 provided for the Administration to "aid in assisting cooperative and self-help associations for the barter of goods and services."[21] Seven cooperatives received grants of between $5,000 and $10,000 in the early months of the New Deal, under the supervision of a Joint Committee on Self-Help in conjunction with the Subsistence Homesteads Division of the Department of the Interior. By May of 1934, over two hundred self-help cooperatives of various kinds had received financial assistance from the government.[22] Administrators examined a variety of possibilities for promoting cooperatives, including asking State Commissioners of Education to explore the possibility of using school shops for self-help groups wanting to produce goods for barter.[23] Private enterprise quickly recognized this as a major threat; Washington received a flood of protests from manufacturers throughout the country who foresaw government entering into direct competition with private industry, especially in consumer goods.[24] Hopkins received reports that business interests were launching a drive for government economies, but their "more serious drive [was] . . . on self-help production activities."

For the time being, the attack focused on mattress-making, but Hopkins's agent Willis Wissler believed that it would fan out to other cooperative ventures. The manufacturers' major grievance centered on damage being done to future markets, but Wissler believed that their true concern lay in the desire to "capture for themselves the increasing volume of relief supported markets for consumptive [sic] goods as an increasingly large source of profits underwritten with federal subsidies."[25] Manufacturers also feared that any large-scale transition to cooperatives would eventually mean the demise of the free market system as they knew it, and certainly the evidence indicates that some of the most ardent non-administrative supporters of cooperatives, and even some administrators, did indeed have precisely this end in mind. One attorney wrote to FERA administrator Aubrey Williams that he supported the Ezekiel plan because

> it would set up a cooperative system in competition with our capitalist system. In short, it might be the means of a quite painless transition from competition and rugged individualism to what the socialists term a 'cooperative commonwealth' . . . This plan may be loaded with dynamite insofar as

*Mordecai Ezekiel, Assistant Secretary of Agriculture, was the major administration figure behind the cooperatives in the early months.

its ultimate effects on our present system, but then it at least offers a means whereby the transition may be made under the guidance of constituted authority—that is to say, the rule of the middle class.[26]

Williams's warm response may not indicate approval for all of the sentiments expressed in the letter, but he certainly did not find them repugnant, nor did many other New Dealers: and the writer hit the nail on the head when he identified the programs as middle-class.

Massive business opposition ultimately curtailed cooperatives and, as happened in Ohio, the groups were even forbidden to use power-driven machinery in the production of goods.* Here as in the building industry, government policy favored more primitive, labor-intensive techniques rather than more "efficient" ones. (Tugwell recalls hearing Roosevelt and New York Mayor Fiorello La Guardia enthusiastically discuss banning power equipment, including bulldozers, from the construction of La Guardia airport in New York on the grounds that hand tools would allow more men to be employed. Tugwell intervened and sarcastically suggested that they use only hand trowels, which would allow *many* more men to be employed.[27])

When the prospects for cooperative industrial activities dimmed, the Administration groped for ways in which people on subsistence and cooperative farms could supplement their income by labor in industry. W. A. Julian of the Treasury Department suggested to Secretary of Commerce Daniel C. Roper a system of rewards to promote the decentralization of industry, particularly through loans and payroll subsidies for industries willing to move from urban centers to industrially "stranded" rural communities.[28] Resettlement files bulged with such proposals, most of which never saw the light of day, but decentralizing industry remained a cherished dream of the Administration. That this might only lead to further "stranded communities" in the future seems to have occurred to no one. Government support for cooperatives began to center on groups planning to build cooperative farms along the lines sketched by Wallace in March 1934. That the most successful independent cooperatives, many of which pre-dated the New Deal, seemed to have established a connection with the soil argued for continuing this model, and the older cooperatives were even eligible both for grants of working capital and for loans from the Subsistence Homesteads Division.[29]

In addition to supporting existing or new self-organized cooperatives, the Subsistence Homesteads Division also encouraged several demon-

*Wissler also charged that men "inbred with conventional business philosophy who sit in the state ERA boards and commissions" were also responsible for the halting progress of cooperatives; such men "more or less consistantly [sic] and effectively obstruct the easy spread of self-help programs." Wissler to Baker, 16 August 1934 (FERA OSS Field Reports, 278), 2.

strational cooperatives organized and managed by government. The broad resettlement, subsistence, and cooperative program gradually took shape, with the California projects among the earliest attempted. As Tugwell remarked, Roosevelt had always supported rural over urban life, and as governor of New York he had promoted investigations into rural industrial groups, enterprises which were something of a fad during the 1920s.* Since no one really knew what it would take to end the Depression, Roosevelt was willing to try many things, and several versions of subsistence homesteads, cooperative farms, rural-industrial communities, and rural resettlement programs seemed promising as relief experiments that might also help effect some needed reforms in America. Roosevelt gave a number of New Deal activists and theorists an opportunity to put their ideas into practice.

One ardent proponent of the subsistence homesteads idea was Milburn L. Wilson, a farm economist experienced in resettlement-type farms in Montana during the 1920s. With the help of Henry C. Taylor and Richard T. Ely, Wilson established Fairway Farms, Montana, in 1924 as an experimental tenant rehabilitation and land management program. During the Hoover Administration Wilson also worked in the Department of Agriculture, and he eventually came into contact with Henry A. Wallace, future Secretary of Agriculture, with whom he was to enjoy a long and rewarding friendship. In the wake of the Depression, Wilson believed that the only answer for America lay in long-range land-use planning, and he especially promoted industrial decentralization and resettlement to subsistence homesteads; he also fought for soil conservation, land retirement, reforestation, and rehabilitation programs. He may have been more farsighted about future problems than others, but in the end he proved to be overly optimistic about the ability and willingness of Americans to alter their living patterns.

In 1933, Ickes designated Wilson head of the new Division of Subsistence Homesteads. Although Wilson believed major changes were necessary if America was to survive, he also realized that reform took time and could not be hurried. Moreover, the government could not impose reforms from above; Wilson argued that reforms had to come from the people and that no subsistence homesteads would survive if they were part of a centralized, government-controlled program. Like many other New Dealers, Wilson had a vision of a new society based upon a spirit of cooperation, but he was no starry-eyed idealist. He recognized that it would take time, patience, and thoughtful work with local groups and

*Among the many experiments in colonization were the Little Landers colonies in California, which began in 1908 and lasted until after World War I; like the later Subsistence Homesteads, these settlements for "a little land and a living" included small plots of land and cooperative enterprises for groups of families. Henry S. Anderson, "The Little Landers' Land Colonies: A Unique Agricultural Experiment in California," *Agricultural History*, 5 (1931), 140–42. Another great promoter of back-to-the-land enterprises was the Roman Catholic Church, which, through the Catholic Rural Life Conference, sponsored Granger Homesteads in Iowa—one of the first federally financed programs. National Catholic Rural Life Conference, *Manifesto on Rural Life* (Milwaukee, 1939).

communities to turn around the way people lived and thought about their communities. In fact, Wilson's industrial-type subsistence homesteads— planned so that the tenants could find employment in nearby industries— were among the most successful of the New Deal communities. However, some of his plans suffered major setbacks, as when the agency lost its bid to provide a furniture factory for stranded coal miners at Arthurdale in 1934, or when the Comptroller General, John R. McCarl, effectively forced the federal government to take control of subsistence homesteads. Ickes and Wilson clashed repeatedly over the issue of local control, and Ickes finally federalized the entire program in May 1934, stripping the local subsistence corporation of any power. Wilson subsequently re-signed and returned to the Department of Agriculture, for he realized that however sincere and even idealistic federal employees might be, the homesteads would be doomed if the settlers were not allowed to take control of their lives themselves. In the long run events proved Wilson right.[30]

Another key figure in the resettlement and subsistence programs was Rexford Guy Tugwell, a member of the "brains trust," who was Under-secretary of Agriculture and later Director of the Resettlement Administration. Although he was an economist with a primarily urban back-ground, Tugwell developed an early and profound interest in land management and resettlement. Tugwell rejected what he believed was an outdated individualism and proposed instead a cooperative mentality and a collectivist economic policy. These could be achieved, he believed, through planning and public controls on the economy. Tugwell ran the RA for only about a year, but he had had serious doubts about the sub-sistence idea from the beginning. He believed that the suburban resettle-ment program as embodied in the Greenbelt towns was a far more real-istic enterprise and corresponded more closely to the habits and aspirations of Americans.[31] Unlike Wilson, however, Tugwell was un-willing to wait; reform could not come too soon for him, and he bluntly and often tactlessly proposed a collectivist vision of a new society to an America constantly on the alert against "Reds." He came to be labeled— unfairly—a "Red" himself, and by 1936, pilloried in the press, Tugwell had become a political liability for Roosevelt. The New Deal was under attack from enough quarters that the President wanted to avoid any un-necessary problems—and, given the tenor of the day, Tugwell's very public views certainly created them.[32]

Both Wilson and Tugwell were experimentalists willing to try a variety

3.1 Rammed-earth house, Gardendale Homesteads, near Birmingham, Alabama, 1937 (photo by Arthur Rothstein).

of solutions and to adapt programs to local needs. For this very reason they aroused enthusiastic participation from clients and employees alike, but this also earned them the distrust of men like Ickes, who worried above all about the financial soundness of the programs. Tugwell was particularly interested in building technology and in the development of construction methods that would take advantage of a variety of materials and mass-production techniques. The concrete-slab construction he tried at Jersey Homesteads failed (the concrete cracked), but the rammed-earth houses at Mount Olive Homesteads in Alabama and elsewhere were more successful [Fig. 3.1], even though at the time critics feared that they would not survive the rains (they did, for years).*

Tugwell's hopes lay not with rural resettlement but with suburban resettlement, which he believed was more consistent with trends then under way and which offered greater hopes for employment because of their proximity to large cities: in this, too, time would prove him right.[33] Initially Tugwell proposed twenty-five Greenbelt towns, loosely modeled on the English Garden City, adjacent to existing cities which offered good future prospects for employment.[34] In the end, only three towns were built: Greenbelt, Maryland (between Baltimore and Washington); Greenhills, Ohio (near Cincinnati); and Greendale, Wisconsin (near Milwaukee). Widely publicized at the time and repeatedly examined by planners and historians since, the Greenbelt towns have long been considered one of the real successes of the community program. Certainly Tugwell, who

*Conkin, *Tomorrow a New World*, 120–22. Experiments with pre-cast concrete paneling preceded World War I in the United States, but there were still technical difficulties in the 1930s; what was innovative in Tugwell's scheme was simply that the federal government tried something out of the ordinary in housing.

went to live at Greenbelt himself, believed this was the case. Part of the towns' success, to be sure, derived from the lavish sums spent on them—between $15,000 and $16,000 per unit, while the Casa Grande Cooperatives, for example, cost less than $12,000 per unit counting all of the community and cooperative facilities, and San Fernando Homesteads cost $2,552 per unit. The extra money paid for elaborate infrastructures and community facilities in the Greenbelt towns and for less elaborate ones in the cooperatives; subsequent additions at Greenbelt cost only $3,950 each.[35]

The design strategies for all three towns showed acute awareness of the automobile. The plan of Greenbelt separated pedestrian and automobile traffic around five "superblocks" for the 885 housing units, and included a small community center with a school, fire station, cinema, restaurant and hotel, and small shopping center [Figs. 3.2–3.5]. The designers of Greenbelt combined flat-roofed cinderblock buildings with brick-veneer pitched-roof houses; Greenhills dwellings were terra-cotta blocks with stucco finishes; and Greendale houses were cinderblock and wood frame. The sites alone made the communities quite different from one another: Greenhills, for example, located in an area of sharp ravines, exhibits more extensive development than the others and is as efficient for the automobile today as when first built. Greenbelt became famous for its cooperatives, initially financed by Boston merchandising magnate Edward Filene.[36] Each of the towns opened with the cooperative facilities in place, and all successfully operated their cooperatives at least for the duration of FSA administration. With the end of the FSA and the increasingly outspoken opposition to government ownership the towns were privatized, and all the properties had been sold to tenants or veterans by 1954.[37]

Despite the outpouring of praise for these three suburban communities—and their influence on the planning of suburban developments over the ensuing fifty years—it was the rural resettlement towns that "provided the most complete laboratory for New Deal social and economic theory."[38]

While the Department of the Interior initiated the Division of Subsistence Homesteads, and the Department of Agriculture ultimately inherited them as part of the Resettlement Administration, the FERA also initiated its own communities in 1934. Harry Hopkins selected Lawrence Westbrook and David Williams, two Texans with experience working with rural rehabilitation communities in Texas, to run the program. Although

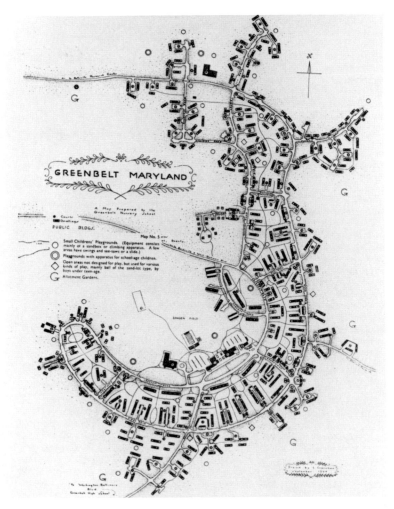

3.2 General plan of Greenbelt, Maryland, ca. 1935. Each Greenbelt town was designed by a different group of designers; the designers of the Maryland town were Douglas D. Ellington, R. J. Wadsworth, and Hale Walker.

quite similar to the Subsistence Homesteads, the Rural-Industrial Communities of the Rural Rehabilitation Division were only one part of a much larger program, and unlike the others they included only relief clients in their communities. Westbrook in particular was interested in promoting the subsistence communities as models for future development. With all of this enthusiasm in Washington, it is not surprising that many new communities got under way during the first two years of the Roosevelt Administration.[39] In his early proposal for Rural-Industrial Communities, Westbrook argued that something must be done

> to protect taxpayers from the burden of a perpetual dole system, free the children of unemployed families from the blighting influence of their present hopeless environment and safeguard the general welfare of all the people.[40]

3.3 Plan of shopping center, Greenbelt, Maryland, ca. 1935. Although the site was a good half-hour from Washington, DC, the plan for Greenbelt provided for only the bare necessities in the urban center; compare this plan with that of the center of Sabaudia, Fig. 2.15.

3.4 Aerial view of Greenbelt, Maryland, ca. 1935. The cinder-block houses appear far less stark fifty years later, when landscaping has softened the austerity of the designs.

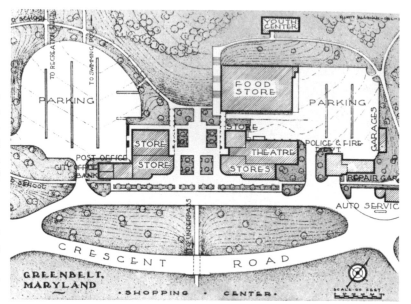

This same rationale—grounded in a paternalistic view of the economy and of the general quality of life—lay behind all of the community programs from migrant camps to Greenbelt towns. In a letter to Harvey Couch, a member of the Board of the Reconstruction Finance Corporation, Westbrook elaborated further, arguing that by setting up some of the unemployed on two- or three-acre plots with a garden, orchard, chickens, and pigs "such a setup could be amortized over a fifteen-year period for less than one-half of the monthly relief grant."[41] A press release of 28 February 1934 put the matter even more succinctly:

> Direct relief as such, whether in the form of cash or relief in kind, is not an adequate way of meeting the needs of able-bodied workers. They very properly insist upon an opportunity to give to the community their services in the form of labor in return for unemployment benefits. The Federal Government has no intention nor desire to force either upon the country or the unemployed themselves a system of relief which is repugnant to American ideals of individual self reliance.[42]

Reducing the cost to the government and putting families on a self-sustaining basis made resettlement and subsistence proposals attractive

3.5 Shopping center, Greenbelt, Maryland, 1942 (photo by Marjory Collins). From the left, the movie theater, apartment buildings, and the pedestrian underpass to keep pedestrian and automobile traffic separate. Public amenities such as the benches were not found in the other resettlement or subsistence homesteads.

to the Administration; in addition, rural living offered benefits less amenable to statistical verification but no less real in the minds of the programs' proponents. In New Deal America as in Fascist Italy, administrators shared an attachment to rural living and a belief in the benefits that supposedly accrued to those who extracted their living directly from the soil; in the main, this reflected a corresponding dislike of urban-industrial agglomerations. Whatever the immediate effects of the Depression, the long-term population shift from rural to urban areas, under way since at least 1870, was at least as troubling to many at the time. By 1910, in fact, fewer than one-third of all Americans were engaged in farming. Farm income steadily dwindled in comparison with other sectors of the economy, and tended to be concentrated in fewer and fewer hands. Despite the shift, an idealized image of rural life still held sway up through the 1930s: an image, as Jacob H. Dorn put it,

> of grass-roots democracy and disinterested citizenship, of interpersonal intimacy and cooperation in a matrix of face-to-face relationships and of local control.[43]

Rural depopulation became a target of church activity (in such bodies as the Commission on the Church and Country Life, 1913), presidential policy (Theodore Roosevelt founded a Country Life Commission in 1908), and sociological study and activism (in, for example, the Bureau of Agricultural Economics of 1922). A mixture of nostalgia, paternalism, anti-industrial and anti-urban sentiment, self-interest, and a belief in the positive effects of scientific management on efficiency and profit formed an unstable compound of motives: but all of the programs emphasized a revitalization of rural life and a corresponding de-emphasis on urban life.

In arguing that the heads of families in the Subsistence Homesteads should be between the ages of 30 and 55, Westbrook noted that "these more mature persons have gone through this depression and have learned by experience the uncertainties and limitations of city life. They will, therefore, appreciate the opportunities available in a rural community." By contrast with city life,

> although life in such a community does not offer possibilities of great riches, it does offer the security, independence and comfort which are so universally desired. It also offers freedom from unemployment, destitution in old age and loss of home through sickness, accident or other misfortune.[44]

How Westbrook could have voiced such an optimistic appraisal of the security of rural life, given the depressed condition of agriculture, the thousands of farmers and farm laborers on relief, and the many others who had lost their farms, is difficult to understand now, but certainly the longstanding American vision of the agrarian ideal played a crucial role, and for Roosevelt and many back-to-the-landers it nicely coupled with a healthy dislike of cities.[45]

The confused compound of wishful thinking and realism which marred Westbrook's proposal also surfaced in those of many other government officials. Nor did the programs themselves ever resolve the conflicting demands. Westbrook argued, on the one hand, that the participants would no longer have to worry about unemployment; on the other, that the settlements should be "rural-industrial" and that the participants would produce only "part of their living from the soil."[46] The program would depend, at least at this early stage, upon the availability of arable land and the presence of opportunities for professional or industrial employment, but industry suffered a malaise at least as severe as that in agriculture. Thus cooperative industrial enterprises for the homesteaders seemed to present the perfect solution.[47]

Some form of employment was a key component of several Resettlement Administration communities, even if sooner or later the factories always failed.* Of all these cooperative industrial projects Jersey Homesteads, one of the earliest, stood the best chance of accomplishing its goals. The Division of Subsistence Homesteads granted a loan in 1933 to a community planned for Jewish garment workers, but nothing was accomplished until 1935, when the Resettlement Administration inherited the project. Despite the unifying elements of religion and employment, Jersey Homesteads ended up no more successful than others: the cooperative factory, the farm, and the consumer cooperatives all lost money, and the families for the most part even failed to plant subsistence gardens.

The Administration by no means enjoyed a mandate for building any kind of housing; resistance from industry supplemented widespread resentment about subsidized housing of any type. Critics pointed out that middle-class tax dollars—often from families of very modest incomes—supported the various housing programs directed toward other moderate-income families. Other government housing subsidy programs stirred little opposition: the Homeowners Loan Corporation (HOLC) refinanced mortgages for delinquent homeowners; the Farmers Home Administration

*See the extensive correspondence between W. E. Zeuch and Ross H. Gast in late 1934 about the possibility of establishing cooperative homesteads near Fresno, California. The correspondence is especially interesting because it is clearly private, and both men are candid about their aspirations for cooperative ventures, about Upton Sinclair (then a candidate for governor in California), about FDR, and about the political situation in general (FSA RG 96 San Francisco, General Correspondence 1940–42, 028). The desire to establish rural-industrial communities persisted until at least 1938; see the typescript of the report for the National Resources Planning Board, "Rural and Urban Ways of Life" (1938), 611 (NRPB RG 187 Reports).

(FHA) insured mortgages for middle-income families and for low-income rental units. It is not difficult to see why these were largely uncontroversial, aimed as they were toward providing security and incentives to private banks and builders and homeowners. These programs helped stabilize existing social and economic patterns; the resettlement, subsistence, cooperative, and migrant programs also sought stability and also reinforced certain existing patterns, but with a difference: they involved the government in new arenas, and they sought to promote changes in living patterns.

Back to the Land

The idea of avoiding the worst excesses of capitalism was an attractive one in the 1930s. Despite Westbrook's assertion that "it is not proposed to make Utopias out of these Rural-Industrial Communities," on an operational level dreams of social improvement and reorganization crept in.[48] Ross Gast explained his involvement in a California-based series of projects, Rurban Homes, to his superiors in Washington with the remark that

> I think you know that the only reason why I am in this work is because I have felt for many years that the subsistence homestead ideal, if soundly approached, is a real palliative for many of the evils of the machine age, and further that it is a stepping stone or vehicle of transition to a new social and economic order which, although not readily obvious, has been in the making for some time.[49]

People living and working in small groups on their own land, growing the food they needed for survival and supplementing their labor with cooperative ventures in manufacturing, seemed vastly preferable to the reality that faced so many Americans during the 1930s: men traveling from one desolate spot to another, seeking work and living on handouts; families despondently living on relief checks with no work opportunities in sight; industries closed and huge quantities of surplus produce destroyed in order to prop up prices. Although Gast saw this as a "new social and economic order," it looks far more like a pre-industrial paradise than anything truly new.

The Division of Subsistence Homesteads developed Rurban Homes projects in El Monte and San Fernando, California, and Ross H. Gast of Rurban Homes located a privately sponsored proposal to build Subsistence Homestead cooperatives in Fresno, which he proposed to bring under the aegis of the Division. Although the Fresno project foundered within a few months and never received government funding, the Division of Subsistence Homesteads actively supported the plan as a model for future cooperatives.[50]

What prompted the government to encourage cooperative ventures, and why did California seem a likely place to establish some of the first government cooperative and subsistence homesteads? The answers to this question are complex and originate with the back-to-the-land movement of the early decades of the twentieth century and with the anti-industrial sentiment that sprang up along with a rapidly increasing pace of industrialization. The homeless—hobos and migrants—came to be seen as potential "Reds," a view that lent support to the thesis (common in both Italy and America) that providing as many people as possible with a piece of land, no matter how encumbered with mortgages, would induce good citizenship and a staunchly capitalist attitude.

California also enjoyed a modest tradition of publicly funded land resettlement programs. In 1917, the California Legislature enacted a settlement program along the lines suggested by Professor Elwood Mead of the University of California, the reigning expert on irrigation and land management. Mead's land resettlement experience in Australia and Palestine had convinced him that a fully planned program for agriculture—including settlement and irrigation—was necessary for a healthy agricultural sector in the future. Mead believed that group settlement had to replace individual settlement and that the government should be actively involved in promoting such settlements and in planning land usage in general.[51] Mead oversaw the development of two experimental communities in California: one (for 110 farms and thirty farm-laborer plots) at Durham in 1917, and the second at Delhi in 1919. The settlers chose house plans and enjoyed electricity and running water in the homes—unusual in rural areas at the time. In exchange for favorable loan terms and fully prepared land, colonists agreed to remain on the land three-quarters of the time for the first ten years. Both colonies ran into financial troubles during the 1920s, although Durham, better planned and more cautious in expenditures, suffered far less than did Delhi.[52]

During the First World War, Mead sold Secretary of the Interior Franklin K. Lane on the idea of undertaking similar projects for returning veterans. This program never got off the ground—largely because most postwar politicians saw it as an improper activity for the government to engage in—but when the Department of the Interior created a Division

127

of Subsistence Homesteads in 1933 Mead served as an advisor to Secretary Harold Ickes and to the Director, Milburn L. Wilson.

One other factor in the development of the California projects was the novelist Upton Sinclair's candidacy for Governor of California in the 1934 elections. A fundamental feature of Sinclair's EPIC (End Poverty in California) platform was a plan to place unemployed people on farms to grow their own food, or in factories to produce their own goods. During a visit to Washington in September 1934, Sinclair called on Charles E. Pynchon, General Manager of the Federal Subsistence Homesteads Corporation, to ask whether the agency would consider six or seven more homesteads if a Governor of California were to submit such an application. Pynchon acknowledged that the Division would give serious consideration to such a proposal.[53] Indeed, when the Division gave tentative approval to the Fresno Security Cooperative Homesteads on 17 September 1934, Sinclair's candidacy figured prominently in the decision. Dr. W. E. Zeuch of the Planning Section of the Division of Subsistence Homesteads, in his letter notifying Gast of the project's tentative approval, commented that "we want to get it through before election as a model for Upton—if he is elected, and so that no one may say the election influenced the decision."[54]

In addition to Mead's projects, California had seen a number of private cooperative community ventures in earlier decades, including the ill-fated Llano del Rio cooperative in Antelope Valley north of Los Angeles.[55] One of the supporters of Llano del Rio, Alice Constance Austin, remained in California when the rest of the group moved to Louisiana; she continued to promote her ideas about cooperatives in Los Angeles.[56] Such cooperatives advertised the benefits of living in idyllic rural settings, and from the late nineteenth century onward they managed to attract many settlers. Members of utopian cooperatives such as Llano del Rio believed that their developments offered them a far better life than they could find in modern cities. Their advertisements made far-reaching claims for the promises of their way of life: "Before Your Very Eyes, Individualism Disintegrates! The Palaces of the Profiteers Crumble and Fall Apart! Be one of the Master Builders! Spread the Cement of Cooperation!"[57]

The minor but nonetheless lively and longstanding tradition of cooperative settlements in America provided one example for possible solutions; but contemporary endeavors under way in Europe were another source. In Italy the government promoted the establishment of building cooperatives among state employees by lending building funds amortized over fifty years, with interest and amortization charges running only 5 percent per year. The Fascist government also encouraged major industries to build rental housing for their employees. Most of these were not subsistence homes, and the government limited its control to selection of land and design of buildings.[58] In Vienna a decade earlier, Josef Frank had designed row houses with subsistence gardens for the *Siedlungsbewegung* (settlement movement), which ultimately failed to become a prototype for further building in Vienna because the municipality found that it needed higher densities to keep costs at a reasonable level.

The policy of creating a "new peasantry" and decentralizing urban areas was as strong in Nazi Germany as it was in Fascist Italy, although the German government committed fewer resources to the program. Between 1933 and 1935, thirty thousand subsistence homesteads had been constructed in Germany by the government, by cooperatives, or by private industry. Handicraft workers formed cooperatives to build homes, and other groups also formed shareholder cooperatives to build apartment blocks or suburban settlements—also a common practice in Italy.[59] As with the American resettlement projects, the German subsistence homes blossomed after 1931 when the government sought to reduce the problems of technological unemployment by offering to unemployed or very poor families both shelter and the possibility of growing their own food.[60] With the Nazi takeover, this policy of offering subsistence homes to the unemployed was abandoned in favor of a similar program available to those who could afford a 20 percent down payment.[61]

Most of these experiments in Germany and Italy pre-dated the American programs, and administrators in Washington were aware of them. In addition to Mead's experiences in Australia and Palestine, Milburn Wilson knew first-hand of a Russian Jewish colony from his trip to Russia as part of an American delegation to help formulate a distribution system for the colony. There is also evidence that low-level administrators in the field had access to information about resettlement, cooperative, and subsistence projects elsewhere. Anthon Wagner of Kiel University (Germany) spent several months with Gast in the Rurban Homes project during 1933–34 and gave him information about the development of subsistence homesteads in Germany, which Gast in turn forwarded to Washington.[62] In addition to perusing consular reports about low-cost housing and subsistence projects in Germany, Italy, the Netherlands, and Norway, administrators culled information from periodicals, including, for example, an article that appeared in *American Forests* in July 1933 about the reclamation of the Pontine Marshes in Italy.*

The aims of the German and Italian examples corresponded with those of the Resettlement Administration: to alleviate overcrowding and unemployment by promoting rural and suburban cooperatives and subsistence settlements. In all three countries, the governments responded to real problems of health and sanitation in urban centers, and all perceived rural resettlement to be one way of handling the crisis of the Depression. A genuine need to increase agricultural productivity—not only to feed the colonists but also for cash crops—underlay the planning of the Italian New Towns, which also accounts for the fully agrarian character of the rural homesteads. In most cases New Deal subsistence homesteads and farm communities (with the exception of the cooperatives) explicitly avoided the presumption that cash crops would be raised, for the settlers simply needed to produce enough to supplement their meager earnings from other sources. Initially Westbrook argued that American families could "work out their destinies" on the land and be better off than they presently were as unemployed urbanites, but eventually most programs depended on the colonists having regular employment elsewhere.[63] Thus, whereas the ONC in Italy enforced a rule against working away from the farm in order to increase national productivity, American settlers received strong incentives to work outside their homesteads. It is difficult to see how the program could have helped the economy as a whole, however, for it simply removed more possible consumers of agricultural projects from the marketplace and permitted depressed prices to remain depressed. Since the object was less to aid other industries than to set up models for a future lifestyle, by the late 1930s reform rather than recovery had become the primary goal of these projects. Recovery was the more pressing concern, and reformist programs never won the kind of Congressional support that relief projects did.

The story of the Security Cooperative Homesteads offers some indications not only of the government's objectives, but also those of lower-level government employees charged with implementing the programs.

Security Cooperative Homesteads began as a private venture by John C. Forkner, Sr., his son John Jr., Kate Richards Cunningham, and a group of real-estate entrepreneurs in Fresno. The Division of Subsistence Homesteads was eager to develop a "demonstrational cooperative project" in California, not only because of Sinclair's election campaign but also because the subsistence projects then under way were planned, or-

*Westbrook, "Rural Industrial Communities." In addition to his own report and the summary of the *American Forests* article about Italy, Westbrook's report included summaries from consulates in Germany, Austria, Canada, and Denmark and articles from books and magazines about Hungary, Czechoslovakia, Greece, and Vienna. All of the material concerned land reform, housing, and subsistence homesteads. Although no substantial evaluation of the various programs appeared, some (such as the article about Italy) seem to have been entirely positive; the range and shape of the various efforts appear to be what primarily interested Westbrook.

ganized, and built by government, with settlers initially renting and then buying the property through a Homestead Association. None allowed homesteaders to build their own homes or to plan the organization of their community. Forkner's proposal offered the positive advantage of having the settlers build their own homes as a communal endeavor, much as participants in earlier utopian communities had banded together to build one another's homes and community buildings.[64] But whereas utopian communities offered an alternative social vision, often buttressed by religion, the Security project trod a thin line between cooperative venture and real-estate gimmick. Forkner already had experience with cooperative developments in which he sold land to settlers who then built their houses as a group.

In an unofficial report to Zeuch, Gast expressed serious reservations about the development precisely because of Forkner's involvement. He believed that the Forkner proposal would not prove useful as a demonstrational cooperative because it included no provisions for cooperation beyond house construction; moreover, there was neither a waiting list of settlers nor an explicit set of selection criteria. Gast based his assessment of Forkner on his own years of experience in dealing with land racketeers, and he cautioned that the development should only proceed in lots of fifty houses to ensure that construction would progress regularly and that the government would retain some control over the project.[65] He believed that one of the sponsors, Kate Cunningham, a social worker with broad experience on cooperatives, sincerely wanted the cooperatives to succeed; but Sinclair's campaign occupied most of her time, so she exerted little influence on the Forkner project. Concern that Forkner would use this cooperative to help him in other land speculation deals prompted Gast to urge strongly that the government require that Forkner not be involved in any other land deals for three years, and also that the Division be responsible for tenant selection.[66]

The Division failed to reach agreement with Forkner on these issues, and the project, according to Gast's later assessment, died even before the Division was transferred to the Resettlement Administration; and when, as Gast predicted in October 1934, Sinclair lost the election, much of the steam went out of the project to develop a demonstrational cooperative in California, even though the urgent need remained.* The fate of this project demonstrates the government's wariness of private speculators' involvement in its subsistence projects, for the government's aspirations embraced more than merely building houses and providing

*Gast to Zeuch, 3 October 1934 (see footnote to p. 25 above). Gast informed Zeuch that he did not believe there was any rush to obtain complete approval for the Fresno project because he believed that Sinclair would not win. Sinclair's campaign was lagging while Merriam's had picked up; and, perhaps most important, Sinclair "had not been able to 'make a deal' with McAdoo and the Democratic group within the state . . . McAdoo wanted the patronage and Sinclair would not agree. It is the opinion of most political observers that Sinclair will lose if he does not get McAdoo's support and if he secures his support through the patronage to McAdoo, his program is lost."

gardens for the poor. Communities in the true sense of the word were the goal: people working together in cooperative endeavors. It began to appear that the only way to assure this was to have the government initiate and run the cooperatives, so the early idea of having settlers build their own homes was soon abandoned.

Although the Fresno venture failed, some cooperatives in California eventually received approval. In 1936, the Resettlement Administration under Tugwell announced an ambitious plan, four hundred Part-Time Farms in the Sacramento, San Joaquin, San Bernadino, Imperial, and Coachella Valleys of California. Each family was to receive a maximum of three and a half acres of land and either a unit in an apartment complex or a single-family home of three to six rooms. Families living in these projects were to supplement their subsistence gardens by engaging in other agricultural labor in the vicinity.[67] Although it never came to fruition as envisioned, the scale of this proposal suggests that the long-range plans of the RA, though targeted on migrant families and not urban residents, exceeded the hopes of even the most ardent back-to-the-landers.

Experiments in Cooperation

Cooperative marketing associations enjoyed a long tradition on the American frontier, and the reverses suffered by agriculture in the depression following World War I stirred interest in establishing cooperative marketing schemes to help restore prosperity on the farm.[68] Throughout the 1920s, the American Farm Bureau Federation encouraged cooperatives as the linchpin of a wider program to organize farms along the lines of industry and business. With the coming of the New Deal, the cooperatives yielded the tasks of production control and marketing programs to the AAA. The fledgling self-help cooperative movement which took root among the unemployed as the Depression wore on also enjoyed assistance from the FERA, through the Division of Self-Help Cooperatives. Ultimately the cooperative idea also underlay the community programs in the Department of the Interior's Division of Subsistence Homesteads as well as the FERA farm colonies.

Elwood Mead organized California's new farm communities as cooperatives, and Milburn Wilson, with his land-use program in Montana during the 1920s and his study of Mormon farm villages, brought the cooperative idea to the Division of Subsistence Homesteads. For both of these

men, and for many other promoters of cooperation, the idea that cooperation would effect a beneficial transformation of character supplemented the goal of meeting emergency needs. Once the FSA took over the homestead program, this transformational aspect became even more pronounced. Typical cooperatives in Region IX (California, Nevada, Utah, and Arizona) included the Camelback, Chandler, and Casa Grande Farms in Arizona, and Mineral King Farms in California [Fig. 3.7].* Casa Grande (which, like Mineral King, drew its members from the ranks of the migrants from the Dust Bowl) was a full-time farming operation in which the members of the cooperative worked most of the time on the farms. These two projects were among the most expensive of all such government settlements (excluding the Greenbelt towns), Casa Grande costing over $12,000 per farm unit and Mineral King over $14,000 per farm unit, as compared with $8,602 for the individually operated farms of Fairfield Bench in Montana [Fig. 3.8].[69] Nearly sixty families farmed 3,265 acres at Casa Grande, and eighteen families worked 503 acres at

3.6 Multi-family units, Greenhills, Ohio, 1938 (photo by John Vachon). Greenhills also boasted a wide variety of single-family homes and duplexes.

*Among other communities, for example, were those for stranded communities (Tygart Valley Homesteads, Elkins, West Virginia); farm communities (Richton Homesteads, Richton, Mississippi); industrial communities (Houston Gardens, Houston, Texas); a garden city for blacks (Aberdeen Gardens, Newport News, Virginia); and farm villages (Two Rivers Farmsteads in Douglas and Saunders counties, Nebraska). Some of these were full-time farms, while others were cooperative or part-time farms.

3.7 Barn, Mineral King Cooperative Farm, near Visalia, California, 1940 (photo by Russell Lee). The FSA provided barns, silos, fences, and the other necessities of farm life.

Mineral King. Settlers at Casa Grande lived in three- to five-room adobe houses, with complete kitchens and baths, electricity, washing machines, and refrigerators. Mineral King housing was a bit more spare: the four-room frame-construction houses did include bathrooms, but the FSA expected settlers to provide the other necessary furnishings.[70]

Theoretically, cooperative farms offered advantages over small individual farms because a group of people could purchase expensive new types of machinery normally beyond the income of a small farmer; and, rather than having twenty to sixty small plots with each family dependent on one or two crops, the cooperatives could parcel out large stretches of land and take advantage of economies of scale. Or, as at Casa Grande, the group could purchase feeder cattle and feeders, and market milk for the group as other small farmers in the area were unable to do.[71] Since the

3.8 School and Community Center, Fairfield Bench Farms, Montana, 1939 (photo by Arthur Rothstein). These two buildings constituted the center of a "scattered homestead development" established by the FSA.

3.9 Community Building, Camelback Farms, Phoenix, Arizona, 1942 (photo by Russell Lee). Amenities such as screens and the covered passageway, concessions to the hot dry climate of Phoenix, were not found in the nearby migrant camps.

Resettlement Administration provided for the construction of houses by hiring relief labor, the cooperative aspects were limited to farming and sharing the ancillary facilities normally unavailable to farmers, including cold-storage lockers, community meeting halls, repair shops, and machine shops [Fig. 3.9].

In short, nothing about the design of cooperative homesteads suggested that they departed from traditional economic and social patterns: no cooperative kitchens, laundry facilities, child care, or other kinds of living arrangements. The imagery of the houses differs not a whit from subsistence houses or, indeed, other houses nearby. In fact, all of these government single-family homes were highly traditional in appearance and disposition: whatever ambitious social goals inspired them, they were garbed in an architecture no less traditional than the houses, public buildings, and towns were in Italy.

Although the prospects appear to have been bright for cooperative farms, on closer examination they reveal a number of shortcomings, of which some replicated problems in the Subsistence Homesteads while others were unique to the cooperatives. The chief problem was that no basis existed for cooperation on the government-initiated ventures; generally settlers had not known one another before coming onto the project, and many would have preferred to operate individual farms. Only their financial straits led them to accept placement on cooperatives.[72] On the whole, enthusiasm for cooperatives seems to have been far stronger among government employees than among settlers. Despite massive federal subsidies, the cooperative farms at Casa Grande, Lake Dick, Arkansas, and Terrebonne, Louisiana, never managed to become self-sustaining operations [Fig. 3.10]. By the time the FSA took over on 1 September 1937, no new cooperative communities were planned, and attention focused on the operation and management of existing communities.

Once settled on the farms, residents expected to participate actively in management. Members could elect a Board of Directors for the Cooperative Association, and only the members could expel another member. But the Resettlement Administration and later the FSA, through the project manager, exercised far greater control in actual operation. Although the Board of Directors approved the project manager's appointment, the FSA chose and paid him, and he answered to the FSA rather than to the Cooperative Association. All too frequently the manager, who allocated chores and granted loans, used his position to force members out either by refusing a loan or by assigning a member all of the most disagreeable

tasks.[73] Serious social tensions prevailed at the Casa Grande Coopera-tive, centering on the manager; among other things, he plowed up the baseball field when he concluded that playing ball after lunch caused the men to arrive late for work. He also announced to the settlers that he admired Hitler and Mussolini and wanted to run things as they did—presumably this meant dictatorially.[74]

Likewise, managers often decided policy and simply ignored Board decisions. This occurred as commonly on the community farms as on those individually held farms which cooperated only with respect to ma-chinery, dairies, and other enterprises. Such problems probably would have been more tolerable had the settlers achieved economic indepen-dence or at least incomes superior to those they had had before entering the cooperative farms; but the only benefit they seemed to derive from the projects was a measure of security—provided they complied with ad-ministrative decisions. In his 1943 report on the Resettlement Adminis-

3.10 Lake Dick, Jefferson County, Arkansas, 1938 (photo by Russell Lee). Lake Dick Cooperative Farms, a Reset-tlement Administration community, in-cluded ninety-seven housing units and the cooperative farm structures shown in the lower part of the photograph.

137

tration, Marion Clawson aptly summed up the cooperative situation with the comment that "these cooperative farms were run as though they were government farms and the members were simply hired laborers."* Settlers who came to the cooperative farms had little other choice, except to remain on relief or, as in California, to settle temporarily in one of the migrant camps. In effect, they were at the mercy of the project manager and the FSA, and unless they were accustomed to being tenant farmers, as in the South, such outside control was something new to stomach. By 1940, administrators in the Community and Family Services Section of the Regional Offices began to realize that the formation of communities— long the goal of reformers—had lagged, and moderate improvements in financial well-being did not compensate for resentment over enforced cooperation.[75] Robert Hardie, chief of Community and Family Services at Regional FSA Headquarters in San Francisco, wrote several strongly worded memoranda to the assistant regional director about the quality of community life on the migratory camps and the cooperative farms. He argued that farm managers had ignored the social aspects of the cooperatives, thus actually slowing down productivity and the process of rehabilitation; the high turnover rate at many of the projects, he argued, provided a telling index of tenant resistance to government control.[76] Tugwell quite simply insisted that the cooperatives failed "not because the conception was bad or because the technique was mistaken but because the people there could not rise to the challenge. It was character which failed."[77]

In the kind and degree of control exerted by the government, American cooperatives differed dramatically from state-initiated cooperatives in Germany and Italy, where, once having completed the buildings, the government stepped out of the picture except when called in to arbitrate disputes.[78] In their day-to-day operation the American cooperatives revealed a pronounced drive to implement drastic social changes through the cooperatives by means of paternalistic and ultimately authoritarian control. Only in the New Towns of the Agro Pontino did government control begin to match that of the New Deal cooperative and subsistence programs, but the Fascist government never billed those Italian communities as cooperatives. When the Fascist government gave financial aid to autonomous building cooperatives, it reasonably expected the members to take charge. By contrast, if the settlers on the American projects were indeed working out their own destiny on the land, the government was nevertheless calling most of the shots. Even the efforts to fashion

*Clawson, "Resettlement Experience" (cited in note 9 above), 73. Banfield later adopted the term "government farm" in his study of Casa Grande to point up the fact that control of the farm remained with the government.

communities through recreation programs missed the point. The priorities of the Administration and those of the settlers simply did not coincide on at least one crucial point: beyond immediate relief goals, the Resettlement Administration wanted to engage in experiments involving different living arrangements as possible models for future development, while what attracted the settlers was security and the possibility of owning a home at low cost. They hoped to improve their economic position rather than change their life-styles, hopes which did not bode well for the future of the cooperatives.

Migrant Camps in the Southwest

Camps for migrant workers were particularly important in California and Arizona [Fig. 3.11]. After the disastrous droughts of 1933 and 1934, increasing numbers of families fled the southern central states because they had lost either their farms or their farm labor jobs, and many of them set California as their goal; John Steinbeck's *The Grapes of Wrath* poignantly recounts their story.[79] The new migrants from the Dust Bowl joined the ranks of Filipinos, Mexicans, and blacks who were already following the crops in the West. The New Deal recognized the need to clothe, house, and feed these people, and as a supplement to direct relief, farm labor camps in selected locations provided one means for the government to address the problems. The Migratory Labor Camps were for families, while the Transient Camps, especially from 1933 to 1935, cared for the staggering number of single men and boys who had taken to the road.[80]

Transiency in the United States increased during the early 1930s to record high numbers; moreover, unemployed professionals and blue-collar workers, boys, women, and girls joined the ranks of the professional hobo on the road. The transient problem in the United States exploded in much the same way that the problem of overcrowding in Italian cities did, and both events caught private and public agencies by surprise. In the 1933 Relief Act, Congress authorized grants to the states worst hit by transiency problems, so that by late July a program was under way. Every state in the union except Vermont had established transient relief organizations by the spring of 1934, accommodating the transients either in shelters or centers within city limits, or in camps well outside the residential communities.[81] By December 1934 there were 269 camps and 300 shelters in operation.

3.11 Migrant worker's camp, Belle Glade, Florida, 1939 (photo by Marion Post Wolcott). The FSA archives overflow with similar photographs of impoverished families living in squalor. The caption by Wolcott reads: "A migrant packing house worker's camp in a swamp cane clearing. Two families from Tennessee are living here. There are no lights nor water, nor privy. Water for cleaning is hauled from a dirty canal and drinking water is hauled from the packing house."

Urban centers and rural camps differed dramatically in the quality of accommodations offered to the homeless unemployed. Lorena Hickok, a roving reporter for Harry Hopkins, visited a Denver shelter in 1934 and announced that it should be abandoned: "the very odor and appearance of the place was enough for me . . . [you'd] have to rope me and give me knockout drops to make me stay in that place."[82] A report by Irving Richter, a Special Assistant in the Transient Division who visited a center in Detroit, declared that the "condition of the rooms and baths was disgraceful . . . [and] at the YMCA Annex, living conditions were worse." Apart from the fact that the structures were firetraps, boys were ill and untreated, went without underwear, and often received no food for

twenty-four hours. When food did arrive, it was sandwiches. Richter compared the behavior of the man in charge of the shelter to that of a prison guard.[83] Many of the buildings were leased out to the agency, which meant that quality varied, and in some cases the government contracted out with the Salvation Army or the YMCA to operate transient centers, which the federal officials claimed also led to problems with standards. The Transient Division gradually tried to move away from centers or shelters located in urban areas and toward rural camps where the transients worked for their keep either in abandoned Civilian Conservation Corps (CCC) camps or in new tent structures supplemented by frame administration buildings and mess halls [Figs. 3.12 and 3.13].

While the camps on the whole provided cleaner and more carefully tended quarters, they also aimed toward some of the same goals that later characterized the migrant camps. First, men in camps no longer disrupted the community—a high-priority objective. From the camps, decisions could be made about where men, boys, or families would go next (for example, back to their hometowns), but whatever the disposition it always involved keeping them segregated from nearby communities. Second, wanderers could be controlled, an end toward which the Transient

3.12 Transient Camp 8, near Wilhoit, Arizona, n.d. The makeshift tents of this camp for men and boys are typical not only of the transient camps but, later, of migrant worker camps.

141

3.13 Mess Hall, Douglas Transient Camp, Arizona.

Division enlisted the support of outside forces as well. Since travel for the transients consisted in part of hopping freights, federal officials urged the railroads to clamp down on this free transportation. Hitchhiking, the other preferred mode of transient travel, dropped dramatically after the police started arresting and jailing hitchhikers.[84]

Part of the zeal for containing the movements of the itinerant unemployed stemmed from fears that cities and towns in America would be overrun by hordes of hoboes. Partly out of a desire to hang on to the transients long enough to rehabilitate them and give them medical attention, and partly out of fear that they were incipient communists about to incite a revolution, the Division tried to chart their movements and to hold them in the centers as long as possible. Any transient who griped or complained, even with grounds, was branded a "radical" or an agitator. But the transient camps had no legal hold over the wanderers, and their only appeal lay in the safety they offered from local police and the promise of a meal.[85] The camps operated as one half of a vise which closed inexorably on the transients: local law enforcement agencies and railroad police zealously arresting and harassing transients formed the other half.

3.14 FSA Migrant Camp, Jefferson County, Oregon, 1940 (photo by Arthur Rothstein).

By 1934, however, administrators began to realize that nearly 40 percent of the transient population consisted of families, many of whom followed the crops as migrant workers.[86] After uncertain beginnings in association with the Transient Division, the care of migrants passed to the Farm Security Administration in 1937 and became Migratory Labor programs.

Most camps were stationary, but numerous mobile units in California and Arizona followed the crops much as the migrants did [Fig. 3.14]. By 1940, about a dozen permanent farm worker communities—long the goal of reformers—had been established in California, consisting of groupings of small apartments or duplexes [Fig. 3.15]. Most of the rest of the camps, whether stationary or mobile, contained tents, and the permanent camps utilized both tents and metal shelters at an average cost to each family of ten cents a day in 1936.[87] Both types of construction presented problems for the residents. Laurence I. Hewes, Jr., Regional Director in California, reported that the mobile unit in Blythe (Riverside County) had "unscreened tents [that were] highly uncomfortable in this hot climate where flies, mosquitoes and gnats [were] numerous."[88] Since these fami-

3.15 FSA Migrant Camp, Yuba City, California, 1940 (photo by Arthur Rothstein). The modern design of these units is the work of Vernon De Mars, a first-rate young designer who continued to design in California after the war.

lies were among the most destitute in the country, even the relatively modest cost of screens strained their limited budgets.

Metal shelters presented an even greater problem [Fig. 3.16]. At the Agua Fria Camp in June 1939, Assistant Camp Manager James T. Collins reported that twenty of the thirty-five families who had moved out in the preceding four weeks did so because of the excessive heat—between 100° and 120°—in the metal shelters. In Westley, California, the same problems drove a family with a sick child to rent a house which they could ill afford several miles away, and other families moved back into jerry-built structures with no sanitary or cooking facilities which at least did not become ovens in the afternoon heat.[89]

In effect, the government-supported migrant camps provided an indi-

rect subsidy to growers: already benefiting mightily from such New Deal policies as price supports, they now no longer had to provide housing. As an added boon, the exemption of farm workers from the National Labor Relations Act of 1935 allowed growers to keep wages low for field workers—a practice which was to persist for decades, until farm workers began to organize their own resistance. And growers used their strength effectively. They customarily united to set wage rates, so that no free market for labor could develop; they also closed ranks during strikes such as the 1933 Cotton Strike in the San Joaquin Valley. Inevitably, the migrant workers became the victims.

Although living conditions were always poor for migrant workers, at times they became unbearable. In 1938, migratory cotton pickers in Arizona suffered extreme hardships when they were stranded in the Salt

3.16 Metal shelter, Westley Migrant Camp, San Joaquin Valley, California, 1939 (photo by Dorothea Lange). The metal shelters would quickly become unbearable in the heat, but this family from Oklahoma, the first occupants of the camp, had yet to learn this on their first day in the camp.

River Valley of Arizona after harvesting the cotton crop. With nowhere else to go for work, they ended up living in squalor and in hunger in camps where typhoid and other diseases broke out. No state relief was forthcoming because in 1937 the Arizona Legislature had set a three-year minimum residency requirement for relief, effectively eliminating those most in need from all but minimal temporary or emergency aid. Ultimately the Farm Security Administration donated $50,000 in emergency funds for the 12,000 needy people (3,500 cases, two-thirds of them families). But how the migrants came to be in such desperate straits is telling. Cotton growers customarily paid lower wages in Arizona than in either Texas or California, but continued to grow more and more fields of cotton. They began to advertise in Oklahoma and Texas for workers, luring them with promises of $14 to $19 a week per worker. The average, including the value of in-kind payments, turned out to be less than $8 a week. And since more and more Arizona growers planted cotton, there were no out-of-season jobs for the pickers to move on to when the cotton ended.[90]

A government report which documented the events in Arizona in 1938 reveals in clear fashion the shortcomings of the New Deal. In response to the outrageous behavior of the growers (who even tried to have all WPA projects suspended during the cotton season in 1937), officials proposed improving living conditions for migrants, both on the camps and in the Dust Bowl regions from which they had fled; allowing migrants to receive relief; and controlling recruitment activities by the growers—all of them compromises that favored the growers. New Deal policies toward migrants were not benign. Only reluctantly did the Roosevelt Administration accept the claims of organized labor with the National Labor Relations Act of 1935, and then only in the wake of labor's implacable opposition to the provisions of the NIRA. Migrants, with their ranks swollen by former freeholders and tenant farmers, lacked the political power to assert their claims against the combined forces of growers, police, and government agencies, as well as the wider public, which treated the migrants as if they were pariahs.[91]

However sympathetic New Deal officials in the field were to the plight of the migrants, they remained firmly committed to a policy of eliminating conflict, in effect robbing migrants of the one mechanism they might have used to press their case. Government-operated camps and programs ended up coopting many of the functions of unions, yet without offering the political perspective and solidarity promised by the unions. In short, whatever they were called, the FSA migrant programs differed in no discernible way from corresponding government programs in Italy: humanitarian impulses provided aesthetic cover for a profoundly conservative scheme which served the vested interests of agribusiness and large landowners and at the same time, in the long run, worked against the interests of the migrants.

Nonetheless, government policies accurately reflected the prejudices of the American public. Although housing conditions in the government camps barely met minimum needs, conditions outside of them were often worse. Migrant families camped wherever they could find vacant land with water and shade, or they lived in tents provided by growers [Fig. 3.17]. Sanitary conditions were crude in the few owner-provided installations by comparison with FSA provisions for showers, toilets, and laundry facilities in the Migratory Labor Camps. Additionally, "Oakies" encountered substantial prejudice from growers, permanent laborers, and residents in nearby towns. One grower near Elk Grove, California, discharged his Oakie laborers as soon as possible, and elsewhere Oakies were taken on only when all local labor reserves had been exhausted.[92]

From the outset, the Resettlement Administration viewed the camps as demonstrational and experimental, with the primary goal of providing adequate (if minimal) housing and sanitary facilities.[93] There is good evidence that agency officials were deeply and genuinely concerned about the migrants, and that they bent their efforts to improving living conditions as much as possible, but their programs were palliative and promised no long-term improvement. The program was not entirely disinterested, however; program administrators also believed that the camps would give the agency the opportunity to introduce health education, home management and general adult-education classes, and they hoped that the camps would help reduce "Red Activity." They reasoned that with acceptable living conditions, education, and government supervision migrants would be less likely to rebel against their financial and social conditions.* Instead of real economic improvements or changes, the government promised better—though always controlled—living conditions. Administrative correspondence is laced with references to the social unrest of the unemployed, unrest often linked with "Red" agitation which might presage a revolution.[94] "Reds" usually referred to anyone associated with unions, but agricultural laborers were still seen as "Red" threats, even though no union recruited them and they were omitted from every government labor program in the 1930s.

*In response to Ernest E. Behr's expression of concern that the migratory labor camps "can easily be made the focal centers of Red Activity," H. E. Drobish, Regional Chief of Farm Labor Projects, responded, "So far as Red Activity is concerned, as you know, we feel there will be less reason for interest in such activity in the government provided camps than in the squatter camps where filth and unsanitary conditions abound" (Drobish to Behr, 20 December 1935. FSA RG 96 SF General Correspondence 1940–42, Box 028).

3.17 California home of Oklahoma drought refugee, 1936 (photo by Dorothea Lange). The makeshift quarters outside of the FSA camps were certainly no improvement, and here even privacy disappeared.

Political motives also dominated the new community program in Italy, no less than in German resettlements. Consul Jefferson Patterson's assessment of the subsistence homes in Germany in 1935 applies equally to the Italian projects and to the American cooperative, subsistence, and migrant programs:

The chief purpose of granting State assistance to city-dwellers to establish themselves in their own homes is to combat social unrest tending toward communism in theory and rioting in practice, by giving persons, of small means, including white collar workers and skilled artisans, a stake in the community through the possession of real property. It was felt that once possessed of such property, the owner would find his personal interest identified with support of the established order and would cease to interest himself in plans for modifying the economic basis of the State.[95]

Dust Bowl migrants did not acquire land through the migrant program, but the Resettlement Administration and the FSA did attempt to induce them to feel part of a community as well as of the larger society by furnishing decent facilities and assistance. Community facilities differed little from camp to camp; most offered nursery schools, health programs, and instruction in gardening. Additionally, equipment might include (as at the Arvin Migratory Camp) a playground, drinking fountains, bulletin boards, a community kitchen, a community center, first-aid stations, and tents for emergency shelter. Residents of the Yuma Camp in Arizona built a library as a community project, and acquired books to stock it from nearby towns. Such features were palliative and promised the migrants no real control nor any substantive economic improvements. The camp at Arvin, for example, replaced the makeshift camps that migrants had set up during the 1933 cotton strike [Fig. 3.18]. Arvin shared with the San Joaquin Valley town of Pixley the distinction of being one of two sites where growers fired on and killed unarmed workers during that strike.[96]

The Migratory Camps were temporary measures, as evidenced by their canvas and metal dwellings [Fig. 3.19]. Several rungs down on the social ladder from permanent FSA settlers, migrants normally could not aspire to ownership of a plot of land, and only in rare circumstances to integration into the larger community. Growers and permanent residents often looked with outright contempt on migrants and, indeed, were unwilling to provide private facilities, while profound suspicion also laced the attitudes of low-level government administrators. A Home Supervisor in Northern California lamented the apparent inequities of rural relief with the comment "there is something wrong when all of these migrants and such get aid and a worthwhile family is turned down every place."[97] "Worthwhile families" exhibited certain key virtues: they were industrious, thrifty, ambitious, cooperative in attitude—and, especially, they were "appreciative of what the FSA has done for them."[98] By virtue of

3.18 Adobe house, Arvin Migratory Labor Camp, Arvin, California, 1938 (photo by Dorothea Lange). Although tiny and hot, these quarters did represent an improvement over the tents and metal shelters. The lower sloped roof covers a screened-in porch for sleeping in the hot weather.

roaming from job to job, following crops, and engaging in the most menial physical labor, migrants seemed to lack these qualities; and with integration into stable communities at best a distant dream, the most reasonable solution seemed to be to isolate them while facilitating a continued pattern of migratory labor.

The camps expressed this attitude both in their location and in the highly provisional quality of their housing and infrastructural systems. To

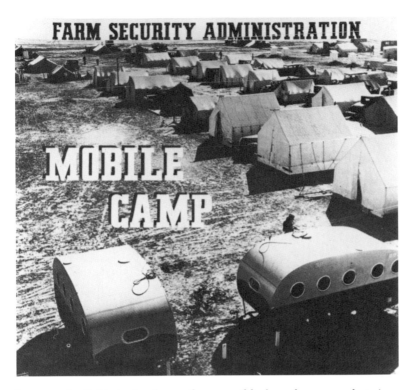

3.19 FSA informational panel, 1941. Typical mobile camp with tents, trailer for manager and office, and portable privies.

be sure, the fields had to be easily accessible from the camps, but since growers normally transported workers in buses there could have been considerable latitude in the location of the camps. However, one priority dominated: the containment of the laborers inside a single, carefully supervised area. The hexagonal plan of the Agua Fria, Westley, and other Migratory Camps expressly contained the migrants within a controlled setting: concentric rows of metal structures lined the hexagon, and all were enclosed within a road delimiting the boundaries of the camp [Fig. 3.20]. The hexagon became the standard footprint for the camps. The administrative buildings stood in the center and at the entrance; their placement gave administrators a clear view of the metal shelters at all times, and thus allowed administrators to control and supervise entrance and egress. Since the individual metal shelters lacked toilets or baths and the communal ones were not necessarily centrally located, no economies derived from grouping the shelters in this fashion; the objective was to create a community turned in on itself, isolated from the nearby town of Westley and the expanse of fields beyond it.

The Rural Rehabilitation Committee in Riverside forwarded a plan for a migrant camp to the FERA in the early days of the New Deal, well

3.20 FSA map of Agua Fria Migrant Camp, Maricopa County, Arizona, 1940 (photo by Russell Lee). The hexagonal plan, with one entrance and with the manager's quarters and offices centrally placed, became a standard one for migrant camps, as at the Westley and Eleven Mile Corner Camps in California and Arizona. This disposition favored control by the management and the separateness of the community from the neighboring towns.

before the Administration had settled upon its own migrant program.[99] The county committee recognized the lack of facilities for migrants, and the corresponding failure of growers to provide adequate housing for them; it also worried about the health problems, school truancy, and crime that seemed to result from the poor conditions in which migrants lived. It was the growers and not the townspeople who needed the migrants, but the growers clearly had no intention of providing housing for them. At the same time, growers were a powerful and stable force in their communities; and townspeople and growers shared prejudices against migrant workers. The committee therefore proposed that the government should bear the cost of building labor camps.[100] The committee proposed to engage the services of Richard Neutra, one of the leading architects in America, to design the housing. Several family units would form a block, and a series of blocks would in turn enclose a court, with a total of fifty family units per court. The homes would be "very small with much glass, no portable furniture, everything built in."[101] Decorative elements such as cornices would be banished precisely to ensure that the units could be steamhosed and fumigated with ease; even the mattresses were to have rubberized covers—hardly the most pleasant sleeping arrangement in a hot climate. Even chairs were omitted: window seats would do the job.

As well as being easy to keep clean, the units would contain nothing to steal or break.

If housing was one important means of improving the migrants' health, a second major benefit acknowledged by the committee was that centralizing laborers and their families in controlled areas would make it easier to police them and keep their children out of local schools. Thus the administrative center contained the church, school, hospital, and indoor recreation center, as well as administrative offices. The committee argued that improving health and raising morale would reduce crime. A basic assumption underlying their proposal was the belief that migrant encampments were crime-infested and that this crime would spill over into nearby settled communities. No statistics confirmed this belief; the planners merely asserted the presence of social unrest, and assumed consensus on both the causes and the proper remedy.[102] Isolation offered several advantages: "The grouping of the labor element away from the centers of population eliminates much of the class friction and makes more accessible the law violators"—presumably only migrants broke laws.[103] Additionally, containing migrants as a coherent body would facilitate the process of "Americanizing" them.

The notion of "Americanizing" the migrants recurs throughout the proposal and certainly figured prominently in educational programs for migrant children. "Americanizing" children seems not to have involved any less propaganda than did "Fascicizing" children in Italy. The Riverside committee proposed to remove migrant children permanently from the local schools, and to install new schools specifically for them. They adduced as an argument in favor of this the constant disruption of classes by the periodic flux of children whose parents had to move with the crops; but in the next breath they commented that recent crop trends allowed migrant families to stay in the same location for at least nine months, which would allow their children to remain in school uninterrupted for the full academic year. If this was indeed the case, no logical argument based on disruption made separate schools necessary, and the committee acknowledged this with the remark that "mass schooling is more effective and less expensive and isolating the migratory classes has other economic and social advantages."[104] The aim, as the report tersely summarized, was quite simply to make the itinerant agricultural laborer "an economic and social asset instead of the present necessary evil."[105] The idea of separate school facilities appealed to the Resettlement Administration and the FSA as well; while children on Subsistence Homesteads and Co-operatives attended local schools, wherever possible those in Migratory Camps were sent to their own schools.[106]

Of all groups assisted in one way or another by the government in the provision of housing, only migrants did not have to submit to lengthy application and screening processes, on the assumption that if they engaged in agricultural labor and followed the crops then they must need housing. Camp managers confined their policing efforts to insuring that the families who appeared were in fact migrant agricultural workers. The manager of the Marysville Camp noticed a "sudden suspicious increase in the number of families registering at camp." In large measure, he discovered, the families had moved in to avoid paying rent and were not "bona fide agricultural families"; once he had determined this, he evicted seventeen of the fifty-five families on the camp.[107]

Despite their low status, migrants were not exempt from certain implied contracts with the camp administrators. Many of the permanent camps provided garden space for residents, and "all families are required to make full use of subsistence garden space provided for them, and to keep accurate records on income and expenditures."[108] Because many migrants had only minimal knowledge of health, nutrition (see the adjoining table), or sanitation, the Community Services and Home Management units offered classes on food preparation, diet, sex, and health-related topics. Administrators encouraged attendance at the classes, and they also encouraged housewives on the camps to participate in mattress-making, quilting, and sewing projects with their neighbors. Local communities donated old clothes and material, which the women could make over for clothes for themselves and their families, and women from local communities even came in to work with the migrant women to teach them these and other skills. The classes in nutrition and food preparation were important, along with those that helped women learn how to achieve the best diets for their families by using surplus commodities. Home management supervisors regularly visited migrant homes, reviewed accounts, suggested garden plans, and discussed nutrition and other family problems, so that even those women who took no part in community activities had some guidance in the conduct of their homes.[109]

Government agencies proved no less directive than in Italy. The ONC concentrated on young girls and teenagers with its formal instructional programs in domestic economy, childcare, sewing, cooking, and gardening, much like the training provided by the FSA Home Management Bu-

Breakfast

Coffee	60%
Bacon, eggs, or pork (pork in surplus commodities)	34%
Hot bread, hot cakes (use considerable syrup)	25%
Toast (some buttered)	13%
Milk	6%

One woman had no breakfast
20% had below maintenance in calories
93% lacked adequate vitamin content and roughage

Lunch

Spaghetti, potatoes (usually creamed), beans	80%
Pie, cake, or cookies	30%
Fruit (mostly surplus canned peaches)	30%
Vegetable (sometimes a woman had two)	30%
Meat (chiefly surplus pork)	26%
Milk	30%

14% inadequate in calories
26% wholly lacking in vitamins

Supper[a]

Vegetables and salads	61%
Potatoes (some creamed)	53%
Meat	40%
Bread	69%
Beans	20%
Pie and cake	30%
Fruit	23%

One family did not eat an evening meal
18% wholly lacking in vitamins or minerals
36% wholly lacking in vitamins except for milk

[a]Supper: based on only 34 reports; others did not have plans for supper.
[Source: "Excerpts from Home Management Supervisors Monthly Reports," 18 February 1941. FSA RG 96 SF General Correspondence 1940–42, 934: Economic Development and Education]

reau. Men and boys learned about farming and animal husbandry, and their wives learned to bake bread (no daily trips to nearby markets from the isolated farmsteads!), to grow vegetables and fruits for home use, and to perform the other duties required of a farm wife. Both programs reaffirmed the role of the woman as the cook, laundress, seamstress, house-cleaner, nurse, and nurturer in her single-family dwelling, although the American women also participated in communal activities. Where migrants in America met as a group for instruction, women in Italy received informal and more irregular instruction in their own homes; only the children met as groups at the ONB headquarters. Manpower demands in Italy militated against such daily instruction as migrant women could receive in America. While isolation in their farmhouses prevented Italian women from socializing much with their neighbors, it also spared them the kinds of daily intrusions by government agents so characteristic of American projects.

As the projects matured and the need to provide housing for homeless migrants diminished, camp administrators began to promote programs that would allow migrant families to share in the operation of the camps. In addition to guiding the activities mentioned above, supervisors organized self-government, recreation, and education study groups on the camps. These groups developed consumer cooperatives on five projects, and school lunch programs and Women's Clubs on most projects. Migrant families at the Tulare Migratory Labor Camp eventually worked with residents of the Mineral King Farms to form the Rochdale Consumer Cooperative Association to purchase food, clothing, and other goods in large quantities and at reduced prices.[110] Most such community activities were geared toward the "ultimate rehabilitation of labor home occupants."[111] Along with these programs, once the migrant camps, subsistence homesteads, and corporate farms were all grouped into farm-labor homes under the Farm Security Administration, the FSA began to construct permanent apartment units adjacent to the temporary tent or metal shelters for migrants [Fig. 3.21]. In the first quarter of 1941, for example, twenty-four families moved into apartments at the Arvin Migrant Camp, thirty-six in Tulare, thirty-six in Firebaugh, and thirty-seven in Ceres. More modest than Subsistence Homesteads or the earlier Cooperative Farms, these units nonetheless represented a step up from tents and metal shelters. Supervisors in these camps reported antagonism between the residents of apartments and those in shelters, probably because many families wanted to move into the new housing but only a few could be accommodated. At the same time, supervisors in the field began to acknowledge that many of the families could not be rehabilitated in agriculture—at least not the way the FSA wanted them to operate.[112]

With war looming ever closer, the FSA began to undertake programs

designed to outfit clients to fulfill National Defense needs which held out long-term prospects of industrial employment. This included training in auto mechanics, welding, and woodwork for both adult males and high school boys. The FSA proved to be no more imaginative about tasks for women and girls than were the ONB and the OND. Several camps established Resident Centers, such as the one at the Eleven Mile Corner Farm Workers community, under the sponsorship of the National Youth Administration (NYA). The girls, all from low-income agricultural families, worked and received training in traditional women's jobs: in hospitals, nursery schools, and school lunch programs, and in gardening and clerical work.

The continuing nationwide agricultural depression also had an impact on the Migrant Camps: Agua Fria was vacant for a year in 1939, and vacancies ran quite high at other camps as well. Only at Yuba City did a manager note that agricultural workers were purchasing lots at a compet-

3.21 Chandler Farms, Maricopa County, Arizona, 1939 (photo by Dorothea Lange). Originally connected with migrant camps, Chandler Farms became a part-time and cooperative project, despite the fact that the FSA provided apartments rather than single-family homes.

ing private subdivision, Bull Tract, at $10 a year for twenty years. However, the FSA manager contended that the thirty-one families on his project (fifty-three units were vacant) were of a "high caliber, and are good publicity for families of a similar community standing who are slowly but steadily applying for homes." The manager believed that eventually only a high class of agricultural workers would occupy the project, and that they would be able to build a successful cooperative community.[113] In any case, the government developed a landlord's mentality quickly and easily, eager to keep units occupied with tidy and well-behaved tenants who paid their rent on time.

Many of these camps continue to provide shelter for migrants nearly half a century later: many of the tents and metal shelters have been replaced by simple frame dwellings, and the community facilities have often disappeared, but the hexagonal footprint persists, occasionally with the same houses and even with descendants of original tenants.

Subsistence Homesteads

The third type of community, industrial or subsistence homesteads, was planned largely by the Division of Subsistence Homesteads, and later passed to the RA and the FSA. The United States boasted thirty-one subsistence projects in seventeen states, with a grand total of 10,938 individual homesteads.[114] The most famous of these, and certainly the one that received the most publicity at the time, was Arthurdale, near Reedsville, West Virginia; it was also the first to get under way in 1933 [Fig. 3.22]. Much of its fame derived from the fact that it was the first, but it was also Eleanor Roosevelt's pet project. The community sat in the depressed coal region of West Virginia, where miners had been out of work for many years and where poverty seemed to be a permanent condition. Mrs. Roosevelt had far-reaching hopes for this community; she argued that "it is not purely a housing problem . . . [the people] must be taught how to live. Therefore this is a resettlement problem."[115] Arthurdale was to have consumer and producer cooperatives, a health and education program, and a handicrafts program [Fig. 3.23]. Ickes later bemoaned the vast sums of money spent at Arthurdale with little or no permanent improvements to show for it; at no time did more than a third of the members of the community find employment in local private enterprises [Fig. 3.24].[116]

Although Arthurdale was the most lavish project, at least in terms of community facilities and in its graceful, curving streets, it followed the general plan of all subsistence projects in setting individual houses on one- to three-acre plots of land, a size that permitted industrious homesteaders to produce sufficient foodstuffs for home consumption. Often the plans included chicken coops and pigsties [Fig. 3.25]. In December 1933 the first cottages were assembled: each measured ten by forty feet and was prefabricated of Oregon cedar frame and cedar siding, with fiberboard and building paper inside. This mode of construction was the project's first mistake, for as initially built the prefabs could not survive the cold West Virginia winters. Expenses soared as the Division began ripping out three of the four walls, expanding and altering the prepared foundations, and changing to a combination of concrete-block and frame construction.

3.22 Arthurdale, near Reedsville, West Virginia, 1935 (photo by Walker Evans). The 165 units line the road that gently curves through the undulating terrain of Reedsville. (The barn in the foreground is not part of the project.)

3.23 Cooperative Store, Arthurdale, West Virginia, ca. 1933.

3.24 Factory, Arthurdale, West Virginia, 1935 (photo by Walker Evans). Although many different ventures were launched in this factory, none was sufficiently stable to provide permanent employment for the residents of Arthurdale.

As modified in early 1934, the homes consisted of four to six rooms with paneled walls, hardwood floors, copper plumbing, brass fixtures, well, septic tank, and barn. Although now roomier and far more livable, the homes needed special oversized furnaces for heating because the original fourth wall was inexplicably left in place. Despite huge cost overruns and considerable adverse publicity, the residents moved into their homes and became the first members of the Arthurdale community. Another one hundred homes were built with similar construction (without the thin fourth wall, of course), but the final group of houses was the most expensive yet: six rooms, with locally quarried stone veneer over frame construction, and fittings that bordered on the luxurious.

The Resettlement Administration later added 108 cellars and fifty-six storage houses to the community's resources. Many of the future residents supplemented the income from their garden produce and relief checks by working on the housing construction projects until building slowed down in 1935. In the final accounting, the government spent $16,377 on each family, only $8,665 of which paid for the actual structures of the homes and barns. Government largesse had proved comparatively expensive: in the adjacent countryside during those years one could purchase a thirty-five-acre farm with a brand new two-story brick house and barn for only $5,000.

3.25 Home, Arthurdale, West Virginia, 1935 (photo by Walker Evans). Interior spaces were generous, and the frame-with-concrete-block construction fitted in well with local housing types.

Thus far Arthurdale was little more than a sleepy bedroom community. Planners had envisioned the community as a mini-town in which only the most basic needs of residents would be met. Grouped around a small town square were a community center, barbershop, forge, furniture shop, cooperative store, and administration office. Apparently it was assumed that other necessities and services would be taken care of by existing businesses in Reedsville. But this also meant that local businesses would not provide sufficient new part-time employment for residents once building slowed down in 1935.

Initially, the Resettlement Administration planned to set up a plant to manufacture equipment for the U.S. Post Office. Despite heavy politicking by Administration officials, Congress blocked the proposal on the grounds that it would involve the government in operating a business in direct competition with private industry. As its next strategy, the RA induced a vacuum cleaner company to operate a factory in the unused building. When the venture proved unsuccessful and the company pulled out, a succession of other manufacturing organizations followed: a collar factory, a farm equipment company, and finally a radio company. All folded within a year or so, each time throwing the residents out of work and back on relief again. Only with the onset of war did stable employment come to Arthurdale, as the Hoover Aircraft Corporation occupied the plant and manufactured defense materials.

Another subsistence project for stranded populations was Cumberland Homesteads in Tennessee [Fig. 3.26], originally an FERA project, with 253 masonry houses with steeply pitched roofs set on sixteen-acre plots. The residents, children and adults alike, attended classes at the stone and masonry Homestead school and enjoyed performances at the ubiquitous New Deal outdoor amphitheater.

California and Arizona received three suburban resettlement projects, all initiated under the Division of Subsistence Homesteads and taken over by the Resettlement Administration in May 1935. The Division was determined not to repeat the expensive errors of Arthurdale. Phoenix Homesteads, situated in suburban Phoenix, provided homesteads for seventy-five families, El Monte and San Fernando in California for one hundred and for forty respectively. Whereas in the East, as at Arthurdale, the housing provided often consisted of two-story frame houses, in Arizona and California the houses were all three- to five-room bare pine or redwood boxes; all had interior baths, garages, and storage space. Of the forty houses at San Fernando, five had three rooms, thirty-three had

four rooms, and two had five rooms; at El Monte, fifty-six had three rooms, thirty-two had four rooms, ten had five rooms, and two had six rooms [Figs. 3.27 and 3.28].

Like the first residents of the cooperative farms and migrant camps—and like settlers in the Agro Pontino—the homesteaders arrived to find the houses already built; the planners had preempted many decisions regarding disposition of services, placement on the lot, choice of elevation facing the street, number of rooms, and other considerations. Prospective tenants passed through the selection process while construction was under way, long after the stage at which individual families could express preferences in these matters. And there were few options in any case; project architects designed facilities with an eye on the construction bill, meeting family needs at minimum cost. At San Fernando, for example, architects calculated that by cutting twelve inches off the bed-

3.26 Cumberland Homesteads, Crossville, Tennessee, 1937 (photo by Arthur Rothstein). These attractive masonry houses have become choice housing, and, as at many of the other projects, nearly fifty years of tree and vegetation growth have enhanced the desirability of the houses.

163

3.27 Gardening at El Monte Subsistence Homesteads, California (photo by Dorothea Lange).

3.28 San Fernando Homesteads, California, 1936 (photo by Dorothea Lange). Homesteaders were wholly responsible for the preparation of the land they would cultivate.

room hallway width in each of forty houses they could save enough on materials to add a total of four bedrooms to the project as a whole for the same price.[117] Ceiling heights dropped, and closets lost doors; porches were vestigial. The obvious financial benefits of such precise care were offset by the prospective tenant's loss of control in the design of his new home, not to mention simple livability. The houses were plain pine or redwood boxes with porches and pitched roofs—no "frills" anywhere.

The techniques adopted by New Deal planners for their communities mirrored those of Italian town planners. They took the typical elements of suburban speculative housing in the United States, enlarged the lots, and called the result Subsistence Homesteads. Italian designers adapted the characteristic single-family farmhouse for use in the Agro Pontino and at Carbonia (Sardinia). Sometimes, as at Arthurdale and Carbonia, the undulating terrain dictated a softer approach, with roads snaking around hillocks and houses raised above them [Fig. 3.29]. But this was unusual. Where the surface was flat, as in California and Arizona or, indeed, in the Agro Pontino, designers reverted to strings of single-family houses along a simple grid, echoing the pattern established in imperial Roman *coloniae* or in settlements built during the American pioneers' westward migration. The grid layout, though non-hierarchical, was far from neutral, for its assertion of the designer's power over the vagaries of topography corresponded to the government's implied assertion of power over the lives of the future settlers. In both countries, the settlements managed to escape total monotony only with variations in the placement of houses on the lots and in setbacks from the street [Figs. 3.30 and 3.31]. In the Subsistence Homesteads the house was typically placed directly in the middle of the plot, set well back not only from neighboring houses but also from the street [Fig. 3.32]. Although planners declared that the houses were so located in order to leave the maximum area for garden production, such an arrangement also prevented further subdivision of the plots (short of tearing down or moving the houses) and so forestalled the speculation that planners feared might ensue.

Accommodation to local building traditions surfaced in the dwellings themselves: adobe construction in the American Southwest; frame structures, often with pitched roofs and gables, in the Southeast [Fig. 3.33]; hipped-roof frame houses in the West; and traditional Roman materials in the Agro Pontino [Fig. 2.8]. The blandness of the formalized vernacular design and lack of interest in anything more architecturally adventurous emphasized the way in which the settlements, rather than looking

3.29 Westmoreland Homesteads, near Greensburg, Pennsylvania, 1936 (photo by Edwin Locke). A total of 255 homes were clustered in small groups, with adjacent farm buildings.

toward the future, took refuge in known, reassuring formulas from the past.

Just as Italian planners carefully defined the agricultural and animal husbandry objectives for each of the farms, so American planners meticulously set forth the subsistence aims of the homesteads. At El Monte, "these lots are laid out for five purposes: vegetable gardens, home orchards, berries and small fruits, poultry, and home ornamentation [governmentese for lawns and flowers]."[118] On most of the subsistence projects nothing was left to chance. Designers of the Ashwood Plantation in Lee County, South Carolina, carefully listed the fruit trees, berries, and flowers for the homesteads, and specified precisely where each plant or tree should be placed on each plot [Figs. 3.34 and 3.35].[119]

The subsistence units were among the best-equipped of all of the government housing programs; but even so, the houses in California had concrete floors, which, although durable, left much to be desired both in comfort and in aesthetics. Within, the houses included "all modern conveniences, having gas, hot water heaters, built-in gas stoves, electric lights, running water, kitchen sinks, complete bathrooms, laundry tubs,

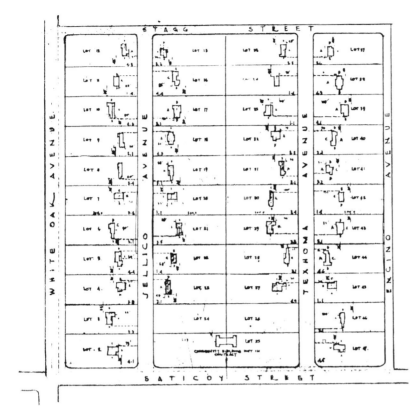

3.30 Plan of San Fernando Subsistence Homesteads, 1935; Joseph Weston, architect. In the grid of the subsequent surrounding tracts, San Fernando still stands out, distinguishable by the generous size of its lots. Variations in house placement and orientation do little to relieve the monotony of the general plan.

and three built-in cabinets in the kitchens."[120] Houses in the Italian New Towns lacked these features, but it had traditionally been the province of tenants in Italy to provide such things.*

In certain respects, the subsistence homes marked a major improvement over any previous housing that most of the families had known. Of twenty-one families surveyed at San Fernando Homesteads, only one had ever had both electricity and gas before; eight families had only had electricity, and twelve families had lived with neither. Homesteaders also got more for their money; in the first year on the San Fernando project they paid an average monthly rent of $12.90, while the rent for their previous housing averaged $22.50, ranging from a low of $15.00 to a high of $27.49.[121] Clearly residents in New Deal communities enjoyed a higher standard of living than did their Italian counterparts. To some degree this renders comparisons of their situations more difficult, but only in an item-by-item comparison. Cars, gas, and electricity simply did not exist on the farms of the Agro Pontino; but this was also true of most homes even in major Italian cities. Comparisons of the architectural and urban

*Even today, a new apartment in Italy comes without closets, cupboards, or kitchen equipment, so the absence of these features in the 1930s indicates not stinginess but simply a different tradition.

3.31 Mineral King Cooperative Farm, near Visalia, California, 1940 (photo by Russell Lee). Members' homes are set out in a long row behind the barn (cf. Fig. 3.7), with the cooperative fields on either side.

arrangements, the treatment of the settlers, and the aims of the specific programs are nonetheless still possible, for the absence of certain conveniences in Italy merely indicates a different degree of development from that in America.

Cooperative and Subsistence Homesteads projects served markedly different constituencies than did the Migrant Camps, particularly in the early years, and the guidelines for tenant selection reflected the Resettlement Administration's aspirations for the homesteads. Tenant selection on the Cooperative and Subsistence projects aimed to locate settlers who already had some kind of income, whose net worth was at least $1,200, and who stood a reasonable chance of succeeding at part-time or full-time farming. As the early head of the Subsistence Homesteads Division, Milburn Wilson, remarked, it was a middle-class movement for people neither at the top nor at the bottom of the social structure.[122] Normally, this meant that settlers had experience in farming and had survived the Depression in fairly good shape. Only the FERA farm communities and migrant camps directly addressed relief clients. Administrators envi-

sioned these projects as long-term settlements, with the renters eligible to buy their homes after one year. The Project Description Book from Region IX spelled this out clearly: El Monte homesteaders would be

3.32 San Fernando Homesteads, California, 1936 (photo by Dorothea Lange). A family prepares the footpath next to the front garden.

> low-income families employed, full or part time, in the industrial and commercial establishments located in and about the city of Los Angeles. Purpose is to provide better housing and living conditions, and the opportunity to increase real income through home production of a large portion of food requirements.[123]

Since the average annual income of families at El Monte before the sales contracts were offered was $1,020 (ranging from a low of $600 to a high of $1,700), while the maximum on farm projects was $750 per year,

169

3.33 FSA Homes, Eatonton, Georgia (photo by Walker Evans). These homes under construction are raised on blocks in a manner typical of the region.

3.34 Plan 104-K, Ashwood Plantation, South Carolina. Planners have meticulously designated types of trees and the complete organization of the homestead.

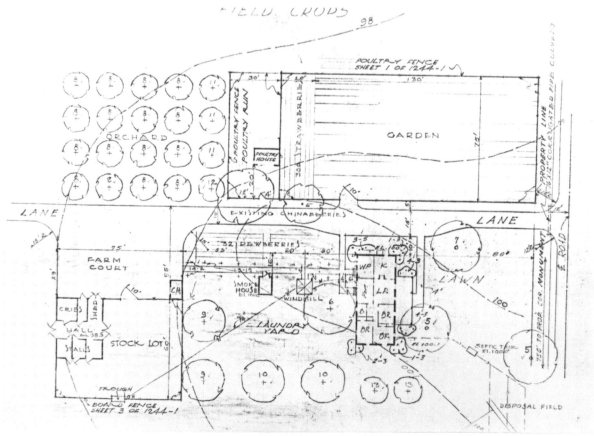

170

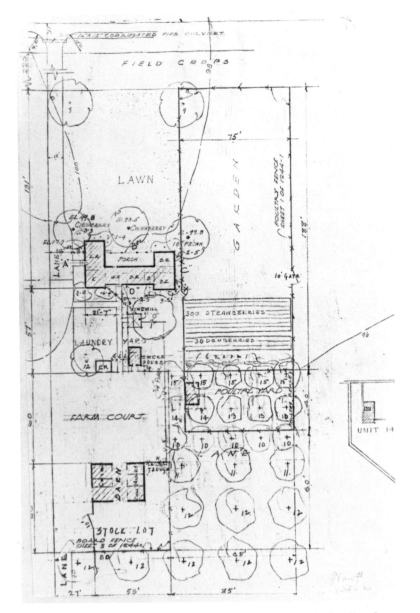

3.35 Plan 127-K, Ashwood Plantation, South Carolina. This farm community, planned by the Federal Emergency Relief Administration, included 161 homes; each unit cost over $11,000.

clearly it was not the lowest income groups—those who had suffered most from the Depression—who benefited from the project.

Financial status was only one of a number of criteria that guided tenant selection. The administrators of the Subsistence Homesteads program used the following selection procedures, which were originally formulated for the homesteads at Three Rivers, Texas, but were subsequently adopted as guidelines for all Subsistence projects:

1. Preference will be given to families whose residence in a given region has been sufficiently stable to meet the requirements of the project. Emphasis will be laid upon economic and social boundaries rather than upon fixed state and county lines.

2. There will be no discrimination based on nationality, race, or creed, but consideration will be given to the homogeneity within the group. [In practice, at the very least, this sanctioned racial discrimination.]

3. Heads of families (man and wife) must be at least 21 years of age. Preference will be given applicants under 55.

4. Preference will be given to married couples with one or more children or other dependents.

5. Families must be free from infectious diseases and from disabilities that can obstruct fulfillment of obligations.

6. Families with occupational, agricultural or other special experiences or training will be given preference where such qualifications make them desirable for the project.

7. Families selected must give reasonable assurance of attaining economic stability sufficient to permit them to meet the rental or other payments on their homesteads for which they are proposing to obligate themselves.

8. In general, families selected will be those unable to obtain the necessary loans for homes from other governmental agencies or private funds.

9. Preferential consideration, other things being equal, will be given to veterans. Extra preference will be given to disabled veterans.

10. Those applicants who cannot meet all these requirements, yet who have some exceptional qualification, may be considered.[124]

What do these selection criteria reveal about the aims of the Administration? For one thing, the government attempted to hedge its bets on the people selected for the projects: the possession of a skill, a job, a family, and a good work history might not always ensure reliable tenants, but it would certainly weed out most people affected by the Depression. In memorandum after memorandum, administrative officials made reference to helping "good families," and as the guidelines suggest, administrators had a firm idea of just who the "good families" were. As the agencies responsible for the Subsistence Homesteads refined the criteria over a nine-year period through 1944, it became clear that in addition to insisting upon families who were regularly employed and in perfect health, the agency wanted families with "the reputation for honesty and integrity," who would "show promise of ability to enter into community life and to profit from residence on the project."[125]

To ensure that an applicant met these criteria, local administrators conducted careful checks of the family's financial, employment, and health history, and the local manager held at least one or two personal interviews with the family. Employers, landlords, and personal references all received a questionnaire about the cooperativeness of the applicant. This insistence on a cooperative attitude echoes the comments from local administrators over the years when they remarked on families in the various programs; the ones who earned praise were invariably cooperative and "appreciative" of what the government was doing for them.

Concern about an applicant's financial stability was linked with the demonstrational character of the projects. Since Congress and the Administration never gave sufficient support to enable the Rural Resettlement and Subsistence programs to operate on a massive scale or for more than one year at a time, the administrators feared that any hint of problems or major financial losses on the projects would count heavily against them in annual Congressional hearings. The impact of legislative and political realities upon these and many other New Deal agencies was both to impose limitations on their size and to render them ineffective in resolving larger housing and relief problems. Had the projects not been billed as demonstrational, administrative supporters would have found it far more difficult to obtain Congressional approval, particularly after 1936, for this was an entirely new type of activity being underwritten by the government; but it was precisely the demonstrational and ultimately utopian character of the projects that led to many of the problems. As one observer wrote in 1940,

> When the government stepped in . . . planning was done for, rather than with, prospective homesteaders. Perfection rather than reality became the goal. There is much testimony and ample evidence that as the perfectionist idea grew the zeal of homesteaders diminished until it became an attitude of grateful resignation.[126]

Given the length and severity of the Depression, it seems unreasonable to think that those who applied for the programs did not need them or that none of them would have either questionable credit or uneven work records. The emphasis on cooperativeness and appreciation also reflected the views of administrators at the site, and (as we shall see) the penalties for breaching this code were swift and final.

By contrast, Italian tenant selection procedures were at best haphazard; to administrators, apparently, the formation of stable communities depended less on the people than it did on the constitution of the surrounding physical elements. The towns were important props for propaganda theatricals—indeed, they were themselves theaters provisioned with elaborate stage settings down to the most minute details—but they tended to focus less on the future actors and the dramas to be enacted against them. American settlements were stages of Brechtian sparseness; their puritan simplicity yielded primacy to the program of sifting through the applications of prospective actors and ensuring that they knew their lines and played their parts according to highly precise criteria.

Restrictions in tenant selection were sufficiently stringent that at San Fernando, for example, of seventy-seven applications for forty homes only thirty-eight were accepted. In December 1935, twenty-one families occupied their homes on a temporary licensing basis, and the Community Manager compiled an initial census of the families. Ages of heads of households ranged from twenty-five to fifty-three. Ten of the twenty-one had not gone to school beyond elementary school, six had not gone beyond high school, and four had some college education although none had a degree. Their occupations ranged from truck driver to mechanic; all were blue-collar workers or salesmen, with the exception of one woman, a former teacher unemployed at the time the family moved to San Fernando. The two women who did work were laundresses. Of the twenty-one families nineteen had cars, only four had radios, and eighteen had life insurance. Only two men worked in seasonal occupations, and only one man was unemployed (a retired fireman). Fifteen husbands and twelve wives had had previous farm experience.[127] Later additions to the project included nine studio workers in the movie industry, several more construction workers, and truck drivers. Although none of the men held high-status jobs, these were clearly stable and solid people; significantly, many had lived and worked in the area for some time.

The tenants signed on to live in the Subsistence tracts with the idea that they could eventually purchase the land and house; in California and Arizona they initially signed temporary licensing agreements. But they were doing more than merely inhabiting the land, as they might expect to do in a private development. They were participating in an experiment in living, and that experiment was controlled by the government through its local administrators. The government's decision six months after the first occupancies to give title to the homesteads through an intermediary corporation (the Homesteaders Association) only minimally altered the government's control of the project. The manner in which the government and local administrators oversaw the operation of the Subsistence Homesteads at El Monte and San Fernando will reward closer scrutiny in this respect.

In the early months of their tenancy, the homesteaders began to ready their land for the gardening programs. This was not an activity that the Resettlement Administration allowed them to undertake if they chose, but a responsibility to which they had committed themselves when they entered into their lease or purchase agreements. The project administrators determined the amounts and types of foodstuffs the homesteaders could reasonably be expected to produce, and by June 1936 the monthly report at San Fernando indicated that about half of the residents were producing their "vegetable requirements." But, as the report noted,

> Some families do not seem to be getting the results and a few do not appear to be trying. While the enthusiasm on this project dropped considerably after the announcement of the plan for selling the properties and this had a tendency to delay plantings, it is very evident which families came to the project solely for a home where they could supplement their earnings by making use of the ground, and those who came for cheap rent. This latter type will be culled out when the sales contracts are offered.[128]

The lapse of several months between actual occupancy and the government's announcement of the plans for incorporating the communities allowed local administrators to take stock of the various families to determine which ones would be able to make a go of the farming operations, and which would be suitable members of the community. Additionally, a number of families in the Phoenix, El Monte, and San Fernando homesteads earned inadequate incomes to manage the higher payments that would be required under the sales contract, while others were unemployed: the government would not be able to offer either group sales contracts.[129] Although Dr. E. E. Agger, Assistant Administrator of the Resettlement Administration, admitted that Gwen Geach (Regional Representative) was correct in her observation that if some of the poor but deserving families were forced to move from the projects, the Administration would have to admit "that the projects are not for those earning less than $1,000 per year," Agger nonetheless insisted that the government had to be assured that its investment would be repaid.[130] At the time, this meant that "several" of the twenty-five families at Phoenix, eight of the hundred at El Monte, and five of the forty at San Fernando did not earn sufficient income to afford the higher payments.

In April 1936, the tenants received the news that the government planned to create an intermediary corporation, the Homesteaders Association, in which the homesteaders would be shareholders and which would hold title to the homesteads for a period of forty years. Average rents increased from $12.90 to $23.86.[131] Although the homesteaders were unclear about the exact details of the sales contracts, they reacted immediately and angrily. At El Monte a disgruntled group of twelve to fourteen homesteaders called a meeting of all homesteaders; at San Fernando, a petition circulated by unhappy tenants gathered twenty-seven signatures out of forty homesteaders; and at Phoenix, though there was no organized protest, there was clearly some worry and discontent. Local Subsistence Homesteads administrators assessed the unrest at San Fernando, El Monte, and Phoenix as resulting from

> the interference in personal affairs and attempts at persuasion by a certain few against plans for incorporation . . . The homesteaders have concerned themselves too much with whether or not their neighbors can afford the payments under the sale contract; whether they will be 'good pay' and keep up their payments, and whether they will have to carry the other thirty-nine families.[132]

Local managers believed that the problems they faced were agitation by a few and fears about whether the poorer members of the community would be able to keep up their payments. Discontent did diminish when it became clear that if a homesteader failed to pay his assessment he would be evicted and replaced by another homesteader.

But there were other aspects of the new arrangement that were disturbing. Although homesteaders received homes and land for low prices and interest rates (4.3 percent), the provisions of the tenant agreement and deed of conveyance made it clear that there was a price to pay for this financial package. The Homeowners Association had to submit monthly reports to the government, and the government retained the right to visit and inspect the properties whenever it chose, in order to ensure that the subsistence activities continued as the program had originally intended. And the right of inspection was no empty proviso. Although homesteaders could elect their Board of Directors, "it was the wish of the Government that two of the directors be from the [Resettlement] Administration," and the Resettlement Administration instructed the homesteaders to elect Regional Representative Gwen Geach and Community Manager Arline Chewning.[133]

Additionally, in the deed of conveyance from the Resettlement Administration to Community Corporations the government retained the right to approve any and all persons to whom the Corporation intended to lease or sell property. This restraint against alienation was an unusual provision and, in the opinion of General Counsel Monroe Oppenheimer, was almost always illegal and void under English and United States common law. He believed that three considerations might differentiate the Subsistence Homesteads from other privately deeded properties: the grantor was the United States; the grantee would not have paid for the property for forty years, and therefore the restraint could be calculated as protecting the security interest of the United States; and it was not a commercial or private transaction but a governmental enterprise to maintain a certain community organization. Oppenheimer placed particular emphasis on the last point, commenting that if the people were not qualified or "desirable" or did not enter into the organized activities proposed "the entire plan of the project might be defeated. Proper selection of the homesteaders is vitally essential to its success. Furthermore, the statutory purpose of these projects is the rehabilitation of a particular class of persons." Nonetheless, Oppenheimer hoped that it would not be tested in court; he believed that the government would lose.[134]

The tenant agreements were equally explicit about the ways in which the government intended to maintain control over the homesteads. Tenant Form A, "Agreement to Purchase Land," specified that homesteaders could not prepay the final installment on their homes in advance of the termination of the forty-year mortgage without the consent of the government; the government specifically wanted this provision so that it would be "insured control over the land for the full period of the contract."[135] Paragraphs five through ten limited the tenant's use of his property in several ways. The farm lands had to be used continuously as a farm, and the tenant "had to conduct his farming operations in accordance with approved organization and management."[136] The land and buildings had to be kept in good repair, and the homesteader could not demolish, modify, or erect buildings without the consent of the government.[137] Administrators at the site emphasized this last requirement repeatedly. One resident of El Monte, Kenneth Greene, undertook to build a three-room house for his mother-in-law without the consent of either the Association or the government. He received an eviction notice, but "because of his willingness to make amends and do anything the Board might suggest to reinstate himself as a homesteader," the Board gave him sixty days to remove the small dwelling.[138]

The desire to build additional structures on the land appears to have been a persistent problem, especially at the two California projects. Both the local administration and administrators in Washington fretted about this almost as much as they did about delinquencies. In either case, Edward Stone observed "that it might be necessary to deal drastically with families at the El Monte and San Fernando projects."[139]

In the Tenant Form, the settler had to consent to the government's right to inspect and enter the property when it chose, precisely so that the government could ensure that only authorized changes were made and that the house and land stayed in good repair; the homesteader also had to agree to give the government the final say on leases or sales. Such restraints seldom applied to individually owned property, but the aim of the Resettlement Administration and later the FSA was to promote subsistence communities; if they were to ensure that the money invested at the outset was not wasted—that is that the subsistence communities remained exactly that—the government had to retain effective control in as many ways as possible, including those mentioned above.[140]

Government involvement did not end here. It would seem that with two seats on the Board of Directors, control over the physical landscape in the design and building stage and for forty years afterwards, the right to visit the premises at any time, and control over tenant selection, the government had already taken extraordinary precautions to protect its interest. In fact, since the homesteads were demonstrational projects, and since their intent was to form a particular type of community, the government was determined to exercise control over both physical and social aspects. The news of the proposed incorporation galvanized some of the homesteaders into action; the features to which they reacted with particular violence were the forty-year mortgage, with no possibility of prepayment, and the near doubling of monthly payments. Administrators scoffed at these objections and declared that if the settlers had received adequate information about monthly payments when they originally came to the project there would have been few problems at El Monte and San Fernando (Phoenix was far more docile). But so great was the outcry that eventually Dr. Agger traveled from Washington to California to meet with the homesteaders. Regional Attorney Fred Weller attended the meeting with him, and both dismissed the objections to a forty-year mortgage as evidence of a "real estate broker's psychology" typical of Los Angeles; the administrators tried to convince the homesteaders that the government's plan gave them special security—though of what sort none of the documents makes clear.[141] Just what the special benefits might have been, other than that most of the families probably would not have received mortgage credit elsewhere, is not easy to discern.

The notion of a forty-year mortgage was appalling at a time when five- and ten-year mortgages were the rule (even in the 1970s Americans were just beginning to accept mortgages of twenty-five and thirty years). For these settlers, the penalty clause that would make prepayment a practical impossibility was perhaps even more disturbing; they expected their financial condition to improve and apparently hoped to acquire legal title as soon as possible. When the final contracts appeared it became clear that tenants were being held to a quasi-feudal contract within a system that, whatever its merits, rested upon their willingness to submit to government policy. Within a period of six months, three families were evicted from El Monte for failure to care for their property "properly," for arrearages, or for "improper attitude."[142] Among those evicted, administrators considered the Drackett family especially difficult; they refused to remove some trees on their property and were lacking in "appreciation and cooperation."[143] This hardly gave assurance of government equity in the future.

In response to the sales contracts, some homesteaders formed a 40 Year Club, much to the dismay of administrators.

> A homesteader with political aspirations appears to have organized a 40 Year Club among the homesteaders, which causes a lot of difficulties, and those of us who go down to attend the [4 January 1937] meeting will have to make them understand that regardless of what the 40 Year Club resolves, the homesteaders are still bound by their agreement with the government.[144]

In response to this, Agger reminded local administrators of the policy for eviction and cautioned that they might have to deal "drastically" with homesteaders on the two California projects. Local administrators admitted that the club was a problem, but they also argued that different family selection procedures would not have prevented it: "Those people from whom one would expect a favorable reaction have been the leaders of the group who desire changes in the plan."[145] Far from being malcontents, the leaders of the opposition were among the stable elements in the community, which suggests that the protests were serious and thoughtful, and represented many settlers' feelings.*

The government actively discouraged such privately organized homesteader ventures; as Stone advised Agger, there should be one community

*One homesteader, whom the administrators called a "ringleader," threatened to call the Hearst papers if he was forced to move; he would ask the paper—famous for its yellow journalism—to photograph his furniture out in the street and would lay the blame squarely on the government (Project Book, San Fernando Homesteads, Miscellaneous. FSA RG 96 Project Records 1935–40, California, SH-CF-3).

organization so as to avoid "a multiplicity of homesteader organizations and consequent dispersion of interests."[146] But in defiance of the government the 40 Year Club continued in operation for several months. The President of the El Monte Association, Theodore Drake, notified homesteaders that the Club was a "competitive and parallel organization . . . and could not, therefore, be recognized."[147] Two of the organizers insisted that they had every right to have a club of their own, but Drake argued in return that since it was an outgrowth of three separate "indignation meetings" it was not "organized in the right way."[148] He then resigned because of "lack of cooperation," and although he was persuaded to remain, Geach rebuked the homesteaders with a stern lecture. She "admonished the group for their actions, their lack of cooperation, and appreciation," reminded them that they had to abide by the terms of their contracts, and urged them to continue as "the gem of the subsistence homesteads."[149] Clearly this status depended on close adherence to government rules and regulations, concerning not only their property but their behavior as well.

Marion Clawson's 1943 report compiled the results of interviews and studies at nine resettlement projects. His summary reveals some of the shortcomings as the participants at other projects saw them. Their cash income was low—as was that of their Italian counterparts—and settlers were unable to pay for adequate clothing and furnishings, much less to amass savings.[150] Many people felt uncomfortable about living in houses more lavish than they would normally have been able to afford, and for which their indebtedness mounted steadily, especially on the farm projects. Although the settlers received favorable terms—deferred principal payments, low interest, little collateral—they had effectively handed over control of much of the operation of their homes to government administrators.[151] The character of supervision was the most frequent reason settlers gave for leaving the various projects, and those who remained commonly believed that "lack of cooperativeness was a major factor in eviction."[152] They were not wrong; and even when settlers left voluntarily it was often because project personnel made it clear that they would find it unpleasant to remain.[153]

Supervision persisted as a constant problem on all of the Resettlement projects, principally because final authority rested with the supervisor or manager, although whether the issue was crop choices, expenditures, debt contraction, or allocation of time or other resources it was the settler who had to live with the decision. The home plans to which the women on all projects had to submit touched even more sensitive nerves, since they invaded the domain of the home itself—and, as with the farm plan for individually operated farms, too often decisions came from administrators rather than settlers. At Fairfield Bench, the FSA required residents to purchase refrigerators because they could be obtained at low cost in bulk, and some settlers only learned about them when they appeared on their doorsteps. On the other projects, settlers appealed to outside political forces or to administrators in Washington for assistance against local managers.[154] Sometimes settlers had to sign a "Pledge of Cooperation," or they had to agree to chattel mortgage on personal goods or to joint checking accounts with project supervisors. Settlers rightly felt that they were surrendering entirely too much freedom simply to obtain a loan or to remain on a project, and some "felt that they were being spied upon, and that their privacy was unreasonably invaded."[155]

The actual results of the efforts to construct rural communities differed dramatically from those envisioned by administrators. Despite the rejection of urbanism implicit in the projects (and explicit in the proposal and documentation), Subsistence Homesteads and some cooperatives depended on the availability of industry, and all were tethered to urban centers or towns. Motivated in part by cost, in part by a de-institutionalizing emphasis, planners chose not to indulge in the costly venture of creating fully equipped towns. This stands in sharp contrast to the Italian settlements, where the most publicized—and certainly the most discussed—aspect was the creation of a formal town. In theory, at least, it should have been possible for communities to blossom in America even in the absence of formal physical structures. This did not happen except insofar as communities of interest developed to oppose management policies or personnel.

There are several possible explanations for this failure. For one thing, in most cases the only thing the settlers in a community had in common was some degree of economic need. Only migrant laborers shared an additional prior interest or experience in agriculture. On the cooperatives, although most families had some farming experience, the cooperative ownership of land or farm industries was a novelty that contradicted the tradition with which they were most familiar, that of private ownership. Additionally, neither the government nor the settlers managed to invest sufficient funds in the projects to make them thriving enterprises. Agriculture was not a particularly healthy sector of the economy in any case, and the attempt to promote small family farms was an uphill struggle against the trend toward large, mechanized corporate farms that took advantage of economies of scale. Such economies might eventually have been possible on the cooperative projects, but their land was generally too poor, and their resources too limited. The principal reason for the failure of new communities to flourish lay in their system of administration, which was flawed in conception. The nature and degree of control exerted by the government simply did not allow the settlements or the individual settlers any significant degree of autonomy and, indeed, actively suppressed or eliminated moves by settlers in the direction of independent initiatives. Such control would have been impossible in established communities where there were no project managers and government administrators with command over housing, job finances, group activities, and selection and eviction. Only acute need and the lack of prospects elsewhere induced settlers to stay on the projects; even need was insufficient to hold many of them. The turnover rate ranged up to 22 percent per year, with an equally high vacancy rate.[156]

In the Italian New Towns, the Fascist government discouraged autonomous organization by farmers simply by failing to provide a meeting place and by ensuring that farmers were sufficiently far apart to hinder their meeting even in one another's homes. This was an architectural and planning decision; in the Resettlement projects, although the government sometimes provided a community center, the administrators carefully controlled group organization by a combination of threats, promises, and constant supervision. Such infringements of traditional rights boded ill for the survival of the communities.

4. Afterword

What became of these bold ventures in community planning?

By the end of World War II the U.S. government no longer operated most of the New Deal communities; by 1954, all had been sold to occupants or to new tenants. The Greenbelt towns are still occupied and have even grown significantly with subsequent development. Some of the subsistence settlements, such as the Cumberland project, have become extremely desirable housing. Elsewhere, the homesteads have been swallowed up by urban sprawl: this has happened to (among others) San Fernando and El Monte, which are distinguished from neighboring communities only by having unusually large lots. Houston Gardens for black families affords vivid evidence of how little has improved for the blacks in fifty years: poorly maintained city services help keep Houston Gardens isolated from the larger community. The direction of growth has been toward the south and the west, while the northeast, with Houston Gardens, has changed little. And the strategy of removing black families from the heart of urban Houston persists, too.[1]

Significantly, in most cases the "community" buildings quickly disappeared; even in the Greenbelt towns, they were soon turned over to private management. The new communities as such simply never emerged.

In Italy most of the New Towns have flourished. Sabaudia is a thriving summer resort, Littoria a bustling provincial capital; Pomezia and Aprilia have enjoyed the benefits of the expansion of light industry south of Rome, and Guidonia has benefited from the expansion to the east. Only Pontinia remains a sleepy backwater. Because of the taint of Fascism, these towns were poorly maintained through the 1970s; only as their fifty-year anniversaries approached did the communities undertake to spruce up the buildings [Figs. 4.1 and 4.2].

Predappio is also a thriving little rural community, but its efforts to celebrate its best-known native son have met with staunch resistance. The centennial of Mussolini's birth saw national television specials and local celebrations, but no state support for the local plan to have a first-day-of-issue stamp honoring Mussolini. The curious still come to Predap-

4.1 Seaside Colony XXVIII Ottobre, Marina di Massa, 1937; Ettore Sotsass and Alfi Guaitoli, architects (photo by author, 1979).

4.2 Interior of Casa del Fascio, Predappio, 1937; Eng. Elio Danesi and Ing. Adolfo Volpi, designers (photo by author, 1985). Both of these buildings reveal decades of neglect; until the recent anniversary celebrations, many of the new towns contained similarly neglected buildings.

pio, some to visit the Duce's birthplace and his tomb; the Mussolinis also still live there.

In short, communities did take root in Italy, and the physical testimony to the success of the Italian enterprise surrounds the visitor in a way that never happens even in the Greenbelt towns in America. The spacious piazza in Sabaudia which Mussolini intended for outdoor rallies still serves for public political events, and it also hosts the weekly outdoor market. Even through decades of neglect the Agro Pontino towns grew and prospered. Shrewd choices of location in part account for this success, as well as the fact that the towns artfully adapt traditional Italian town models which have proven to be responsive to Italian living patterns. Even if some piazze are overscaled (such as the one at Sabaudia and the central piazza in Littoria), this has not hindered their development.

With the exception of the Greenbelt towns, the New Deal communities were never intended to be separate towns—closely knit communities, yes, but not true towns. And on the whole their identities, fragile to begin with, have been swallowed up by encroaching suburbs. The larger goals of part-time farming, rural resettlement, and "reform" of urbanites largely vanished with postwar prosperity and the sale of the units to tenants. Once the government stepped out of the picture, in other words, they became suburban tracts.

But assessing the success or failure of the communities may be the least interesting of the possible analytical approaches. For example, the New Deal has long enjoyed a reputation for being leftist and even revolutionary, despite the revisionist work of New Left historians.[2] Liberals regard Roosevelt's New Deal as a triumph for the lower classes and as an administration which oversaw a significant curbing of the power of big business. For the benefit of low-income groups, they argue, the Roosevelt Administration initiated several forms of social insurance against the problems of unemployment, disability, and old age, as well as public housing and rural resettlement programs.[3] Other historians have already established that these programs were limited in scope and regressively financed, and that they failed to effect a redistribution of income or a significant shift of power in America.[4] It also gives one pause to note that the U.S. Catholic bishops, a notably conservative body, had proposed in their "Bishops' Program for Social Reconstruction" (1919) a minimum wage; unemployment, old-age, and health insurance; the legalization of labor unions; public housing; and a number of other reforms—all of which the Roosevelt Administration cautiously backed fifteen years later. Fewer than 200,000 low-cost housing units went up during the 1930s, which barely made a dent in the housing needs of the lowest economic groups. If the facts do not bear out the radicalism of the 1930s, what accounts for the persistence of the New Deal's left-wing image, and what contribution does a comparison with Fascist Italy make to our understanding of the New Deal?

During the 1930s, many of those who opposed Roosevelt Administration policies did so by characterizing them as "communist," because they perceived the mere fact of government intervention into traditionally private spheres of activity as evidence of creeping socialism. With the onset of the Cold War after World War II, and especially during the heyday of Joseph McCarthy, a historical veil dropped over the 1930s. Earlier charges about the purportedly socialist imperatives of the New Deal resurfaced, while McCarthy singled out a number of Roosevelt's civil servants as communists and the House Committee on Un-American Activities indulged in extensive redbaiting campaigns. American liberals found themselves in the awkward position of denying that the New Deal was inspired by communist principles while maintaining, on the other hand that New Deal programs had a radically new character. Their political image of the 1930s emphasized the magnitude of the economic crisis and the novelty of government intervention on such a scale, particularly with measures directed toward relieving the distress of the lowest economic groups, and the real progress made in ensuring that people received food and the bare necessities of life. Even while conceding the obvious flaws and shortcomings in New Deal programs, historians such as William Leuchtenberg and Carl Degler chose to emphasize positive aspects, especially the break with previous policies and the alleviation of acute distress for millions of Americans. Most of these historians attach the liberal or leftist image to the New Deal as much for the fact of massive government intervention as for the way that intervention sharply differentiated the Roosevelt Administration from previous administrations.

But comparing the New Deal with the Hoover or Coolidge Administrations tells only part of the story. In that context, it is arguable that liberal reforms did characterize the New Deal; in comparison with events in other countries, on the other hand, the New Deal appears less radical and far more cautious and conservative. There is little question that big business found the New Deal on the whole at least as congenial and responsive to its concerns as big business in Italy found Fascism.[5] Provisions for old age, disability, and unemployment insurance in the United States came several years after Mussolini had inaugurated such a program in Italy, and decades after similar measures in Germany. Guided by an ethos which stressed the responsibility of the individual for his/her own well-being, the United States only slowly and reluctantly accepted that in a modern and complex industrial economy the individual has little power to control the forces which impinge upon daily life. And support for allowing individuals to combine for greater force through unions came equally reluctantly.

While historians acknowledge the superficial similarities between the programs of Mussolini's Italy and Roosevelt's United States, because Fascism and democracy seem irreconcilable the tendency has been to avoid exploring any of the specific programs to determine how far the parallels extend. In fact, at least in the new towns, the parallels are extensive indeed. Both administrations spent far more money on politically "safe" building enterprises—public buildings—than on tampering with politically explosive issues such as land expropriation or significant direct intervention in the housing industry; and, as we have seen, the new communities were profoundly conservative in impulse.

In the most general terms, the governments of Fascist Italy and New Deal America sought to preserve rather than destroy capitalist economic relations in the building industry, and especially in the housing industry. Many historians would probably concede that much; but with the traditional reading of the 1930s still dominant, most would balk at finding the operations of the programs comparable on a closer level: democracy and Fascism could not have that much in common. Yet the way the American programs were operated, their immediate and long-range goals, and even very specific characteristics did match those of the Italian examples. Among other shared features were the attempts to ruralize urbanites, to stem the movement of the lowest socio-economic groups, to isolate low-income or welfare tenants in urban and suburban enclaves, to intervene massively in the day-to-day lives of new town residents, to reduce them to the status of sharecroppers for the state, to reinforce traditional social patterns and sexual and racial prejudices, to supervise and control the recreational activities of new community residents, and to discourage residents from seizing the initiative in organizing their own communities. In Greenbelt, the government even denied entry to families in which the wife worked outside the home.[6]

More than half a century separates us from the programs and events examined in this book. Our vantage point offers us the luxury of detachment and of insights and knowledge unavailable to contemporaries. But as with all perspectival renderings, vantage and distance distort: in particular, they efface the power and urgency of the problems Italy and America faced, the distress and fear that gripped their populations, and the very real sense in both countries that they stood on the brink of terrifying, catastrophic changes. New communities were one response to these problems, these fears, these tensions. In their broadest lineaments, the new community programs in the two countries—whether rural, subsistence, cooperative, industrial, or migrant—represented a retreat from present troubles by turning to the solutions of a more stable past.

The appeal of ruralism during the 1930s derived from obvious doubts about the consequences of industrialization. In Italy and the United States, as well as in Germany, the turmoil of the Depression and the inability of modern industrial cities to provide for all of their residents led to the knee-jerk reaction that people should find their own sustenance on the land, as they had done for centuries. Instead of accepting industrialization as a condition of the modern world, those who held this view sought refuge in the known certainties of an easier, less complicated arrangement borrowed from the past: specifically, the traditional nuclear family diligently at work on its own plot of land in a traditional farmhouse, uninvolved in strikes or demonstrations. The back-to-the-land movement was more of an anachronism in the United States, an advanced industrial economy, than in Italy, where increased agricultural productivity was a condition of further modernization; but even in Italy the program clearly preserved anachronistic social and economic relationships. Fears of a radicalized urban working class also fueled the ruralization campaign in both countries.

Once the two governments began to fund projects meant to accomplish this return to the land, they behaved in virtually identical fashion. Not surprisingly, government administrators who believed that they had engineered good programs for living had little tolerance for modifications or deviations proposed by settlers. Neither particularly "Fascist" nor especially "democratic," this pattern of response directly reflects how a large capitalist government bureaucracy with centralizing tendencies handles its programs, especially when they are intended as models for future development.

In part, the control over the colonists resulted from the bureaucratic imperative to have the projects work smoothly and fulfill the goals of the programs, both to protect investments and to demonstrate the viability of the new living arrangements. But the government's notion that it had the right to demand of the homesteaders an attitude of perpetual subservience is one of several telling clues to understanding the Depression in America. The government's emphasis on cooperation, appreciation, and "worthy" families threw the responsibility for unemployment or financial distress back onto the individual: for there to be "worthy" families there also had to be "unworthy" ones, and they were the unemployed. By acting in a certain way and by following the government's guidance in home management, a family could expect to improve its condition, and failure to do so by implication meant the reverse: the fault lay with the client, not the government.* Tugwell affirmed as much with his remark that he regarded problems in the new settlements as due to a failure of character on the part of the homesteaders.[7]

When a project aimed to alter living patterns dramatically, as the Subsistence Homesteads and Cooperative Farms programs did, an additional utopian element crept in, leading to an emphasis on "model" families and "model" communities. The lively if marginal tradition of utopian communities in America and Europe during the nineteenth century shared with its twentieth-century descendants the basic assumption that a controlled physical setting coupled with certain social arrangements could improve individuals and make them better—and less rebellious—

*"A confidential report is secured on each family together with a short history of the family and its ability to perform the labor necessary to make the crops and maintain the home. In this way each family is adjudged a good risk or a poor risk. With those who pass this test, a farm and home management plan is developed by the County Farm and Home Supervisor." Connie Bonslagel, FSA, "Rural Rehabilitation," American Home Economics Convention, Seattle, Washington, 9 July 1936. FSA RGH 96 SF General Correspondence 1940–42, File 530.

members of society. A similar underlying assumption had characterized many of the organized movements against squalid tenements during the Progressive era in the United States. By the 1930s this notion found expression in Italy and America in town plantations and settlement programs, but when such enterprises came under the aegis of the state several other aims, chiefly propagandistic ones, were attached to them.

Good citizens in pleasant communities, producing food and earning a livelihood, were glowing advertisements for the benefits possible under their respective countries' political systems. For Italian Fascism, such communities afforded vivid proof at home and abroad that benefits accrued to ordinary Italians under the corporate state, that Fascism was an energetic and positive force, and that noble agrarian virtues (dignified by Cincinnatus in the days of ancient Rome) were alive and well and living near the New Towns. Legitimacy figured no less prominently in the propaganda goals of the American settlements. In opposition to the economic and psychological crisis of the Depression, New Deal settlements asserted the ability of the government to generate living arrangements and even working situations which upheld not only the traditional value of private property but also those of community [Fig. 4.3]. The settlements responded to the often conflicting claims of recovery and reform without fully satisfying either, largely because they chose to moderate distress and control unrest without threatening the market system and private interests.

The actual characteristics of "model" communities differed between Italy and the United States. In Italy the architecture and urban plans gave physical expression to a complex and rigid hierarchy of classes, houses, and government authority, all based on highly traditional models. In the United States, hierarchy did not dominate the layouts of Resettlement projects, but—as in the Italian settlements in Africa—the program rigidly segregated blacks from whites and class from class. Crude distinctions separated permanent settlements from temporary shelters for migrants, as well as principally rural developments from urban ones, and sale housing from rental housing. Hierarchical order flourished in the relationship between government agencies and clients, as well as in the formal and informal criteria for tenant selection and management programs. Attempts were made, through devices such as the use of different roof types, varieties of shrubbery and trees, and different orientations on the street, to stress the individuality of each home, but they were

4.3 (*Overleaf*) Gee's Bend, Alabama, 1939 (photo by Marion Post Wolcott). Little Pettway's family sits on the porch of the new home provided by the FSA; their old home is to the left. The porch of another FSA home is visible in the background. Of a similar sharecropper's

house in Alabama, James Agee wrote: "The houses are built in the 'stinginess,' carelessness, and traditions of an unpersonal agency; they are of the order of 'company' houses. They are furnished, decorated and used in the starved needs, traditions and naiveties of profoundly simple individuals. Thus there are conveyed here two kinds of classicism, essentially different yet related and beautifully euphonious. These classicisms are created of economic need, of local availability, and of local-primitive tradition: and in their purity they are the exclusive property and privilege of the people at the bottom of that world" (*Let Us Now Praise Famous Men*).

patently illusory: not only the inhabitants' conduct but the environmental and ornamental variations themselves were governed by rules that made it clear that real control rested with the government.

Stripped of propaganda, the goal of planning every aspect of life exemplified by the Italian New Towns—from the arrangements of roads for the various social classes in Carbonia to the coordination of tower heights in the Agro Pontino to the control over exactly which shrubs and trees would be planted—signals a desire to leave nothing to chance. For the social and architectural experiments to work, they could harbor nothing random. Perhaps this is the most telling inversion of the medieval prototypes upon which so much of the architecture in the Italian towns drew. The beauty of a medieval city such as San Gimignano is in the chaotic and even cumbersome arrangements that sprang not from an ideal plan but from often abrasive social interaction, determinedly individualistic impulses, and a periodic need to fulfill changing functional needs. The

Fascist *arengario* and its relationship to its medieval ancestor is emblematic of the way in which order would replace disorder in the Fascist state. The spacious medieval *arengario* provided a meeting hall for the citizens of the commune to debate public issues. It accommodated instances of pettiness and narrowness as well as unified, common action; it offered, in a sense, a forum for the best and worst in human behavior when two or more people meet to resolve conflicts and settle grievances. Clearly these were not the features of medieval models that appealed to the Fascist state or to the architects who designed its buildings and cities. The possibility of conflict is simply read out of the cities and the architecture by the imposition of self-consciously integrated, hierarchical, and highly ordered plans at every point. In its twentieth-century incarnation, the *arengario* is simply an appendage of the Casa del Fascio's towers, appropriately dimensioned not for several hundred people but for one. No debates, no arguments, no making difficult policy decisions in common: one man handed down policy, submerging potential strife with the weight of his dictates.

Totalitarianism? Paternalism? The two may not be very far apart. Perhaps it is in the migrant camps, those painfully neglected sites for the refugees from the economic failures of American capitalism, that the contradictions of the New Deal emerge most clearly. Launched and sustained by a rhetoric which criticized the excesses of capital, the unfairness of contemporary economic practices and institutions, and the inadequacies of public and private agencies to cope with the problems of the "little guy"—in other words, a rhetoric which seemed to challenge bourgeois relations—the New Deal in practice promoted policies which directly augmented and rationalized the mechanisms and arrangements of a conservative capitalist bourgeoisie. Landowners and commercial farms needed migrant laborers, combined to pay them low wages, and met their efforts to unite with arms, evictions, and law-enforcement support. Government stepped in not to equalize the disputants' positions, but to erode union power among the migrants through the government-operated camps and through the government's self-appointed role as broker between the two groups. Clean and well-managed migrant camps "Americanized" their clients, improved on the squalid grower-provided camps, and contained the migrants in tight formation well away from neighboring communities. They also kept the inhabitants under the watchful eye of the government, and effectively depoliticized living and working conditions for the migrants.

And what the schemes promote informs us in a concrete fashion of what was believed to have been lost: modernization had robbed the individual of self-reliance, independence, self-respect, and pride in workmanship, as well as the close-knit cooperation of the family; hence the emphasis on the home and the small farm as the means of meeting all needs. On a larger scale, the very size of cities and the complexity of modern industrial life led to increasingly tenuous ties within communities and in the nation as a whole: from the breakdown of the family and the community seemed to loom the threat of a breakdown of the entire social order. For both countries, the government's answer to this disruption entailed a change in lifestyles rather than a change in political relations.

The *borgate* on the outskirts of Rome offer yet another example of the attempt to control dissent. Bound by poverty, by limited hours of public transport, and by the distance from the bus lines, the residents of Primavalle were effectively contained within the boundaries from dusk to dawn. Beyond this unofficial control, on special occasions the Fascist government passed to more stringent measures. Because Primavalle was home to a large number of anarchists and opponents of the state, on the occasion of major ceremonies, visits of foreign heads of state, or important propaganda events, the *borgata* was surrounded by armed soldiers who permitted no one to leave until the event had ended.

The plan to relocate urbanites to rural settlements, coupled with an attempt to tame the effects of industrialization, appealed to national leaders even after the onset of World War II. The Allies incorporated these proposals as a punitive measure in the short-lived Morgenthau Plan for postwar Germany, whereby the Saar and the Ruhr would become internationalized industrial regions and the rest of Germany would be rural. Since this proposal aimed to neutralize and depoliticize Germany, it is a telling indication of the sentiments which similar plans for the poor must have represented in pre-war Italy and America. All of these resettlement programs reflected understandable but, ultimately, profoundly reactionary responses to the social, technological, and economic changes wrought by modernization and industrialization, and arguably the resettlement programs succeeded precisely here: even the trauma of Depression and major social dislocations failed to raise political consciousness. What the programs also do not evince is a developing understanding of how the political economy of capital affects those most touched by its excesses.

Appendix A
New Communities in Fascist Italy

(provinces identified in parentheses)

Founded by Arsa Anonima Società Carbonifera

Arsia (Istria)

Founded by Azienda Carboni Italiani

Carbonia (Cagliari)
Pozzo Littorio (Istria)

Founded by Azienda Tabacchi Italiani

Tigrinna (Libya)

Founded by Ente Ferrarese di Colonizzazione

Fertilia (Sassari)

Founded by Ente per la Colonizzazione della Libia

Baracca (Libya)
Battisti (Libya)
Beda Littoria (Libya)
Breveglieri (Libya)
Crispi (Libya)
D'Annunzio (Libya)
El Fager (Libya)
Filzi (Libya)
Garibaldi (Libya)
Gedida (Libya)
Gioda (Libya)
Giovanni Berta (Libya)
Luigi di Savoia (Libya)
Mahamura (Libya)
Mameli (Libya)
Naima (Libya)
Oberdan (Libya)
Oliveti (Libya)
Primavera/Luigi Razza (Libya)
Sauro (Libya)
Umberto Maddalena (Libya)
Zahra (Libya)

Founded by Istituto Autonomo Fascista per le Case Popolari

Guidonia (Rome)

Founded by Istituto Nazionale Fascista per la Previdenza Sociale

Michele Bianchi (Libya)
Giordani (Libya)
Micca (Libya)
Mazzoli (Libya)
Corradini (Libya)

Founded by Mvsn della Legione Cirenaica

Colonia Libica del Fascio Milanese—
    E. Crespi (Libya)

Founded by Opera Nazionale per i Combattenti

Provincial capital:
Latina (formerly Littoria)

Communal centers:
Aprilia (Latina)
Pomezia (Rome)
Pontinia (Latina)
Sabaudia (Latina)

Rural borghi:
Alberese (Grosseto)
Appio (Caserta)
Bainsizza (Latina)
Carso (Latina)
Cervaro (Foggia)
Colonia Elena (Latina)
Coltano (Pisa)
Domizio (Caserta)
Ermada (Latina)
Faiti (Latina)
Giardinetto (Foggia)
Ginosa Marina (Taranto)
Grappa (Latina)
Grappa (Lecce)
Incoronata (Foggia)
Isonzo (Latina)
Montegrosso (Bari)
Montello (Latina)
Montenero (Latina)
Pasubio (Latina)

Perrone (Taranto)
Piave (Latina)
Piave (Lecce)
Porto Cesareo (Lecce)
Sabotino (Latina)
San Cesareo (Lecce)
San Cesareo (Rome)
Segezia (Foggia)
Vittoria (Bolzano)
Vodice (Latina)

Borghi *in Ethiopia:*
Biscioftù

Olettà

Founded by Società Agricola Industriale Cellulosa Italiana
Torviscosa (Udine)

Founded by Società Bonifiche Sarde
Mussolinia (Oristano)

Founded by Unione Coloniale Italo Araba
El-Guarscia (Libya)

Appendix B
New Communities in New Deal America

[Based on Conkin, *Tomorrow a New World*, pp. 332–37, drawing primarily on U.S. House of Representatives, Select Committee of the Committee on Agriculture, *Hearings on the Farm Security Administration* (78th Congress, 1st Session, 1943–44).]

Planned and initiated by Division of Subsistence Homesteads

Stranded communities:
Arthurdale (Reedsville, West Virginia)
Cumberland Homesteads (Crossville, Tennessee)
Tygart Valley Homesteads (Elkins, West Virginia)
Westmoreland Homesteads (Greensburg, Pennsylvania)

Cooperative industrial community:
Jersey Homesteads (Hightstown, New Jersey)

Farm communities:
Penderlea Homesteads (Pender County, North Carolina)
Piedmont Homesteads (Jasper County, Georgia)
Richton Homesteads (Richton, Mississippi)

Resettlement communities:
Shenandoah Homesteads (five counties in Virginia)

Industrial communities:
Austin Homesteads (Austin, Minnesota)
Bankhead Farms (Jasper, Alabama)
Beauxart Gardens (Beaumont, Texas)
Cahaba (Trussville Homesteads) (near Birmingham, Alabama)
Dalworthington Gardens (Arlington, Texas)
Dayton Homesteads (Dayton, Ohio)
Decatur Homesteads (Decatur, Indiana)
Duluth Homesteads (Duluth, Minnesota)

El Monte Homesteads (El Monte, California)
Granger Homesteads (Granger, Iowa)
Greenwood Homesteads (near Birmingham, Alabama)
Hattiesburg Homesteads (Hattiesburg, Mississippi)
Houston Gardens (Houston, Texas)
Lake County Homesteads (Chicago, Illinois)
Longview Homesteads (Longview, Washington)
Magnolia Homesteads (Meridian, Mississippi)
McComb Homesteads (McComb, Mississippi)
Mount Olive Homesteads (near Birmingham, Alabama)
Palmerdale Homesteads (near Birmingham, Alabama)
Phoenix Homesteads (Phoenix, Arizona)
San Fernando Homesteads (Reseda, California)
Three Rivers Gardens (Three Rivers, Texas)
Tupelo Homesteads (Tupelo, Mississippi)
Wichita Gardens (Wichita Falls, Texas)

Garden City (for blacks):
Aberdeen Gardens (Newport News, Virginia)

Planned or initiated by Federal Emergency Relief Administration

Farm communities:
Ashwood Plantation (Lee County, South Carolina)
Bosque Farms (Valencia County, New Mexico)
Chicot Farms (Chicot and Drew Counties, Arkansas)
Dyess Colony (Mississippi County, Arkansas)
Irwinville (Irwin County, Georgia)

Roanoke Farms (Halifax County, North Carolina)

Ropesville Farms (Hockley County, Texas)

St. Francis River Farms (Poinsett County, Arkansas)

Scuppernong Farms (Tyrell and Washington Counties, North Carolina)

Skyline Farms (Jackson County, Alabama)

Wichita Valley Farms (Wichita Valley County, Texas)

Wolf Creek (Grady County, Georgia)

Farm and rural industrial communities:

Cherry Lake Farms (near Madison, Florida)

Pine Mountain Valley (Harris County, Georgia)

Stranded communities:

Burlington Project (Burlington, North Dakota)

Red House (Red House, West Virginia)

Industrial communities:

Albert Lea Homesteads (Albert Lea, Minnesota)

Arizona Part-Time Farms (Phoenix, Arizona)

Farm Villages:

Fairbury Farmsteads (Jefferson County, Nebraska)

Fall City Farmsteads (Richardson County, Nebraska)

Grand Island Farmsteads (Hall County, Nebraska)

Kearney Homesteads (Buffalo County, Nebraska)

Loup City Farmsteads (Sherman County, Nebraska)

Scottsbluff Farmsteads (Scotts Bluff County, Nebraska)

Sioux Falls Farms (Minnehaha County, South Dakota)

South Sioux City Farmsteads (Dakota County, Nebraska)

Two Rivers Farmsteads (Douglas and Saunders Counties, Nebraska)

Woodlake Community (Wood County, Texas)

Initiated by Resettlement Administration

Garden cities:

Greenbelt (Berwyn, Maryland, near Washington, DC)

Greendale (Milwaukee, Wisconsin)

Greenhills (Cincinnati, Ohio)

Ironwood Homesteads (Ironwood, Michigan)

Forest homesteads:

Drummond Project (Bayfield County, Wisconsin)

Sublimity Farms (Laurel County, Kentucky)

Cooperative farms:

Casa Grande Valley Farms (Pinal County, Arizona)

Lake Dick (Jefferson and Arkansas Counties, Arkansas)

Cooperative plantation:

Terrebonne (Terrebonne Parish, Louisiana)

Farm communities:

Biscoe Farms (Prairie County, Arkansas)

Christian-Trigg Farms (Christian County, Kentucky)

Clover Bend Farms (Lawrence County, Arkansas)

Desha Farms (Desha and Drew Counties, Arkansas)

Escambia Farms (Okaloosa County, Florida)

Flint River Farms (Macon County, Georgia)

Gee's Bend Farms (Wilcox County, Alabama)

Hinds Farms (Hinds County, Mississippi)

Kinsey Flats (Custer County, Montana)

La Forge Farms (New Madrid County, Missouri)

Lakeview Farms (Lee and Phillips Counties, Arkansas)

Lonoke Farms (Lonoke County, Arkansas)

Lucedale Farms (George and Greene Counties, Mississippi)

McLennan Farms (McLennan County, Texas)

Mileston Farms (Holmes County,
  Mississippi)
Mounds Farms (Madison and East
  Carroll Parishes, Louisiana)
Orangeburg Farms (Orangeburg and
  Calhoun Counties, South Carolina)
Osage Farms (Pettis County, Missouri)
Pembroke Farms (Robeson County,
  North Carolina)
Plum Bayou (Jefferson County,
  Arkansas)
Prairie Farms (Macon County, Alabama)
Sabine Farms (Harrison County, Texas)

Saginaw Valley Farms (Saginaw County,
  Michigan)
Sam Houston Farms (Harris County,
  Texas)
Tiverton Farms (Sumter County, South
  Carolina)
Townes Farms (Crittenden County,
  Arkansas)
Transylvania Farms (East Carroll Parish,
  Louisiana)
Trumann Farms (Poinsett County,
  Arkansas)

Notes

Introduction

1. Franklin K. Lane, *Annual Report of the Department of the Interior for the Fiscal Year Ended June 30, 1918* (Washington, DC, 1919), 11.

2. For an account of attitudes toward the city, see Morton and Lucia White, *The Intellectual Versus the City* (Cambridge, MA, 1962).

3. Sigfried Giedion, *Space, Time, and Architecture: The Growth of a New Tradition*, 5th ed. (Cambridge, MA, 1967), 820.

4. Henry A. Millon, "Some New Towns in Italy in the 1930s," in Henry A. Millon and Linda Nochlin, eds., *Art and Architecture in the Service of Politics* (Cambridge, MA, 1978), 326–41.

5. Robert R. Taylor, *The Word in Stone: The Role of Architecture in National Socialist Ideology* (Berkeley and Los Angeles, 1974), 231–34; Barbara Miller Lane, *Architecture and Politics in Germany: 1918–45* (Cambridge, MA, 1968, 1985), 206–211. Considerable public building characterized some other countries as well; see for example Mina Marefat's forthcoming Ph.D. dissertation "Aesthetics of Power: Reza Shah and the Reconstruction of Teheran 1920–1940," MIT.

6. Paul Conkin, *Tomorrow a New World: The New Deal Community Program* (Ithaca, NY, 1959), 49–54.

1. Italy and the United States During the 1930s

1. Studs Terkel, *Hard Times* (New York, 1978), 241.

2. William E. Leuchtenberg, *Franklin D. Roosevelt and the New Deal, 1932–1940* (New York, 1963); Carl Degler, *Out of Our Past: The Forces that Shaped Modern America* (New York, 1970); Otto L. Graham, Jr., ed., *The New Deal: The Critical Issues* (Boston, 1971).

3. Enzo Santarelli, *Storia del Fascismo*, vol. 2 (Rome, 1981), 215ff; Alberto Aquarone, *L'organizzazione dello stato totalitario* (Turin, 1965), 540ff.

4. Helen Rosenau, *The Ideal City: Its Architectural Evolution in Europe*, 3rd ed. (London and New York, 1983), 2.

5. For general information on the Fascist New Towns, see Diane Ghirardo and Kurt Forster, "I modelli delle città di fondazione in epoca Fascista," in Cesare De Seta, ed. *Storia d'Italia*, Annali 8: *Insediamenti e territorio* (Turin, 1985), 627–674; Riccardo Mariani, *Fascismo e città nuove* (Milan, 1976); R. Martinelli and L. Nuti, "Le città nuove del ventennio da Mussolinia a Carbonia," in *Le città di fondazione*, Atti del II Convegno Internazionale di Storia Urbanistica (Lucca, 1977), 271–93; idem, "Città nuove in Sardegna durante il periodo Fascista," in *Storia Urbana*, 2/6 (1978), 291–323; idem, *Le città di strapaese: La politica di "fondazione" nel ventennio* (Milan, 1981); A. Mioni, *Le trasformazioni territoriali in Italia nella prima età industriale* (Venice, 1976).

6. For general studies of Italian Fascism, see Alberto Aquarone and Maurizio Vernassa, eds., *Il regime Fascista* (Bologna, 1974), Alan Cassels, *Fascism* (New York, 1975); Alexander De Grand, *Italian Fascism: Its Origins and Development* (Lincoln, NB, and London, 1982); Renzo De Felice, *Mussolini il Fascista*, vol. 2, *L'organizzazione dello stato Fascista* (Turin, 1968); idem, *Mussolini il Duce, I: Gli anni del consenso, 1929–1936*

A note on archival sources: When this book was being written, the ONC archives for the Italian communities on the mainland had not been opened for consultation. From time to time it has been possible to obtain some documents from the file, many of which have been cited in this study. Because of the provisional nature of the collocation of these documents, however, at this point it is not clear whether their permanent organization will conform to the style in which I have cited them. I have therefore given dates and as many particulars of a document as possible for the benefit of future researchers. As the ONC archives for Africa Orientale Italiana have not yet been reorganized, that material is cited under the criteria established by the ONC itself; the eventual reorganization of these files may differ from the citations here. Again, I have given as much relevant information as possible to guide future researchers.

(Turin, 1974); Edward R. Tannenbaum, *Fascist Italy: Society and Culture, 1922–1945* (London, 1973).

7. Diane Ghirardo, "Italian Architects and Fascist Politics: An Evaluation of the Rationalists' Role in Regime Building," *Journal of the Society of Architectural Historians*, 39/2 (May 1980), 109–27.

8. Matthew H. Elbow, *French Corporative Theory 1789–1948: A Chapter in the History of Ideas* (New York, 1953); Taylor Cole, "Corporative Organization in the Third Reich," *Review of Politics*, 2 (1940), 438–52; Gordon A. Craig, *Germany 1866–1945* (New York, 1978), 602–37.

9. Roland Sarti, *Fascism and the Industrial Leadership in Italy 1919–1940: A Study of the Expansion of Private Power under Fascism* (Berkeley, 1971); P. Ciocca and G. Toniolo, *L'economia italiana nel periodo Fascista* (Bologna, 1976).

10. Marco Maraffi, "State/Economy Relationships: The Case of Italian Public Enterprise," *British Journal of Sociology*, 31/4 (December 1980), 507–24.

11. Ellis W. Hawley, *The New Deal and the Problem of Monopoly: A Study in Economic Ambivalence* (Princeton, 1966); Douglas North, *Growth and Welfare in the American Past: A New Economic History* (Englewood Cliffs, NJ, 1974).

12. G. Taratta, "Cerealicoltura e politica agraria durante il Fascismo," in G. Toniolo, ed., *Lo sviluppo economico italiano 1861–1940* (Bari, 1973), 385–86.

13. John Maynard Keynes, *The General Theory of Employment, Interest, and Money* (London, 1936), 87–113, 387–89.

14. John Maynard Keynes, letter to Franklin D. Roosevelt, 1 February 1938; now in Richard N. Current and John A. Garraty, *Words that Made American History* (Boston, 1962), 374.

15. Marriner Eccles, Testimony before the Senate Finance Committee, 24 February 1933; in Current and Garraty, *Words*, 333–46.

16. Keynes, *General Theory*, 388.

17. Terkel, *Hard Times*, 49.

18. A.F.K. Organski, "Fascism and Modernization," in S. J. Woolf, ed., *The Nature of Fascism* (New York, 1969), 19–41; Henry A. Turner, Jr., "Fascism and Modernization," *World Politics*, 24 (1972), 547–64; A. James Gregor, *The Fascist Persuasion in Radical Politics* (Princeton, 1974).

19. Mussolini, address to the Senate, 18 March 1932; in Paolo Orano, ed., *Le direttive del Duce sui problemi nazionali: I lavori pubblici* (Rome, 1937), 84.

20. Marcello Piacentini to Antonio Muñoz; in "Marcello Piacentini parla di Roma e di architettura," *L'urbe*, 2/4 (April 1937), 25.

21. Michele Bianchi, message to the Blackshirts, 28 October 1928; in Orano, *Le direttive: I lavori pubblici*, 71.

22. Col. E. W. Clark, speech at Richmond, Virginia, 18 September 1939.

23. E. Lipson, *Europe 1914–1939*, 5th ed. (London, 1949), 422–23.

24. Renzo De Felice, *Le interpretazioni del Fascismo* (Bari, 1977), 244–47.

25. Degler, *Out of Our Past*, 379–413.

26. John A. Garraty, "The New Deal, National Socialism, and the Great Depression," *American Historical Review*, 78/4 (October 1973), 907–44.

27. Lane, *Architecture and Politics in Germany*; Taylor, *The Word in Stone*.

28. Among the recent books on some of the new towns, see Carlo Taormina, ed., *Il territorio: Latina 1932/82*, Atti del Convegno Nazionale (Ancona, 1982); Richard Burdett et al., *Sabaudia città nuova Fascista* (London, 1982); Feliciano Iannella, *Il territorio pontino e la fondazione di Sabaudia* (Rome, 1975); *Le Paludi Pontine: Mostra antologica di pittura* (Latina, 1982); Riccardo Mariani, *Latina: Storia di una città* (Florence, 1982); Giuseppe Pasquali and Pasquale Pinna, *Sabaudia 1933–34* (Milan, 1985); Tommaso Stabile, *Agro Pontino Romano 1700–1971* (Latina, 1971); idem, *Latina una volta Littoria: Storia di una città* (Latina, 1982); Pio Zaccagnini, *Storia di Latina dal diario di un medico* (Latina, 1982).

1. Foreign press coverage of the New Towns was remarkably detailed: see the *London Daily Mail*, 14 December 1932; *Kölnische Zeitung*, 24 April 1932; *Action Française*, 23 December 1932. Italian newspapers issued reports and commentaries almost constantly; on Littoria, for example, see Luigi Bottazzi, "Nascita del Grano a Littoria," *Corriere della Sera*, 7 January 1933; Gino Carocci, "Notte di Natale nella pace di Littoria," *La Nazione*, 28 December 1932.

2. Riccardo Mariani, "Le città nuove del periodo Fascista. Com'erano, perchè furono costruite, come sono adesso," *Abitare*, October 1978, 76–91. The only American discussion of the New Towns is Millon, "Some New Towns in Italy in the 1930s."

3. Benito Mussolini, "Breve preludio," in *Tempi della Rivoluzione Fascista* (Milan, 1930), 13ff; Mussolini, *Dottrina politica e sociale del Fascismo* (Milan, 1932), 20ff.

4. Mariani, *Fascismo e città nuove*, 144ff.

5. Mussolini, 1 August 1931; in Orano, *Le direttive: I lavori pubblici*, 79.

6. "La cronaca dello storico avvenimento," *La Conquista della Terra* (special issue devoted to Littoria), 3/12 (December 1932), 86.

7. Mussolini, "La nascita di Littoria," 18 December 1932, in B. Mussolini, *Opera omnia*, vol. 25: *Dal dodicesimo anniversario della fondazione al Patto a quattro (24 Marzo 1931–7 Giugno 1933)* (Florence, 1958), 184–85.

8. Denis Mack Smith, *Mussolini's Roman Empire* (New York, 1976), 107.

9. Mussolini, 1 August 1931, in Orano, *Le direttive: I lavori pubblici*, 79.

10. Ebenezer Howard, *Garden Cities of Tomorrow* (London, 1902; reprinted Cambridge, MA, 1965).

11. Charles-Edouard Jeanneret [Le Corbusier], *Urbanisme* (Paris, 1925); for a cogent discussion of Le Corbusier's urban theory, see Stanislaus von Moos, *Le Corbusier: Elements of a Synthesis* (Cambridge, MA, 1979), 187–220.

12. Nello Mazzocchi Alemanni, "La conquista rurale," in Opera Nazionale per i Combattenti, *L'Agro Pontino al 29 ottobre anno XVI E.F.* (Rome, 1937), 56.

13. On Roman town planning, see John B. Ward-Perkins, *Cities of Ancient Greece and Italy: Planning in Classical Antiquity* (New York, 1974).

14. Orano, *Le direttive: I lavori pubblici*, 7–8.

15. Commissione per lo Studio della Sistemazione dell'Abitato di Predappio, 12 February 1925, 2–3; "Relazione," 2–3: ACS, Seg. Part. Duce, C.O. Busta 937, Fasc. 501.028/II–2.

16. "Relazione," 2.

17. Giovanni Giuriati to Benito Mussolini, 7 March 1925. ACS, Seg. Part. Duce, C.O. Busta 937, Fasc. 501.028/II–2. For an entertaining account of Predappio during the Mussolini era, see Vittorio Emiliani, *Il paese dei Mussolini* (Turin, 1984), esp. 36–37.

18. Mussolini to Giuriati, 18 March 1925. ACS, Seg. Part. Duce, C.O. Busta 937, Fasc. 501.028/II–2. Mussolini notified the Prefect of Forlì of the decision in a telegram dated 3 June 1925: "Consiglio Superiore Lavori Pubblici ha deciso trasporto Comune e abitato Predappio a Dovia vicino a Varano [palazzo]. Questa soluzione è stata da me caldeggiata e trova il mio plauso. Il nuovo paese che sorgerà bello e igienico in posizione non franabile si chiamerà Nuova Predappio. Comprendendosi frazione Dovia. Prevenga Sindaco. Lavori possono cominciare subito. Se necessario io riceverei sindaco e Giunta per convincerli utilità soluzione problema. Gradirò notizie. Mussolini." ACS, Seg. Part. Duce. C.O. Busta 937, Fasc. 501.028/II–2.

19. Giorgio Ciucci, "Il dibattito sull'architettura e le città fasciste," in *Storia dell'Arte Italiana*, VII: *Il Novecento* (Turin, 1982): 263–378.

20. Giovanni Ercolini, "I bisogni più urgente del paese," 15 April 1923. ACS, Seg. Part. Duce, C.O. Busta 937, Fasc. 501.028/II–1.

21. Ercolini, "I bisogni." See also Pietro Baccanelli, "Promemoria," 18 August 1926. ACS, Seg. Part. Duce, C.O. Busta 937, Fasc. 501.028/II–2.

22. Podestà di Predappio, "Promemoria," 23 July 1927. ACS, Seg. Part. Duce, C.O. Busta 937, Fasc. 501.028/II–2.

23. Pio Teodorani to Giovanni Marinelli, 17 September 1936. ACS, PNF Fed. Prov. 590, Busta 280, Forlì Servizi Tecnici.

24. Victoria De Grazia, *The Culture of Consent: Mass Organization of Leisure in Italy* (Cambridge, 1981); Philip V. Cannistraro, *La fabbrica del consenso: Fascismo e mass-media* (Rome and Bari, 1975).

25. Commissario Rinaldo Braschi, "Relazione," 23 April 1930. ACS, Seg. Part. Duce, C.O. Busta 585, Fasc. 201.376, 2.

26. Renzo De Felice, *Mussolini il rivoluzionario 1883–1920* (Turin, 1966); Emiliani, *Il paese*, 36ff.

27. See Luciana Firelli and Sara Rossi, *Pienza, tra ideologia e realtà* (Bari, 1979); Ludwig Heydenreich and Wolfgang Lotz, *Architecture in Italy 1400 to 1600* (Harmondsworth, 1974), 43–45. Kurt Forster kindly reminded me of the parallel with Pienza in an early discussion of Predappio.

28. L. C. Gabel, *The Commentaries of Pius II*, books I–IX (Northampton, MA, 1931–51).

29. Aurelio Moschi to Donna Rachele Mussolini, September 1938. ACS, Seg. Part. Duce. C.O. Busta 278, "Predappio GIL," Fasc. 153.830/2; "Appunto," 25 October 1935. ACS, PNF Fed. Prov. 590, Busta 278.

30. Osvaldo Sebastiani to Prefect of Forlì, 10 September 1938. ACS Seg. Part. Duce, C.O. Busta 937, Fasc. 150.904.

31. "Appunto per S.E. Il Capo del Governo," 23 July 1935. From his seaside retreat in Riccione, Mussolini penciled his response in the margin: "Ballino pure—io non andrò." ACS, Seg. Part. Duce, C.O. Busta 585, Fasc. 201.376.

32. "Oggi Ingegnere Capo Genio Civile provincia Forlì mi ha presentato progetti costruzione Predappio Nuova. Linee severe edifici pubblici faranno della Predappio Nuova una cittadina che avrà un sicuro avvenire. Prego V.S. prendere visione dei progetti per convincersi che costituire un nuovo paese è come dissi una delle più nobili imprese spirito fascista." Mussolini to Decurione Raggi, Sindaco di Predappio, 17 June 1925. ACS, Seg. Part. Duce, C.O. Busta 937, Fasc. 501.028/II–2.

33. For a complete discussion of the "liberation" of the mausoleum of Augustus, see Spiro Kostof, "The Emperor and the Duce: The Planning of Piazzale Augusto Imperatore in Rome," in H. Millon and L. Nochlin, eds., *Art and Architecture in the Service of Politics* (Cambridge, MA, 1978), 270–325; see also William L. MacDonald, "Excavation, Restoration, and Italian Architecture of the 1930's," in H. Searing, ed., *In Search of Modern Architecture* (Cambridge, MA, 1982), 298–320.

34. Prefect of Forlì to Mussolini, 25 November 1925. ACS, Seg. Par. Duce, C.O. Busta 937, Fasc. 501.028/II–2.

35. See the publications of the Commissariato per le Migrazioni e la Colonizzazione Interna, *Le migrazioni interne in Italia nell'anno 1932–X* (Rome, 1933); idem, *Le migrazioni interne in Italia nell'anno 1934–XII* (Rome, 1935); and Anna Treves, *Le migrazioni interne nell'Italia Fascista* (Turin, 1976).

36. Mariani, *Fascismo e città nuove*, 24.

37. Constantino Andruzzi, "Le Paludi Pontine nella storia," *La Conquista della Terra*, 3/4 (April 1932), 41–53.

38. Ibid., 45.

39. Ibid., 43. This history is a bit fanciful, because the lagoon had silted up by the fourth century B.C., long before any imperial expansion. See Fulco Pratesi, "L'agro-pontino: Storia, trasformazioni, prospettive," in Taormina, *Il territorio: Latina 1932/82*, 267.

40. Andruzzi, "Le Paludi pontine," 42.

41. Ward-Perkins, *Cities of Ancient Greece and Italy*, 39.

42. Arrigo Serpieri, *La guerra e le classi rurali italiane* (Bari, 1930), 39–40.

43. In addition to Mariani, *Fascismo e città nuove*, 40–44, see Cannistraro, *La fabbrica*

del consenso; Adrian Lyttleton, *The Seizure of Power: Fascism in Italy 1919–1929* (London, 1973). See also the publications of the Commissariato per le Migrazioni e la Colonizzazione Interna cited in note 35 above, and Treves, *Le migrazioni interne.*

44. Oscar Uccelli, Prefect of Forlì, to Osvaldo Sebastiani, 4 March 1938. "Forse, oggi, sembra opportuno non insistere su tale trasferimento se non si desidera urbanizzare, troppo, la nuova Predappio. Lasciare attaccati al vecchio centro di Predappio—e quindi alla terra—gli abitanti del vecchio piccolo centro rurale è—per questo e per molte altre considerazioni d'ordine economico e sociale—preferibile." ACS, Seg. Part. Duce, C.O. Busta 937, Fasc. 501.028/II–3.

45. "Prospetti dei movimenti avvenuti dal 1 gennaio al 31 dicembre 1939 nella popolazione residente e calcolo mensile di essa," undated. ACS, Seg. Part. Duce, C.O. Busta 937, Fasc. 501.028/II-1.

46. Benito Mussolini, *Discorso sull'Ascensione* (Rome, 1927), 22; cf. ibid., 9.

47. In addition to the work by Anna Treves cited above, see also her "La politica antiurbana del Fascismo e un secolo di resistenza all'urbanizzazione industriale in Italia," in Alberto Mioni, ed., *Urbanistica Fascista: Ricerche e saggi sulle città e il territorio e sulle politiche urbane in Italia tra le due guerre* (Milan, 1980), 313–30.

48. Regio Decreto 4 March 1926, no. 440; Legge 24 December 1928, no. 2961; Legge 9 April 1931, no. 358; Legge 5 July 1939, no. 1082.

49. ISTAT, *Annuario Statistico Italiano 1934,* 1935, 178–91, 237.

50. Dino Cinel, "Conservative Adventurers: Italian Migrants in Italy and San Francisco," Ph.D. dissertation, Stanford University, 1979.

51. Mariani, *Fascismo e città nuove,* 10–11.

52. Emilio Sereni, *La questione agraria nella rinascita nazionale italiana* (Turin, 1975), 220–30.

53. For the story of the success of the PNF in Ferrara, see Paul Corner, *Fascism in Ferrara, 1915–1925* (London, 1975), 137–69. See also R. Cavandoli, *Le origini del Fascismo a Reggio Emilia 1919–1923* (Rome, 1972); S. Sechi, *Dopoguerra e Fascismo in Sardegna. Il movimento autonomistico nella crisi dello stato liberale (1918–1926)* (Turin, 1969); M. Bernabei, *Fascismo e nazionalismo in Campania (1919–1925)* (Rome, 1975); Raffaele Colapietra, *Napoli tra dopoguerra e Fascismo* (Milan, 1962); Alice Kelikian, *Town and Country under Fascism: The Transformation of Brescia 1915–1926* (New York, 1986). On sharecropping, see S.N.S. Cheung, *The Theory of Share Tenancy* (Chicago, 1973); P. K. Bardhan and T. N. Srinivasan, "Cropsharing Tenancy in Agriculture: A Theoretical and Empirical Analysis," *American Economic Review,* 61/1 (March 1971); and J. D. Reid, "Sharecropping as an Understandable Market Response," *Journal of Economic History* 33/1 (March 1973).

54. The ONC was established by decree no. 1970, 10 December 1917. Commissioni per la Fondazione dell'ONC, 30 October 1918.

55. Alberto Beneduce, *Relazione sull'ONC* (1921), 15–18. ONC AR (no file numbers available).

56. ONC AR (no file numbers available).

57. Opera Nazionale per i Combattenti, *L'Opera Nazionale per i Combattenti* (Rome, 1926), 69.

58. Opera Nazionale per i Combattenti, *36 Anni dell'Opera Nazionale per i Combattenti 1919–1955* (Rome, 1955), gives the agency's report on expropriations, donations, and purchases.

59. Memorandum from ONC to Mussolini, "Fabbisogno finanziario," undated (1935), ACS, Pres. Cons. Min. 1934/36, 1.1.8.1. 3575.

60. Alemanni, "La conquista rurale," 56.

61. Atti Parlamentari, Camera dei Deputati (1929–30), n. 692, 3.

62. Interview with Dino Cinel, Palo Alto, California, 2 January 1979.

63. Report from Prefect of Potenza, 1 January 1930. ACS, Pres. Cons. Min. (1930); cited in Mariani, *Fascismo e città nuove,* 122.

64. Luigi Razza, memo to Fed. Prov., 1932. ACS, Pres. Cons. Min., 11.4.94.

65. Report of Commissioner V. Orsolini Cencelli, 22 March 1935. ACS, Pres. Cons. Min., 1931–33, prot. 12455, 3.1.1.10089.

66. Alemanni, "La conquista rurale," 82.

67. Mariani, *Fascismo e città nuove*, 122; Pino Riva, *Fascismo, politica agraria, ONC nella bonificazione pontina del 1917 al 1943* (Latina, 1983), 155–58.

68. Mussolini to Serpieri, 5 March 1933; response 14 March 1933. ACS, Seg. Part. Duce, C.O. 132.862.

69. Cencelli, Report.

70. Alemanni, "La conquista rurale," 121.

71. Cencelli to Mussolini, August 1933. ACS, Seg. Part. Duce, C.O. 132.862.

72. Cencelli, Report.

73. "Udienza di S.E. Il Capo del Governo," 8 February 1933; Appendix 4 in Mariani, *Fascismo e città nuove*, 278.

74. Ibid.

75. Sergio Nannini, "Le migrazioni e la colonizzazione," *La Conquista della Terra* 6/12 (December 1935), 93.

76. Alemanni, "La conquista rurale," 122.

77. Ibid., 121–22.

78. Ibid., 122–23.

79. "Relazione del 14 luglio 1936," n. 6672. ONC AR.

80. "Udienza," 8 February 1933.

81. Mariani, *Fascismo e città nuove*, 175–77.

82. ACS, Seg. Part. Duce, C.O. 509.831, 20 December 1938.

83. Mariani, *Fascismo e città nuove*, 309–10.

84. ACS, Pres. Cons. Min. 1931–33, 3.1.1.10089; and Mussolini to Cencelli, 30 January 1933, Seg. Part. Duce C.O., 132.862.

85. ACS Pres. Cons. Min. 1931–33, 3.1.1.10089.

86. Alemanni, "La conquista rurale," 123.

87. Ibid., 123–25.

88. ONC AR 1933–35.

89. ONC AR "Lettere anonime al presidente Crollalanza," undated.

90. "Udienza," 8 February 1933.

91. Nannini, "Le migrazioni e la colonizzazione," 38.

92. Brian Pullan, *Rich and Poor in Renaissance Venice: The Social Institutions of a Catholic State, to 1620* (Oxford and Cambridge, MA, 1971).

93. Conkin, *Tomorrow a New World*, 265.

94. "Work Report and Description of Arizona Transient Camps," May 1934 (file: Arizona), and W. J. Plunkert, "Report on California," 10 July 1934 through 15 July 1934 (file: California); in FERA Transient Division Files, Camp Facilities, Minimum Requirements, 1935, Alabama–California.

95. Alemanni, "La conquista rurale," 89, 92, 119–20, 126.

96. Cencelli, Report (see note 65 above).

97. Ugo Todaro, "L'edilizia urbana e rurale," in ONC, *L'Agro Pontino* (see note 12 above), 28.

98. Ibid.

99. Ibid., 36.

100. ONC, *36 anni* (cited in note 58 above), 144.

101. Todaro, "L'edilizia," 39.

102. Ghirardo and Forster, "I modelli," 631–63.

103. Interview with Carlo Belli, December 1986.

104. In addition to Ward-Perkins, *Cities of Ancient Greece and Italy*, see his *Roman Architecture* (New York, 1977); Ernest Nash, *Roman Towns* (New York, 1944); F. Casta-

gnoli, *Orthogonal Planning in Antiquity* (Cambridge, MA, 1972); Leon Homo, *Rome Impériale et l'urbanisme dans l'antiquité*, 2nd ed. (Paris, 1972).

105. See Article 4 of the competition rules published in the *Gazzetta Ufficiale del Regno*, no. 225 (25 September 1940).

106. "La città giardino Aniene," *Architettura e Arti Decorative*, 1/8 (1920), 359; I. Costantini, "Le nuove costruzioni dell'Istituto per le Case Popolari in Roma. La Borgata Giardino 'Garbatella,' " *Architettura e Arti Decorative*, 2/3 (1922), 119–37.

107. Charles Higgonot, "Les terrenuove florentines du XVIᵉ siècle," in *Studi in onore di A. Fanfani*, vol. 3 (Milan, 1962), 3–17.

108. For a brief overview of Northern Italian communes, see Daniel Waley, *The Italian City-Republics* (New York, 1969).

109. See E. Ruffini Avondo, *I sistemi di deliberazione collettiva nel medioevo italiano* (Turin, 1927); and V. Franchini, *Saggio di ricerche su l'istituto del podestà nei comuni medievali* (Bologna, 1912).

110. Jürgen Paul, *Der Palazzo Vecchio in Florenz* (Florence, 1969), discusses the typology of the town halls.

111. Howard Saalman, "Early Renaissance Architecture and Practice in Filarete's Trattato di Architettura," *Art Bulletin*, 41/1 (1959), 98–106.

112. ONC AG Sabaudia, 2.6.22 (1 March 1934).

113. Mariani, *Fascismo e città nuove*, 249.

114. A. Schwartz, "La bonifica delle Paludi Pontine e la nuova città di Littoria," *Rassegna di Architettura*, 4/2 (1933), 59–60.

115. Filarete (Antonio Averlino), *Trattato di Architettura*, fascimile edition, ed. J. R. Spencer, *Filarete's Treatise on Architecture* (New Haven, 1965).

116. Pierre Lavedan, *Histoire de l'urbanisme, Renaissance et temps modernes* (Paris, 1959), 90–92.

117. Ervin Y. Galantay, *New Towns: Antiquity to the Present* (New York, 1975), 13–14.

118. For Frezzotti's design for the Municipio, see ACS, PNF Dir. B. 276; information concerning financing the project, regulations, visits, etc., can be found in B. 277.

119. See the unsigned article on Littoria, "La nuova città di Littoria nell'Agro-Pontino," *Architettura*, 12/9 (September 1933), 580–85.

120. Caio Savoia, "Appoderamento dell'Agro–Pontino," *La Conquista della Terra* 3/4 (April 1932), 55–79.

121. Ibid., 65.

122. *Telegrafo*, Livorno, 6 April 1932.

123. Giuseppe Nicolosi, "Le case popolari di Littoria nel quadro degli attuali orientamenti della edilizia popolare in Italia," *Architettura*, 16/1 (January 1939), 21–35.

124. Ibid., 26–27.

125. See M. Piacentini, "Sabaudia," *Architettura*, 13/6 (June 1934), 321–58. Mariani recounts the debates in *Fascismo e città nuove*, 95–101; see also Giulia Veronesi, *Difficoltà politiche dell'architettura in Italia 1920–40* (Milan, 1953). Giuseppe Pagano also reported the debate in "Mussolini salva l'architettura italiana," *Casabella*, no. 78 (June 1934), 2–3, now in Cesare De Seta, ed., *Giuseppe Pagano: Architettura e città durante il Fascismo* (Rome and Bari, 1976), 19–24. Of modern historians, only Mariani and Manfredo Tafuri, in *Ludovico Quaroni e lo sviluppo dell'architettura moderna in Italia* (Milan, 1964), 34–35, seem to have grasped what Edoardo Persico understood long ago: that the much-praised Rationalist plan of Sabaudia differed from the others only in style, not substance. See also Ghirardo, "Italian Architects and Fascist Politics," 124–25.

126. Piacentini, "Sabaudia," 321–23.

127. See Mariani, *Fascismo e città nuove*, 101–105; and Pagano, "Architettura nazionale," *Casabella*, no. 85 (January 1935), 2–7, for a critical evaluation of the plan.

128. Franco Biscossa, "Dalla casa del popolo alla Casa del Fascio," in M. De Michelis, ed., *Casa del Popolo* (Venice, 1986), 211.

129. Cencelli, "Littoria provincia rurale," *La Conquista della Terra*, 5/12 (December 1934), 5.

130. Piacentini, "Aprilia," *Architettura*, 15/5 (May 1936), 193–212; idem, "Aprilia," *Architettura*, 17/7 (July 1938), 393–94. Mioni, *Urbanistica fascista*, 256, provides a complete bibliography; see also Mariani, *Fascismo e città nuove*, 329–36.

131. Francesco Fariello, "La casa in Italia," *Architettura*; 14/8 (August 1935), 506.

132. Mussolini, "3a riunione della Commissione Suprema per l'Autarchia," 31 October 1938, in B. Mussolini, *Opera omnia*, vol. 29: *Dal viaggio in Germania all'intervento dell'Italia nella Seconda Guerra Mondiale (1 Ottobre 1937 – 10 Giugno 1940)* (Florence, 1958), 197–97; see also 180–81.

133. Smith, *Mussolini's Roman Empire*, 64.

134. Martinelli and Nuti, "Città nuove in Sardegna," 313. For information on Carbonia, see ACS, Min. Cul. Pop. 467, b. 14 and 19; also "Carbonia, nuova città della Sardegna," *Architettura*, 19/9 (September 1940), 435–52.

135. ACS, Div. Pol. Pol., n. 176, cat. n. 29. Martinelli and Nuti offer a more detailed discussion of Torviscosa in *Le città di strapaese*, 79–90.

136. Giuseppe Reitani, "Politica territoriale e urbanistica in Tripolitania, 1920–1940," and Alberto Boralevi, "Le città dell'impero: Urbanistica fascista in Etiopia 1936–1941," both in Mioni, *Urbanistica Fascista*; Paolo Sica, *Storia dell'urbanistica* II: *Il Novecento* (Bari, 1978), especially 493–520.

The most recent brief study of the Libyan colonization program is Federico Cresti, "Edilizia ed urbanistica nella colonizzazione agraria della Libia (1922–1940)," in *Storia Urbana*, 11/40 (July–September 1987), 189–231.

137. Renato Mori, *Mussolini e la conquista dell'Etiopia* (Florence, 1978); Giorgio Rumi, *L'imperialismo Fascista* (Milan, 1974).

138. Robert L. Hess, *Italian Colonialism in Somalia* (Chicago, 1966), 163–66.

139. Alberto Sbacchi, *Il colonialismo italiano in Etiopia 1936–1940* (Milan, 1980), 245ff.

140. Ibid. For a lucid discussion of early-twentieth-century theories of imperialism, see chapter 4 of Vincent P. Pecora, *Self and Form in Modern Narrative* (Baltimore, 1989). For contemporary Italian views on imperialism, see Virginio Gayda, *Construzione dell'impero* (Rome, 1936).

141. Alessandro Lessona to Araldo Crollalanza, 24 November 1935. ACS, ONC AOI b.1.

142. Lessona to Crollalanza, 20 October 1936. ACS, ONC AOI, b.1.

143. G. Taticchi, "Relazione Settimanale," 23 November 1936, 1. ACS, ONC AOI b.3, f.a.

144. Taticchi, "Relazione Settimanale," 23 November 1936, 2–3. ACS, ONC AOI b.3, f.a. Events proved Taticchi correct: the eventual cost of just 100 of the originally planned 400 farms came in well over six million *lire*. Ing. Mazzucato to ONC headquarters, "Situazione lavori al 31 Maggio 1939," ACS, ONC AOI b.3, f.b.

145. Taticchi, "Relazione," 23 November 1936, 3. ACS, ONC AOI b.3, f.a.

146. See the report of Nello Mazzocchi Alemanni, "Relazione sui programmi di Colonizzazione demografica nell'Impero da parte dell'ONC," 22 April 1938, 3–4. ACS, ONC AOI b.11, f.c.

147. Mazzucato to ONC headquarters, "Situazione lavori al 31 Maggio 1939," ACS, ONC AOI b.3, f.b.

148. Dr. Benigno Fagotti, "Esperimenti culturali eseguite nell'Azienda Agraria di Biscioftù dell'Opera Nazionale Combattenti, 1937–38," 8 November 1938, 5. ACS, ONC AOI b.3, f.a.

149. Dr. Angelo Ponzetti, "Tecnica dell'orticultura a 2500 metri," October 1938. ACS, ONC AOI b.3, f.a.

150. Fagotti, "Esperimenti culturali," 8–9; Taticchi, "Relazione del mese di settembre 1937," ACS, ONC AOI b.3, f.a.

151. Fagotti, "Esperimenti culturali," 8–13.

152. Ing. A. Balconi, "Materiali da costruzione in Addis Abeba, possibilità presenti e future," 9 December 1936. ACS, ONC AOI b.3, f.a.

153. Taticchi, "Relazione," 23 May 1937, 2; "Relazione Attività," 6 August 1937, 2. ACS, ONC AOI b.3, f.a.

154. Despite Taticchi's repeated solicitations, Crollalanza held firm. Crollalanza to Taticchi, 22 March 1937, 2. ACS, ONC AOI b.3, f.a.

155. Dr. Sergio Fornari to ONC headquarters, 10 November 1939. ACS, ONC AOI b.5.

156. See the map of the Biscioftù agency and farm plots in ACS, ONC AOI b.5, f.b.

157. Taticchi to ONC headquarters, 15 December 1936, 1; Crollalanza to Taticchi, 20 April 1940, 3. ACS, ONC AOI b.3, f.b and f.a.

158. N. Mazzocchi Alemanni, "Appoderamento Azienda AO," 22 April 1938, 13. ACS, ONC AOI b.1, f.c.

159. Taticchi, "Famiglie coloniche della Azienda Agricola Opera Nazionale Combattenti," 15 October 1940; idem, "Relazione mese Agosto 1940"; idem, "Relazione mesi di Dicembre 1940 e Gennaio 1941"; idem, "Relazione mese di Settembre 1940"; Daodiace, Governatore Generale, "Famiglie coloniche dell'Azienda Agricola Opera Nazionale Combattenti," 11 October 1940. ACS, ONC AOI b.3, f.a.

160. Alberto Lombardi, "Prestigio di razza e colonizzazione demografica," *Rassegna Sociale dell'Africa Italiana* 2/5 (May 1939), 530–31.

161. Boralevi, "Le città dell'impero," 243.

162. Consociazione Turistica Italiana, *Guida dell'Africa Orientale Italiana* (Rome, 1938), 477–78.

163. Gianluigi Banfi, Ludovico Belgioioso, Enrico Peressutti, and Ernesto Rogers, *Relazione per il piano regolatore di Pavia* (1933), cited in Ezio Bonfanti, *Città museo e architettura: Il Gruppo BBPR nella cultura architettonica italiana 1932–1970* (Florence, 1973), 49.

164. Federico Chabod, *Storia della politica estera italiana* (Bari, 1951, 2nd ed. 1962), 295ff.

3. American New Towns

1. United States Department of Commerce, *Subsistence Gardens: Some Brief Reports on Industrial, Community, and Municipal Projects Prepared from Reports Received from States and Local Communities* (Washington, DC, 1932).

2. Ibid., 1.

3. Ibid., 3–4.

4. Ibid., 4.

5. National Industrial Recovery Act, 48 Stat. 195, 205, 1933.

6. Press release of 28 February 1934. FERA Old Subject Series General, CWA Administrative Correspondence.

7. Ibid.

8. Lawrence Westbrook to David Ross, 25 September 1934. FERA OSS Rural Rehabilitation, General, Box 65.

9. Marion Clawson, "Resettlement Experience on Nine Selected Resettlement Projects," *Agricultural History*, 52/1 (January 1978), 1–92 (reprint of a report originally prepared in 1943).

10. Leonard J. Arrington, "The Sagebrush Resurrection: New Deal Expenditures in the Western States, 1933–1939," *Pacific Historical Review*, 52/2 (February 1983), 1–16; Gregory M. Hooks, "A New Deal for Farmers and Social Scientists: The Politics of Rural Sociology in the Depression Era," *Rural Sociology*, 48/3 (Fall 1983), 386–408.

11. Lawrence Westbrook, "Rural Industrial Communities for Stranded Families," 7. FERA OSS Rural Rehabilitation, General, Box 65.

12. Harry Hopkins to Henry Wallace, 5 March 1934. FERA OSS Rural Rehabilitation, Administrative Correspondence.

13. Wallace to Hopkins, 12 March 1934. FERA OSS Rural Rehabilitation, Administrative Correspondence.

14. Wallace to Hopkins, 19 March 1934. Ibid.

15. Roosevelt made this comment to relief administrators on 14 June 1933. Franklin D. Roosevelt, *Public Papers and Addresses of Franklin D. Roosevelt*, 2, compiled by Samuel I. Rosenman (New York, 1938), 240.

16. For an overview, see Theodore Saloutos, "New Deal Agricultural Policy: An Evaluation," *Journal of American History*, 61 (September 1974), 394–416; also Kenneth Finegold, "From Agrarianism to Adjustment: The Political Origin of the New Deal Agricultural Policy," *Politics and Society*, 2/1 (1981), 1–27.

17. Tugwell, "The Resettlement Idea," *Agricultural History*, 33 (October 1959), 161–63.

18. Edward C. Banfield, "Ten Years of the Farm Tenant Purchase Program," *Journal of Farm Economics*, 31 (August 1949), 469–74.

19. Westbrook, 25 March 1934. FERA OSS Rural Rehabilitation, General.

20. Ibid.

21. Jacob Baker to Mrs. Ewing, 6 December 1933. FERA OSS Barter, General, File 47, Box 17.

22. "Not a Cent for Oregon," *Oregon Journal*, 10 May 1934, 10.

23. John M. Carmody to Commissioners of Education, 21 April 1934. FERA OSS Barter, General, File 47, Box 17.

24. Henry F. Harriman, President, Chambers of Commerce, to Harry Hopkins, 1 September 1934. FERA OSS Barter, General, Box 17.

25. Wissler to Jacob Baker, 21 September 1934. FERA OSS Field Reports, 278.

26. Thomas R. Amlie to Aubrey Williams, Field Representative, 9 November 1933. FERA OSS Barter, General, File 47, Box 6.

27. Rexford Guy Tugwell, *Roosevelt's Revolution: The First Year—A Personal Perspective* (New York, 1977), 45.

28. Julian to Roper, 11 January 1935. FERA OSS Rural Rehabilitation, Administrative Correspondence, 331.1.

29. Baker to Jessie Lummis, 16 October 1933. FERA OSS Barter, File 47, General.

30. M. L. Wilson, "A Land-Use Program for the Federal Government," *Journal of Farm Economics*, 15/2 (April 1933); U.S. Department of Interior, Division of Subsistence Homesteads, "General Information Concerning the Purposes and Policies of the Division of Subsistence Homesteads," Circular No. 1 (Washington, DC, 1933).

31. Tugwell, *Roosevelt's Revolution*, 246.

32. Rexford G. Tugwell, *The Democratic Roosevelt* (Garden City, NY, 1957); idem, "The Sources of New Deal Reformism," *Ethics*, 64 (1954), 266.

33. Tugwell, *Roosevelt's Revolution*, 246; also Bernard Sternsher, *Rexford Tugwell and the New Deal* (New York, 1964), 270.

34. For Tugwell's ideas on the Greenbelt towns, see his "The Meaning of the Greenbelt Towns," *The New Republic*, 90 (1937), 43; his Foreword to Edward C. Banfield, *Government Project* (Glencoe, IL, 1951), 9–13; and the excellent discussion in Sternsher, *Rexford Tugwell*, 262–306. On the Greenbelt Towns, the best study remains Joseph L. Arnold, *The New Deal in the Suburbs: A History of the Greenbelt Town Program 1935–1954* (Columbus, OH, 1971); also Clarence Stein, *Toward New Towns for America* (New York, 1957); George A. Warner, *Greenbelt: The Cooperative Community* (New York, 1954); and Conkin, *Tomorrow a New World*, chapter XIV.

35. Conkin, *Tomorrow a New World*, 322.

36. Warner, *Greenbelt*, 72–74.

37. Conkin, *Tomorrow a New World*, 322–24.

38. Phoebe Cutler, *The Public Landscape of the New Deal* (New Haven, 1986), 119.

39. Westbrook, "Rural Industrial Communities" (cited in note 11 above), 3.

40. Ibid.

41. Westbrook to Couch, 27 April 1934. FERA OSS Rural Rehabilitation, Box 65.

42. Press release, 28 February 1934. FERA OSS Rural Rehabilitation, Box 65.

43. Jacob H. Dorn, "Rural Ideal, Agrarian Realities: Arthur E. Holt, the Vision of a Decentralized America in the Interwar Years," *Church History*, 52/1 (March 1983), 50–65.

44. Westbrook, "Rural Industrial Communities," 34.

45. J. Philip Campbell, AAA, "Memorandum Regarding Visit to Southern States in the Interest of Rural Rehabilitation," April 1934, 4. FERA OSS Rural Rehabilitation, Administrative, 331.1.

46. Westbrook, "Rural Industrial Communities," 3.

47. Ibid.; also Jacob Baker to Frank Bane, 13 March 1934. FERA OSS Rural Rehabilitation, Box 65.

48. Westbrook, "Rural Industrial Communities," 5.

49. Gast to Zeuch, 23 September 1934 (see footnote to p. 25 above), 1.

50. Zeuch to Gast, 18 September 1934; and see note 66 below.

51. Paul Conkin, "The Vision of Elwood Mead," *Agricultural History*, 34 (April 1960), 88–97.

52. Ibid., p. 91.

53. Zeuch to Gast, 9 September 1934, 1–2.

54. Zeuch to Gast, 18 September 1934, 1–2.

55. Dolores Hayden, *Seven American Utopias: The Architecture of Communitarian Socialism, 1790–1975* (Cambridge, MA, 1978), 289–309.

56. Ibid., 310–11.

57. Ibid., 311.

58. Malcolm F. Hooper, Trade Commissioner, Rome, "Summary of the Commercial Attache's Report of 9 March 1936; Housing Problems in Italy," 1–2. NRPB RG 187, Central Office Correspondence, 1933–43, Box 415.

59. Roland Welch, Assistant Trade Commissioner, Berlin, "Housing Problems in Germany," 27 March 1936, Special Report No. 82. NRPB RG 187, Central Office Correspondence, 1933–43, Box 415. These and other consular reports were amassed by the Bureau of Foreign and Domestic Commerce for a planned study of housing throughout the world.

60. Consulate General, Berlin, "Alleviation of Unemployment in Germany," 31 October 1934, Report No. 22. NRPB RG 187, Central Office Correspondence, 1933–43, Box 415.

61. Consulate General, Berlin, "Recent Developments in Germany Regarding Suburban Settlements," 27 April 1935, Report No. 205. NRPB RG 187, Central Office Correspondence, 1933–43, Box 415. The law affecting subsistence settlements was enacted by a decree of the Reichspräsident, 8 October 1931.

62. Gast to Zeuch, 23 September 1934.

63. Westbrook, "Rural Industrial Communities," 4.

64. See Hayden's discussion of Llano del Rio in *Seven American Utopias*.

65. Gast to Zeuch, 3 October 1934, 1.

66. Gast to Pynchon, 2 October 1934 (see footnote to p. 25 above), 7; Gast to Zeuch, 3 October 1934, 2.

67. Region IX Project Development Report, Resettlement Administration Project Description Book, 13 June 1936, project RR-CF-24. FSA RG 96, Resettlement Administration, Project Books.

68. Joseph G. Knapp, *The Advance of American Cooperative Enterprise 1920–1945* (Danville, IL, 1973), 35–53.

69. Clawson, "Resettlement Experience," 30. See also Banfield's study of Casa Grande, *Government Project*.

70. Clawson, "Resettlement Experience," 39.

71. Ibid., 28–29.

72. Ibid., 71. Banfield, *Government Project*, 65.

73. Clawson, "Resettlement Experience," 55ff.

74. Ibid., 74. Banfield, *Government Project*, 75.

75. Rolent Hardie, Report of 18 November 1940, 1. FSA RG 96 SF General Correspondence 1940–42, Box 934.

76. Hardie, 17 December 1940, 266. FSA RG 96 SF General Correspondence 1940–42, Box 934.

77. Tugwell, foreword to Banfield, *Government Project*, 12.

78. Consulate General, Berlin, "Recent Developments" (27 April 1935).

79. *The Grapes of Wrath* (New York, 1939).

80. See the files on transient problems in FERA OSS Transient Division Files.

81. "Summary Report of the Transient Program," December 1934, 1, 2. FERA OSS Transient Division Files, Narrative Reports and Correspondence, 1934: Arkansas/Nevada.

82. Lorena Hickok to Harry Hopkins, 25 June 1934, 6. FERA OSS Transient Division Files, Narrative Reports and Correspondence, 1934: Arkansas/Nevada.

83. Irving Richter to Howard O. Hunter, 31 January 1935, 1. FERA OSS Transient Division Files, Box 80, General, File H.

84. Oscar W. Behrens to William J. Plunkert, 14 June 1934. FERA OSS Conferences, Transients.

85. William J. Plunkert, "Report on Transient Camps in California and Arizona," 10–15 July 1934: Arkansas–Nevada. Edna T. Hawley to Elizabeth Wickenden, 18 September 1934. FERA OSS Transients, Box 80, General, File M.

86. William J. Plunkert, memorandum, "The Transient Program," 1934, 4. FERA OSS Transient Division Files, General, M.

87. "Excerpt from Monthly Report—Region IX—December [1936]," 3. FSA RG 96 SF Correspondence 1935–42, 183.01, Region IX.

88. Hewes to Mason Barr, Director, Management Division, 4 April 1942. FSA RG 96 SF General Correspondence 1940–42, Box 028.

89. Reports to R. W. Hollenberg, Assistant Regional Director, from Milen Dempster and James T. Collins, June–July 1939. FSA RG 96 SF General Correspondence 1940–42, 913.01.

90. Malcolm Brown and Orin Cassmore (United States Work Projects Administration), *Migratory Cotton Pickers in Arizona* (Washington, DC, 1939), documents the 1937–38 season in Arizona. Donald Worster, *Rivers of Empire: Water, Aridity, and the Growth of the American West* (New York, 1985), 194–256, provides a rich and provocative account of land, labor, and water politics in the Southwest in the 1930s.

91. Brown and Cassmore, *Migratory Cotton Pickers*, xvii–xviii.

92. F. N. Mortensen to J. C. Henderson, Chief of Migratory Labor Program, 4 September 1940. FSA RG 96 SF General Correspondence 1940–42, Box 028.

93. Jonathan Garst, Regional Director, USDA, to Ray Richard, 15 March 1937. FSA RG 96 SF General Correspondence 1940–42, Box 028.

94. See, for example, references in letters from Lorena Hickok to Harry Hopkins, especially 29 December 1933. FERA OSS Field Representative Reports, Box 10, File "Lorena Hickok."

95. Jefferson Patterson, Consul, Breslau, Germany, "Housing Settlement Projects in Silesia," 10 July 1935. NRPB RG 187, Central Office Correspondence 1933–43, 415.

96. See Cletus E. Daniel, *Bitter Harvest: A History of California Farmworkers, 1870–1941* (Ithaca and London, 1981), esp. pp. 141–285.

97. Chastain Thomas, Home Supervisor, Yuba, Sutter, Nevada, and Sierra counties, in "Excerpts from Home Supervisors' Weekly Reports," 25 July 1938. FSA RG 96 SF California Rural Rehabilitation Division, General Correspondence 1940–42, file 934.

98. Ida Gene Payne, Home Supervisor, San Joaquin, Contra Costa, and Alameda counties, "Excerpts from Home Supervisors' Weekly Reports," 25 July 1938. Ibid.

99. R. Foraker to Harry Hopkins, "Proposed Rural Rehabilitation Project," 4 December 1934. FERA OSS California Work Relief, Box 57.

100. Ibid., letter, 1.

101. Ibid., attachment 2, 1.

102. Ibid., attachment 1, 2.

103. Ibid.

104. Ibid., attachment 1, 3.

105. Ibid., attachment 2, 3.

106. Hollenberg to Barr, 16 April 1941, "Report on Activities of Community and Family Services Section, 1 January 1941 through 31 March 1941." FSA RG 96 SF General Correspondence 1940–42, Box 934, Economic Division.

107. "Excerpt from Monthly Report—Region IX—December [1936]," section on Marysville Migratory Labor Camp, 1. FSA RG 96 Correspondence 1935–42, 183.01, Region IX.

108. Hollenberg to Barr, 16 April 1941, 4.

109. Ibid.; Robert S. Hardie to Harvey M. Coverley, Assistant Regional Director, 17 December 1940. FSA RG 96 SF California Rural Rehabilitation Division, General Correspondence 1940–42, File 934.

110. Lawrence I. Hewes, Jr., to Barr, 6 August 1941, "Report on Activities of Community and Family Services Section, 1 April through 30 June 1941." FSA RG 96 SF California Rural Rehabilitation Division, General Correspondence 1940–42, Box 934, Economic Division.

111. Hollenberg to Barr, 16 April 1941, 5.

112. Jessie H. Home (?), Firebaugh Report, January 1941, "Excerpts from monthly reports," 18 February 1941, 3. FSA RG 96 SF California Rural Rehabilitation Division, General Correspondence 1940–42, Box 934, Economic Division.

113. Hollenberg to Barr, 16 April 1941, 1–2.

114. See the summary of subsistence homesteads in the Greenbelt Homes Manual. PHA RG 196 FRC box 1592, chapters 010–112.

115. Lois Craig, *The Federal Presence: Architecture, Politics and Symbols in United States Government Building* (Cambridge, MA, 1978), 384.

116. Ibid., 385. See also Conkin, *Tomorrow a New World*, 237–55.

117. Project Book, San Fernando Homesteads, undated. FSA RG 96 Project Records 1935–40, California, SH-CF-3.

118. Project Book, El Monte, LP-CF-5.

119. See the plot, house, and outbuilding plans for Ashwood Plantation, Project RF-SC-9, Region 5. Farmers Home Administration (FHA) RG 97, Paper Tracings and Blueprints of Farmstead Units and Buildings of Resettlement Projects 1936–38.

120. Project Book, San Fernando, 2.

121. Edward Stone to E. E. Agger, "Organization of Rurban Homes, San Fernando Unit," 24 February 1936. SF RG 207, El Monte and San Fernando, History Previous to Resettlement Administration, Box 6.

122. Leuchtenberg, *Franklin D. Roosevelt and the New Deal*, 136.

123. Subsistence Homesteads Manual, Chap. 630, Section 1, Eligibility Requirements. PHA RG 196 FRC box 1592.

124. Project Book, San Fernando Homesteads, Section B, Family Selection and Census.

125. Subsistence Homesteads Manual, Chap. 630, Section 1, Eligibility Requirements.

126. Millard Milburn Rice, "Footnote on Arthurdale," *Harper's Magazine*, 180 (March 1940), 411–19.

127. "Statistical Analysis of Families in Occupancy as of December 13, 1935 at San Fernando California," Project Book, San Fernando Homesteads.

128. Monthly report, June 1936. Project Book, San Fernando Homesteads, Occupant Income and Employment.

129. Stone to Agger, 24 February 1936 (cited in note 121 above), 2.

130. Miscellaneous—transcript of letter from Agger to Gwen Geach, 6 May 1936. Project Book, San Fernando Homesteads.

131. Stone to Agger, 28 February 1936.

132. Monthly Report, June 1936. Project Book, San Fernando Homesteads.

133. Ashby C. McGraw, Report of President, San Fernando Community Asssociation, 31 December 1936. SF RG 207, El Monte and San Fernando, History Previous to Resettlement Administration, Box 6, Minutes of Community Association Meetings.

134. Monroe Oppenheimer to Rexford Tugwell, "Legal Analysis," 24 March 1936, 5. SF RG 207, El Monte and San Fernando, History Previous to Resettlement Administration, Box 6.

135. Oppenheimer to Tugwell, "Legal Analysis of Tenure Forms A & B," 20 March 1936, 7. Ibid.

136. See also Oppenheimer to Tugwell, 24 March 1936, 7. Ibid.

137. Ibid., 2.

138. Minutes of meeting, Board of Directors, El Monte Community Association, 5 January 1937. SF RG 207, El Monte and San Fernando, History Previous to Resettlement Administration, Box 6, Minutes of Community Association Meetings.

139. Edward Stone to L. M. Walker, 19 January 1937. FSA RG 96, 183.01.

140. Clawson, "Resettlement Experience," 35.

141. Fred A. Weller, Regional Attorney, to Rexford Tugwell, "Legal—Community Organization," 29 April 1936. SF RG 207, El Monte and San Fernando, Box 6, Incorporation and Transfer.

142. Arline L. Chewning, Report of Secretary, El Monte Community Association, 31 December 1936. SF RG 207, El Monte and San Fernando, History Previous to Resettlement Administration, Box 6, Minutes of Community Association Meetings.

143. Chewning, Minutes of San Fernando Community Association, 17 November 1936, 1. SF RG 207, El Monte and San Fernando, History Previous to Resettlement Administration, Box 6, Minutes of Community Association Meetings.

144. Excerpt from Monthly Report, December 1935, 3. Project Book, San Fernando Homesteads, Miscellaneous.

145. Monthly Report, June 1936. Project Book, San Fernando Homesteads, Miscellaneous.

146. Stone to Agger, 24 February 1936, 2. SF RG 207, El Monte and San Fernando, History Previous to Resettlement Association.

147. Chewning, Minutes of El Monte Community Association, 15 September 1936, 2. SF RG 207, El Monte and San Fernando, History Previous to Resettlement Administration, Box 6, Minutes of Community Association Meetings.

148. Ibid., 4.

149. Ibid., 5.

150. Clawson, "Resettlement Experience," 40. Also Hardie to Coverly, 17 December 1940, 1. FSA RG 96 San Francisco, General Correspondence 1940–41, 934, Economic Division.

151. Clawson, "Resettlement Experience," 54ff.

152. Ibid., 56. See also "Analysis of Occupancy Turnover," 18 July 1940, where the only concerns are better family procedures. FSA RG 96 SF California Rural Rehabilitation Division, General Correspondence 1940–41, 934, Economic Division.

153. Clawson, "Resettlement Experience," 54–56.

154. Ibid., 62–63.

155. Ibid., 62.

156. Ibid., 53–56.

1. See my article "A Taste of Money: Criticism and Patronage in Houston," in *Harvard Architecture Review*, 6 (Fall 1987), 88–95.

2. See, for example, Barton Bernstein, "The New Deal: The Conservative Achievements of Liberal Reform," in Bernstein and Allen J. Matusow, *Twentieth-Century America: Recent Interpretations*, 2nd ed. (New York, 1972), 242–64; Howard Zinn, *New Deal Thought* (New York, 1966); Paul K. Conkin, *The New Deal* (New York, 1967).

3. Degler, *Out of Our Past*, 379–413; Leuchtenberg, *Franklin D. Roosevelt and the New Deal*.

4. See especially Bernstein, "The New Deal," 258–63.

5. Robert M. Collins, *The Business Response to Keynes 1929–1964* (New York, 1981).

6. Arnold, *The New Deal in the Suburbs*, 142.

7. Tugwell, foreword to Banfield, *Government Project*, 9-13. See also Rena Maycock, Chief, Home Economics Division, Region IX, Conference at Canyon Creek Lodge, Washington, 3–5 July 1936. FSA RG 96 General Correspondence 1940–42, File 530.

Selected Bibliography

Abse, Tobias, "Mussolini and His Historical Context," *Historical Journal*, 26/1 (March 1983), 237–54.

Agee, James, and Walker Evans, *Let Us Now Praise Famous Men*. Boston: Houghton Mifflin, 1941.

Alemanni, Nello Mazzocchi, "La conquista rurale," in Opera Nazionale dei Combattenti, *L'Agro Pontino al 29 Ottobre anno XVI E.F.* (Rome, 1937), 55–126.

Anderson, Henry S., "The Little Landers' Land Colonies: A Unique Agricultural Experiment in California," *Agricultural History*, 5 (1931), 140–42.

Andruzzi, Constantino, "Le Paludi Pontine nella storia," *La Conquista della Terra*, 3/4 (April 1932), 41–53.

"Aprilia," *Architettura*, 17/7 (July 1938), 393–4.

Aquarone, Alberto, *L'organizzazione dello stato totalitario*. Turin: Einaudi, 1965.

Arnold, Joseph L., *The New Deal in the Suburbs: A History of the Greenbelt Town Program*. Columbus, OH: Ohio State University Press, 1971.

Arrington, Leonard J., "The Sagebrush Resurrection: New Deal Expenditures in the Western States, 1933–1939," *Pacific Historical Review*, 52/2 (February 1983), 1–16.

Baldwin, Sidney, *Poverty and Politics: The Rise and Decline of the Farm Security Administration*. Chapel Hill: University of North Carolina Press, 1968.

Banfield, Edward C., *Government Project*. Glencoe, IL. The Free Press, 1951.

Banfield, Edward C., "Ten Years of the Farm Tenant Purchase Program," *Journal of Farm Economics*, 31 (August 1949), 469–74.

Bardhan, P. K., and T. N. Srinivasan, "Cropsharing Tenancy in Agriculture: A Theoretical and Empirical Analysis," in *American Economic Review*, 61/1 (March 1971), 48–64.

Baskerville, Stephen W., and Ralph Willett, eds., *Nothing Else to Fear: New Perspectives on America in the Thirties*. London and Doren, N.H.: Manchester University Press, 1985.

Beneduce, Alberto, *Relazione sull'ONC* (1921), 15–18. ONC AR (no file numbers available).

Berkowitz, Edward, and Kim McQuaid, "Businessman-Bureaucrat: The Evolution of the American Social Welfare System 1901–1940," *Journal of Economic History*, 38/1 (March 1978), 120–47.

Bernabei, Marco, *Fascismo e nazionalismo in Campania (1919–1925)*. Rome: Edizioni di Storia e Letteratura, 1975.

Bernstein, M., "A Reassessment of Investment Failure in the Interwar American Economy," *Journal of Economic History*, 44/2 (June 1984), 479–88.

Boralevi, Alberto, "Le città dell'impero: Urbanistica Fascista in Etiopia 1936–1941," in A. Mioni, ed., *Urbanistica Fascista* (Milan: Franco Angeli, 1980), 235–86.

Bordoni, Carlo, *Cultura e propaganda nell'Italia Fascista*. Messina & Florence: G. D'Anni, 1974.

Bower, William L., *The Country Life Movement in America 1900–1920*. Port Washington, NY: Kennikat Press, 1974.

Brown, Malcolm, and Orin Cassmore, *Migratory Cotton Pickers in Arizona*. Washington, DC: USGPO, 1939.

Bruns, Roger A., *Knights of the Road: A Hobo History*. New York: Methuen, 1980.

Selected Bibliography

Cannistraro, Philip, *La fabbrica del consenso: Fascismo e mass-media*. Rome and Bari: Laterza, 1975.

Cannistraro, Philip V. *Historical Dictionary of Fascist Italy*. Westport, CT: Greenwood Press, 1982.

"Carbonia, nuova città della Sardegna," *Architettura*, 19/9 (September 1940), 435–52.

Castagnoli, F., *Orthogonal Planning in Antiquity*. Cambridge, MA: MIT Press, 1972.

Cavandoli, Rolando, *Le origini del Fascismo a Reggio Emilia 1919–1923*. Rome: Editori Riuniti, 1972.

Cencelli: *see* Orsolini-Cencelli, *below*.

Christensen, Carol A., *The American Garden City and the New Towns*. Ann Arbor, MI: UMI Research Press, 1986.

Ciocca, Pierluigi, and Gianni Toniolo, *L'economia italiana nel periodo Fascista*. Bologna: Il Mulino, 1976.

Ciucci, Giorgio, "Il dibattito sull'architettura e le città fasciste," in *Storia dell'Arte Italiana*, VII: *Il Novecento*. Turin: Einaudi, 1982, 263–378.

Clawson, Marion, *New Deal Planning: The National Resources Planning Board*. Baltimore: Johns Hopkins University Press, 1981.

Clawson, Marion, "Resettlement Experience on Nine Selected Resettlement Projects," *Agricultural History*, 52/1 (January 1978), 1–92 (reprint of a report originally prepared in 1943).

Cohen, Jon S., "Fascism and Agriculture in Italy, Policies and Consequences," *Economic History Review*, 32/1 (February 1979), 70–87.

Colapietra, Raffaele, *Napoli tra dopoguerra e Fascismo*. Milan: Feltrinelli, 1962.

Commissariato per le Migrazioni e la Colonizzazione Interna, *Le migrazione interna in Italia nell'anno 1932–X*. Rome, 1933.

Commissariato per le Migrazioni e la Colonizzazione Interna, *Le migrazione interna in Italia nell'anno 1934–XII*. Rome, 1935.

Conkin, Paul, *Tomorrow a New World: The New Deal Community Program*. Ithaca, NY: Cornell University Press, 1959.

Cordova, Ferdinando, ed., *Uomini e volti del Fascismo*, Rome: Bulzoni, 1980.

Corner, Paul, "Agricoltura e industria durante il Fascismo," *Problemi del socialismo*, 3rd Series, 11–12 (1972), 721–45.

Corner, Paul, *Fascism in Ferrara, 1915–1925*. London: Oxford University Press, 1975.

Craig, Lois, *The Federal Presence: Architecture, Politics and Symbols in the United States Government Building*. Cambridge, MA: MIT Press, 1978.

Cutler, Phoebe, *The Public Landscape of the New Deal*. New Haven: Yale University Press, 1986.

Daniel, Cletus E., *Bitter Harvest: A History of California Farmworkers, 1870–1941*. Ithaca, NY, and London: Cornell University Press, 1981.

De Grand, Alexander, *Italian Fascism: Its Origins and Development*. Lincoln and London: University of Nebraska Press, 1982.

De Felice, Renzo, *Mussolini il rivoluzionario 1883–1920*. Turin: Einaudi, 1965.

De Grazia, Victoria, *The Culture of Consent: Mass Organization of Leisure in Italy*. Cambridge: Cambridge University Press, 1981.

De Seta, Cesare, *La cultura architettonica in Italia tra le due guerre*, rev. ed. Rome and Bari: Laterza, 1983.

De Seta, Cesare, ed., *Giuseppe Pagano: Architettura e città durante il Fascismo*. Rome and Bari: Laterza, 1976.

De Seta, Cesare, ed., *Storia d'Italia*, Annali 8: *Insediamenti e territorio*. Turin: Einaudi, 1985.

Dorn, Jacob H. "Rural Ideal, Agrarian Realities: Arthur E. Holt, the Vision of a Decentralized America in the Interwar Years," *Church History*, 52/1 (March 1983), 50–65.

Field, A. J., "A New Interpretation of the Causes of the Great Depression," *Journal of Economic History*, 44/2 (June 1984), 489–98.

216

Finegold, Kenneth, "From Agrarianism to Adjustment: The Political Origin of the New Deal Agricultural Policy," *Politics and Society*, 2/1 (1981), 1–27.

Fremling, Gertrude M., "Did the United States Transmit the Great Depression to the Rest of the World?" *American Economic Review*, 75/6 (December 1985), 1181–85.

Galantay, Ervin Y., *New Towns: Antiquity to the Present*. New York: G. Braziller, 1975.

Garner, John S., *The Model Company Town: Urban Design Through Private Enterprise in Nineteenth-Century New England*. Amherst: University of Massachusetts Press, 1984.

Gayda, Virginio, *Costruzione dell'impero*. Rome: Edizioni Roma, 1936.

Ghirardo, Diane, "Italian Architects and Fascist Politics: An Evaluation of the Rationalists' Role in Regime Building," *Journal of the Society of Architectural Historians*, 39/2 (May 1980), 109–27.

Ghirardo, Diane. "New Deal, New City," *Modulus*, University of Virginia Architecture Review (1985).

Ghirardo, Diane, and Kurt Forster, "I modelli delle città di fondazione in epoca Fascista," in Cesare De Seta, ed., *Storia d'Italia*, Annali 8: *Insediamenti e territorio* (Turin: Einaudi, 1985), 627–74.

Gli Annali dell'Africa Italiana, I, March 1943.

Goglia, Luigi, and Fabio Grassi, *Il Colonialismo italiano da Adua all'impero*. Rome and Bari: Laterza, 1981.

Gregor, A., "Fascism and Comparative Politics," *Comparative Political Studies*, 9/2 (July 1976), 207–22.

Gregor, A. James, *The Fascist Persuasion in Radical Politics*. Princeton: Princeton University Press, 1974.

Hawley, Ellis W., *The New Deal and the Problem of Monopoly: A Study in Economic Ambivalence*. Princeton: Princeton University Press, 1966.

Hayden, Dolores, *Seven American Utopias: The Architecture of Communitarian Socialism, 1790–1975*. Cambridge, MA: MIT Press, 1978.

Henderson, H., "Farewell to the Corporate State," *Business and Society Review*, no. 17 (Spring 1976), 49–56.

Hooks, Gregory M., "A New Deal for Farmers and Social Scientists: The Politics of Rural Sociology in the Depression Era," *Rural Sociology*, 48/3 (Fall 1983), 386–408.

Howard, Ebenezer, *Garden Cities of Tomorrow*. London, 1902; reprinted Cambridge MA: MIT Press, 1965.

Inouye, Arlene, and Charles Susskind, "Technological Trends and National Policy, 1937: The First Modern Technology Assessment," *Technology and Culture*, 18/3 (October 1977), 593–621.

Insolera, Italo, and Luigi DiMajo, *L'EUR e Roma dagli anni Trenta al Duemila*. Rome and Bari: Laterza, 1986.

ISTAT (Istituto Centrale di Statistica del Regno d'Italia), *Annuario Statistico Italiano Anno 1934—XII*, Series 4, 1. Rome, 1935.

Jellison, Charles A., *Tomatoes Were Cheaper: Tales from the Thirties*. Syracuse, NY: Syracuse University Press, 1977.

Katznelson, Ira, "Community, Capitalist Development and the Emergence of the Clan," *Politics and Society*, 9/2 (1979), 203–37.

"Keynesianism: Illusion and Delusion," *Monthly Review*, 28/11 (April 1977), 1–12.

Kostof, Spiro, "The Emperor and the Duce: The Planning of Piazzale Augusto Imperatore in Rome," in H. Millon and L. Nochlin, eds., *Art and Architecture in the Service of Politics* (Cambridge, MA: MIT Press, 1978), 270–325.

Lavedan, Pierre, *Histoire de l'urbanisme, Renaissance et temps modernes*. Paris: H. Laurens, 1959.

Lazzero, Ricciotti, *Il Partito Nazionale Fascista: Come era organizzato, come funzionava il partito che mise l'Italia in camicia nera*. Milan: Rizzoli, 1985.

"La cronaca dello storico avvenimento," *La Conquista della Terra* (special issue devoted to Littoria), 3/12 (December 1932), 5.

Selected Bibliography

L'economia italiana, 1861–1940 Bari: Laterza, 1973.

Leuchtenberg, William E., *Franklin D. Roosevelt and the New Deal, 1932–1940*. New York: Harper & Row, 1963.

Lyttleton, Adrian, *The Seizure of Power: Fascism in Italy 1919–1929*. London: Weidenfeld and Nicholson, 1973.

MacDonald, William L., "Excavation, Restoration, and Italian Architecture of the 1930's," in H. Searing, ed., *In Search of Modern Architecture* (Cambridge, MA: MIT Press, 1982), 298–320.

Mack Smith, Denis, *Mussolini's Roman Empire*. New York: Penguin, 1977.

Maraffi, Marco, "State/Economy Relationships: The Case of Italian Public Enterprise," *British Journal of Sociology*, 31/4 (December 1980), 507–24.

Mariani, Riccardo, *Fascismo e città nuove*. Milan: Feltrinelli, 1976.

Mariani, Riccardo, "Le città nuove del periodo Fascista. Com'erano, perchè furono costruite, come sono adesso," *Abitare*, October 1978, 76–91.

Mariani, Riccardo, ed., *Latina: Storia di una città*. Florence: Alinari, 1982.

Martinelli, Roberta, and Lucia Nuti, "Città nuove in Sardegna durante il periodo Fascista," *Storia Urbana*, 2/6 (1978), 291–323.

Martinelli, Roberta, and Lucia Nuti, *Le città di strapaese: La politica di "fondazione" nel ventennio*. Milan: Franco Angeli, 1981.

McDonald, Michael, and John Muldowny, *TVA and the Dispossessed: The Resettlement of Population in the Norris Dam Area*. Knoxville: University of Tennessee Press, 1982.

Millon, Henry, "Some New Towns in Italy in the 1930s," in H. Millon and L. Nochlin, eds., *Art and Architecture in the Service of Politics* (Cambridge, MA: MIT Press, 1978), 326–41.

Mioni, Alberto, ed., *Urbanistica Fascista: Ricerche e saggi sulle città e il territorio e sulle politiche urbane in Italia tra le due guerre*. Milan: Franco Angeli, 1980.

Misefari, Enzo, *L'avvento del Fascismo in Calabria*. Cosenza: Pellegrini, 1980.

Monteleone, Franco, *La Radio Italiana nel periodo Fascista: Studio e documenti 1922–1945*. Venice: Marsilio Editore, 1976.

Mori, Renato, *L'Imperialismo Fascista: L'impresa etiopica: Appunti dalle lezioni*. Rome: Edizioni Ricerche, 1975.

Mori, Renato, *Mussolini e la conquista dell'Etiopia*. Florence: Le Monnier, 1978.

Mussolini, Benito, "Breve preludio," in *Tempi della Rivoluzione Fascista* (Milan: U. Hoepli, 1930).

Mussolini, Benito, *Discorso sull'Ascensione*. Rome: Libreria del Littorio, 1927.

Mussolini, Benito, *Dottrina politica e sociale del Fascismo*. Milan: U. Hoepli, 1932.

Mussolini, Benito, *Scritti e discorsi*. Edizione definitiva, 13 vols. Milan: U. Hoepli, 1934–40.

"Mussolini salva l'architettura italiana," *Casabella*, no. 78 (June 1934), 2–3.

Nannini, Sergio, "Le migrazioni e la colonizzazione," in *La Conquista della Terra*, 6/12 (December 1935), 93–138.

Nash, Ernest, *Roman Towns*. New York: Augustin, 1944.

National Catholic Rural Life Conference, *Manifesto on Rural Life*. Milwaukee, 1939.

"Giuseppe Nicolosi: Figura, opere, contesto," special issue of *Rassegna di Architettura e Urbanistica*, 19/55 (April 1983).

Nicolosi, Giuseppe, "Le case popolari di Littoria nel quadro degli attuali orientamenti della edilizia popolare in Italia," *Architettura*, 16/1 (January 1937), 21–35.

Opera Nazionale per i Combattenti, *L'Opera Nazionale per i Combattenti*. Rome, 1926.

Opera Nazionale per i Combattenti, *L'Agro Pontino al 29 Ottobre anno XVI E.F.*. Rome, 1937.

Opera Nazionale per i Combattenti, *L'Agro Pontino, anno XVII*. Rome, 1940.

Orsolini-Cencelli, Valentino, "Littoria comune rurale," in *La Conquista della Terra*, 3/7 (July 1932), 11–79.

Orsolini-Cencelli, Valentino, *Le Paludi Pontine attraverso i secoli*. Rome, 1934.

Pagano, Giuseppe, "Architettura nazionale," *Casabella*, no. 85 (January 1935), 2–7.

Paul, Jürgen, *Der Palazzo Vecchio in Florenz*. Florence: L. S. Olschki, 1969.

Pedrocco, G., *Fascismo e nuove technologie: L'organizzazione industriale da Giolitti a Mussolini*. Bologna: Clueb, 1980.

Piacentini, Marcello, "Aprilia," *Architettura*, 15/5 (May 1936), 193–212.

Piacentini, M., "Sabaudia," *Architettura*, 13/6 (June 1934), 321–58.

Pullan, Brian, *Rich and Poor in Renaissance Venice: The Social Institutions of a Catholic State, to 1620*. Cambridge, MA: Harvard University Press, and Oxford: Basil Blackwell, 1971.

Rassegna Sociale dell'Africa Italiana, 3/2 (February 1940).

Rassegna Sociale dell'Africa Italiana, 3/4 (April 1940).

Reid, J. D., "Sharecropping as an Understandable Market Response," *Journal of Economic History*, 33/1 (March 1973), 106–130.

Reitani, Giuseppe, "Politica territoriale e urbanistica in Tripolitania, 1920–1940," in A. Mioni, ed., *Urbanistica Fascista: Ricerche e saggi sulle città e il territorio e sulle politiche urbane in Italia tra le due guerre* (Milan: Franco Angeli, 1980), 219–34.

Rice, Millard Milburn, "Footnote on Arthurdale," *Harper's Magazine*, 180 (March 1940), 411–19.

Rumi, Giorgio, *L'imperialismo Fascista*. Milan: Mursia, 1974.

Sabbatucci, Giovanni, "Fascist Institutions: Recent Problems and Interpretations," *Journal of Italian History*, 2 (Spring 1979), 75–92.

Santarelli, Enzo, *Storia del Fascismo*, 2nd ed. 2 vols. Rome: Editori Riuniti, 1981.

Sarti, Roland, *Fascism and the Industrial Leadership in Italy 1919–1940: A Study of the Expansion of Private Power under Fascism*. Berkeley, CA: University of California Press, 1971.

Savoia, Caio, "Appoderamento dell'Agro-Pontino," *La Conquista della Terra*, 3/4 (April 1932), 55–79.

Sbacchi, Alberto, *Il colonialismo italiano in Etiopia 1936–1940*. Milan: Mursia, 1980.

Schwartz, A., "La bonifica delle Paludi Pontine e la nuova città di Littoria," *Rassegna di Architettura*, 4/2 1933, 59–60.

Sechi, S., *Dopoguerra e Fascismo in Sardegna. Il movimento autonomistico nella crisi dello stato liberale (1918–1926)*. Turin: Einaudi, 1969.

Sereni, Emilio, *La questione agraria nella rinascita nazionale italiana*. Turin: Einaudi, 1975.

Shapiro, Ellen Ruth, "Building Under Mussolini," unpublished Ph.D. dissertation, Yale University, 1985.

Sica, Paolo, *Storia dell'urbanistica, II: Il Novecento*. Bari: Laterza, 1978.

Skocpol, Theda, "Political Response to Capitalist Crisis: Neo-Marxist Theories of the State and the Case of the New Deal," *Politics and Society*, 10/2 (1980), 155–201.

Skocpol, Theda, and Kenneth Finegold, "State Capacity and Economic Intervention in the Early New Deal," *Political Science Quarterly*, 97/2 (Summer 1982), 255–78.

Steinbeck, John, *The Grapes of Wrath*. New York: Viking, 1939.

Toniolo, Gianni, *L'economia italiana 1861–1940*. Rome and Bari: Laterza, 1978.

Tracchia, Ruggero, *Colonia ad Ascari*. Milan: Cerchina, 1939.

Treves, Anna, *Le migrazioni interne nell'Italia Fascista. Politica e realtà demografica*. Turin: Einaudi, 1976.

Tugwell, Rexford G., *The Democratic Roosevelt*. Garden City, NY: Doubleday, 1957.

Tugwell, Rexford G., "The Sources of New Deal Reformism," *Ethics*, 64 (1954), 249–76.

Vaudagna, Maurizio, "Structural Change in Fascist Italy," *Journal of Economic History*, 38/1 (March 1978), 181–201.

Verba, Sidney, and Kay L. Schlozman, "Unemployment, Class Consciousness, and Radical Politics: What Didn't Happen in the Thirties," *Journal of Politics*, 39/2 (May 1977), 291–323.

Waley, Daniel, *The Italian City-Republics*. New York: McGraw-Hill, 1969.

Selected Bibliography

Warner, George A., *Greenbelt: The Cooperative Community*. New York: Exposition Press, 1954.

White, Morton, and Lucia White, *The Intellectual Versus the City*. Cambridge, MA: Harvard University Press, 1962.

Wiedenhoeft, Richard, *Berlin's Housing Revolution: German Reform in the 1920s*. Ann Arbor, MI: UMI Research Press, 1985.

Wilson, M. L., "A Land-Use Program for the Federal Government," *Journal of Farm Economics*, 15/2 (April 1933), 217–35.

Woolf, S. J., ed., *The Nature of Fascism*. New York: Random House, 1969.

Worster, Donald, *Rivers of Empire: Water, Aridity, and the Growth of the American West*, New York: Pantheon, 1985.

Index